Manhattan

Gil Reavill and Jean Zimmerman
Photography by Michael Yamashita

COMPASS AMERICAN GUIDES
An Imprint of Fodor's Travel Publications, Inc.

Manhattan

LIBRARY OF CONGRESS CATALOGING-IN-PUBLICATION DATA
Reavill, Gil, 1953–
    Manhattan/by Gil Reavill and Jean Zimmerman: photography by Michael Yamashita.
    p.   cm. —(Compass American Guides)
    Includes bibliographical references and index
    ISBN 1-878867-37-7 (paper): $16.95
    1. Manhattan (New York, N.Y.)—Guidebooks. 2. New York (N.Y.)—Guidebooks.
    I. Zimmerman, Jean   II. Title   III. Series: Compass American Guides (Series)
F128.18.R43   1994   94-17972
917.47'10443 – – dc20   CIP

Editors: Kit Duane, Julia Dillon, Deborah Dunn   Designers: Christopher Burt, David Hurst,
Managing Editor: Kit Duane   Candace Compton-Pappas
Photo Editor: Christopher Burt   Map Design: David Lindroth

Compass American Guides, 6051 Margarido Drive, Oakland, CA 94618
Production House: Twin Age Ltd., Hong Kong   Printed in China
10 9 8 7 6 5 4 3 2 1

PUBLISHER'S ACKNOWLEDGMENTS
The Publisher gratefully acknowledges the following institutions and individuals for the use of their photographs and/or illustrations on the following pages:
    Culver Pictures, pp. 72, 100; Katsuyoshi Tanaka, pp. 80, 81, 89, 96, 98, 102, 113, 130, 153, 177, 192, 229, 264, 288; Library of Congress, pp. 31, 32, 33, 36, 39, 50, 53, 68, 90, 137, 146, 166, 178, 187, 243, 249, 259; Margaret Clinton Burt, p. 205; Municipal Archives of the City of New York, pp. 271, 304; Museum of the City of New York, pp. 45, 47, 52, 55, 64, 66; National Academy of Design, pp. 215; National Park Service, p. 73; New York Public Library for the Performing Arts, p. 179; New-York Historical Society, pp. 46, 142, 219, 221; Pierpont Morgan Library, p. 75; Underwood Archives, pp. 15, 54, 59, 101, 105, 120, 129, 234, 261, 270, 305.
    Also for their contributions: Marion Dillon, art consultant with Dillon Hardesty; Willard Jenkins of the National Jazz Service Organization; Wayne Tucker for the piece on bicycle messengers; and Laurie Wolfe, art director at *Women's Wear Daily.*

For Our Parents

C O N T E N T S

Maps

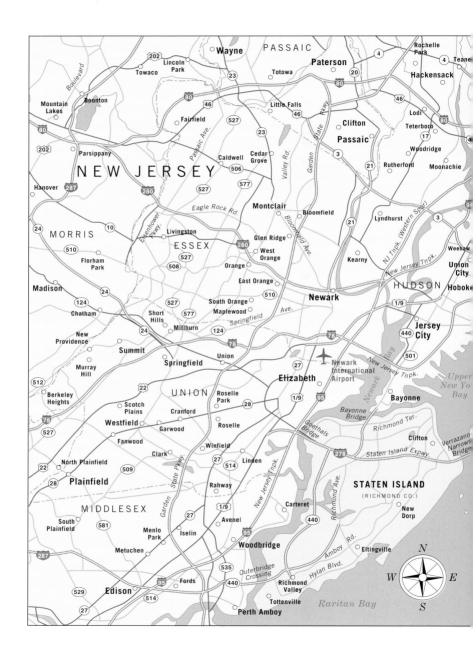

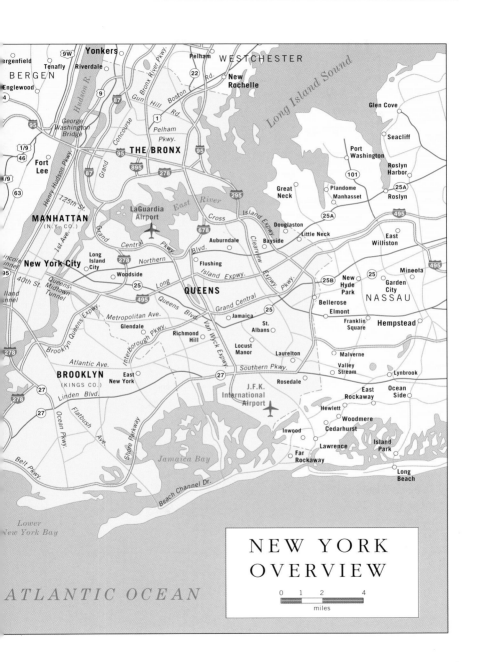

NEW YORK
OVERVIEW

0   1   2   4
miles

Literary Extracts

Essays

AUTHORS' ACKNOWLEDGMENTS

Every book is a collaboration, and this one owes a lot to the efforts of a whole host of people. Chief among them are the staff members at Compass American Guides. Our sincerest gratitude is due to our painstaking and enthusiastic editor, Kit Duane. Tobias Steed and Chris Burt set the tone for the project and gave valuable guidance, Julia Dillon and Debi Dunn helped put it all together.

Mike Yamashita provided the visual balance for a very wordy duo, miraculously getting fresh images out of one of the most photographed places on Earth. Sara Hollister was great at ferreting out historical illustrations.

Special thanks also to Alison Riley, our home office aide-de-camp, who was invaluable on the phone and at the file cabinets. Magalie Gilson was always there for our daughter when deadline pressures got the best of us. Last but far from least, we'd like to thank our Manhattanite friends—those who have stuck it out in The City and those who have regretfully decamped—for their provocative suggestions, inside information, and terrific support.

FACTS ABOUT MANHATTAN

POPULATION OF NEW YORK CITY(1990)

Metro Area	18,087,000
City	7,365,000
Brooklyn (Kings County)	2,358,000
Queens (Queens County)	1,967,000
Manhattan (New York County)	1,488,000
Bronx (Bronx County)	1,172,000
Staten Island (Richmond County)	390,000

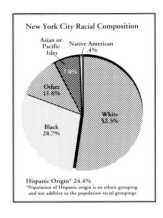

New York City Racial Composition

Asian or Pacific Isles

Native American .4%

Other 11.6%

White 52.3%

Black 28.7%

Hispanic Origin* 24.4%
*Population of Hispanic origin is an ethnic grouping and not additive to the population racial groupings.

✈ 35 million airport arrivals per year
🚶 25 million overnight visitors per year
🚶 5.5 million foreign visitors per year
🚶 2 million convention delegates per year

SIZE OF MANHATTAN
IS 22.2 SQUARE MILES
(NEW YORK CITY IS
301 SQUARE MILES)

*De*Witt Clinton
campaign banner,
governor of New York
1817-1823 & 1825-1828.

HISTORY

Name:	Derivation: After the Algonquian name for the island, "Manahatn."
Discovered:	1524 by Giovanni da Verrazano
Founded:	1625 by Dutch West India Company
Named:	1664 New Amsterdam becomes New York

NOTABLE BUILDINGS:

	Date	Height (each the highest building in the world at the time)	
Flatiron Building:	1903	300 ft.	21 floors
Citibank Building:	1907	741 ft.	57 floors
Woolworth Building:	1913	792 ft.	60 floors
Bank of Manhattan:	1929	927 ft.	71 floors
Chrysler Building:	1930	1,046 ft.	77 floors
Empire State Building:	1931	1,250 ft.*	102 floors
World Trade Center:	1973	1,368 ft.	110 floors

*the mast on the Empire makes it a total of 1,450 ft.

Ethel Merman and dancers from Girl Crazy.

Empire State Building

CULTURE FACTS:

 38 Broadway and 300 Off-Broadway theaters

 150 museums and 400 art galleries

 17,000 eating establishments

 109 newspapers

 183 magazines

 90 book publishers

 13 TV stations

 117 radio stations

 94 universities and colleges

WEATHER RECORDS (AT CENTRAL PARK, EXCEPT FOR WIND RECORD AT THE BATTERY)

Lowest Temp	Highest Temp ☼	Snowiest Day ❄	Rainiest Day 🌡	Highest Wind
-15° 2/4/34	106° 7/10/36	26" 12/26/47	11.3" 9/20/03	113mph 10/13/54

INTRODUCTION

THE ISLAND OF MANHATTAN IS A LITTLE MORE THAN 22 square miles in area, narrow and irregular, posted at one of the greatest natural harbors on Earth, and surrounded on all sides by great rivers and treacherous tidal straits.

The shape of it reminds people of a fish. "New York City is made of five boroughs," states a Depression-era guide, "four of which—Brooklyn, Queens, Richmond, the Bronx—compose like crinkled lily pads about the basking trout of Manhattan." A more contemporary account puts Manhattan in the vast expanse of New York Harbor "like a smelt in a pan."

Its aboriginal inhabitants, Algonquians who used the island chiefly as a summer resort, considered the ground serviceable but nothing special. "Manahatn," they called it, meaning "a place of hills." Their mythology invoked a more particular idea of paradise, which they located somewhere near the modern-day environs of Trenton, New Jersey.

It has been less than 400 years, really, since Manhattan grew from a windswept Algonquian oystering station into the most densely populated place in America. On a purely physical level, the transformation has been extraordinary, a testimony to the almost insane industry of the island's inhabitants. The "place of hills" was leveled, graded, plumbed, bricked over, bored into, and erected upon until it resembled the monstrous hive of a race of hyperactive worker bees.

Yet that's only half the story. There was another transformation afoot, too, one that is harder to place precisely in time and space. As it grew, Manhattan somehow managed to assemble itself from more than just paving stones and granite blocks and steel girders. Dreams, hopes, and ambitions seemed to mark the place.

Dreams of Manhattan came not only from those who lived here, but from those who only imagined the place. In the opening of his 1927 novel *Amerika,* Kafka described the Statue of Liberty without ever having seen it. The island floated in the world's imagination like some golden fantasy. It came to symbolize all that is high and fine about the American experience, and much that is terrible.

This book covers the physical reality of Manhattan, the realm that can be reproduced on a map and talked about in terms of places to go and things to do. We also hope to communicate a little of the meta-Manhattan, too, both good and bad, the ectoplasmic island of people's dreams and the "terrible Jerusalem of the New World," as H. L. Mencken called it.

As overpowering as brick-and-stone Manhattan can be, its mythology has the paradoxical effect of grounding it, keeping it human. "My city!" Walt Whitman apostrophized. For all its pomp and circumstance as a cultural capital, as a center for commerce, fashion, the arts, sports, and tourism, it is still possible for an individual to feel possessive towards it.

There is a secret to approaching the place. Manhattan the Magnificent—the city of Broadway, of Fifth Avenue, of the Financial District—is almost too large and overpowering to love. Admire, yes; respect, certainly, with perhaps an occasional shudder of outright astonishment. People can't live on the whole island at once, so they have broken it down into a series of specific villages, which are more manageable, more livable, and, yes, more lovable than the larger whole.

Manhattan is the "global village," in Marshall McLuhan's original sense of a world brought close and made accessible. It is global in its cultural, commercial, and symbolic scope. It is global because of its amazing collection of peoples, gathered from every nation on the globe.

A 1920s aerial view of Manhattan illustrates how the island rests in New York harbor "like a smelt in a pan." (Underwood Photo Archives)

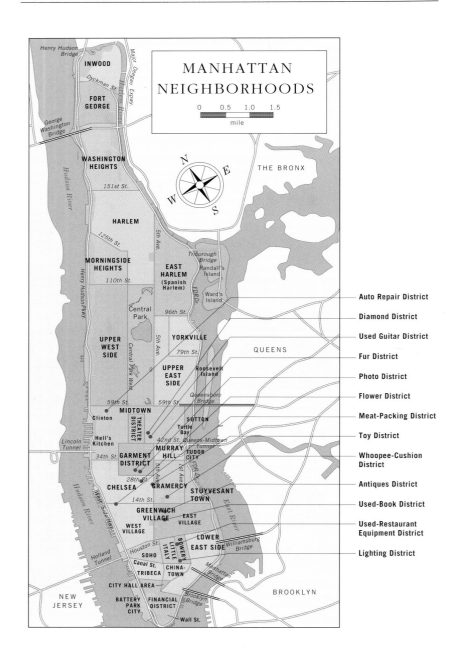

MANHATTAN
NEIGHBORHOODS

0   0.5   1.0   1.5
mile

Auto Repair District

Diamond District

Used Guitar District

Fur District

Photo District

Flower District

Meat-Packing District

Toy District

Whoopee-Cushion District

Antiques District

Used-Book District

Used-Restaurant Equipment District

Lighting District

At the same time, Manhattan is a village, or rather, as Alistair Cooke says, "the greatest collection of villages in the world." The way for a visitor to proceed, then —the way to proceed for anyone who wants to understand this amazing city—is to approach Manhattan the way people who live here do, neighborhood by neighborhood. "We'll have Manhattan," crooned Rodgers and Hart, and the way to have it is not all at once, but in small, manageable bites.

The great luxury that Manhattan extends to everyone is that of nearly inexhaustible choice. Most cities say, "Here's what we have." Manhattan asks, "What would you like?"

Architecture? The array here is staggering, not only in terms of stylistic range. The density of the island's construction is such that the proud ship of Manhattan itself has become one great architectural artifact. "Just the fact of too many buildings in too small a space," says master architect Philip Johnson, "makes it very exciting." As with a handful of other island cities around the world—Hong Kong, most notably—watery boundaries prevented Manhattan from building outward. The only other option for New Yorkers was to build vertically, and Manhattan soars. The Greek word for human means "they who look up," and Manhattan rewards those who lift their eyes with inspiring, hubris-enhancing cityscapes— steel-and-stone extravaganzas like the Empire State Building, slick glass boxes like the Lever Building, hallucinatory terra-cotta confections like Alwyn Court. Throughout the city there are marvelous architectural juxtapositions, the aristocratic Crown Building, for example, just around the corner from the arriviste Trump Tower.

Not passionate about architecture? How about dance? For much of the century, New York has been the world's number one city for dance. The enthralling dramas of George Balanchine and Jerome Robbins revitalizing ballet, Martha Graham's bold definition of modern movement, and the great political-artistic jetés of Russian defectors like Mikhail Baryshnikov during the Cold War were all played out against a Manhattan backdrop. Today, with Merce Cunningham and Paul Taylor both working in Manhattan, with younger modern dance companies goosing things from the edges, with New York City Ballet and American Ballet Theater appearing at Lincoln Center, with the Joffrey and Alvin Ailey and Dance Theater of Harlem—there's something worthwhile to choose from practically every week of the year.

(following pages) "What a glorious garden of wonders this would be, to any who was lucky enough to be unable to read."—G. K. Chesterton, on Times Square signage.

Enjoy
Coca-Cola

Coca-Cola

GET CHERRY COKE,
GET CHERRYFIED.

VAN WAGNER

RENAISSANCE HOTEL

Hungry? How about sausage and peppers in Little Italy, *chow fun* in China-town, or curry in the East Village? Of course, you might choose to nosh on a bagel, or you might prefer a power lunch at Le Cirque or the Four Seasons.

On and on it goes, the dizzying spread that Manhattan lays out all year around, painting and sculpture and photography and antiques, museums and events and historical sites, great restaurants and great shopping and great crowds. You can pick almost any discipline or art form, any pastime or hobby, any human endeavor at all. Manhattan, the gabby, garrulous Walt Whitman of cities, will have some-thing to say about it.

The place is so large and varied that the question for any writer approaching it becomes what to leave out. When Ralph Waldo Emerson said over a century ago that "New York is a sucked orange," he was talking about the fact that even back then, Manhattan had been pawed over pretty thoroughly by a long parade of writ-ers and artists. All art is selection, and everyone who has written about the place —and there have been many—has faced some hard choices.

This book includes the essential stops on the tourist trail, the museums, the shopping districts, the entertainment possibilities, the parks. Our impulse has been to slant the portrait toward the human side, the village side. We might give you an exhaustive tour of the Metropolitan Museum of Art (which gets two votes here for being the greatest art museum in the world), but we won't neglect to tell you about the charming children's playground on its grounds, with great brass bear sculptures.

To enjoy Manhattan you have to enjoy people, all kinds, people en masse, urban hermits, humans at their grandest, and humans at their weirdest. Here the tapestry is fully unrolled. "When you're tired of London, you're tired of life," said Samuel Johnson, and the same could be said of Manhattan. That brilliant phrasemaker, Anonymous, put it another way: "If you're bored in New York, you're boring."

E. B. White, the *New Yorker* writer and chronicler of New York, gives his formu-lation of the three human elements which make up the city's life. There are the com-muters—those millions of rushing workers who flood in and out of Manhattan every day—who give the city its velocity. There are the natives, the people who were born here and will die here. They give the city its solidity and permanence. And there are the transplants, the émigrés, the apprentice actors and writers and artists who come to Manhattan in pursuit of the ineffable. They give the city its dreams.

To E. B. White's formula we must, of late, add a fourth group: the marooned, the thousands of homeless souls who give the city a tang of despair. They are the most distinctive and visible symbol of the failures of urban living in the United States as it approaches the millennium.

What the decay of the streets obscures, however, is the astonishing transformation that New York City has accomplished in the past two or three decades— exactly the timeframe when most people were complaining that America's cities were "falling apart." In the face of fierce competition from other urban centers such as London and Tokyo, Manhattan has managed to become the headquarters of a new global economy, the premier city in a brave new world of international corporations, markets, and communications.

There are a lot of reasons why Manhattan came to prominence on the global and national stage. One is simply the location, beside a harbor that seemed to be designed by some patron saint of ship captains. Another is historical accident, which saw the skies over the city lit by the brilliant dynamo of America's century-long economic boom. Manhattan was simply the right place at the right time.

But today the harbor is moribund, with more shipping going inland to Albany, and the country's boom has long since decelerated, tempered by new economic realities. Why then does Manhattan endure and prosper? We like to think that the real reason for the city's incredible resilience is its devotion to a certain vision of human life that is open, egalitarian, and expansive. It is the embrace of Manhattan, the ability—the insistence, really—to say "Yes!" to whatever is handed it.

By the year 1650, barely 25 years after it was settled, when the population was only 4,500, there were already 18 languages spoken in Manhattan. Today, in what the sociologists call a "conurbation" of 19.7 million people—encompassing the entire metropolitan New York area which includes parts of upstate New York, New Jersey, Long Island, and Connecticut—over 90 languages are spoken, with newspapers in two dozen of them. No other place on the planet boasts such an amazing polyglot of people.

While we can't say all 90 of those tongues are heard in this book, we try to emulate the open, expansive vision of Manhattan. "It's a nice place to visit but I wouldn't want to live there," is an oft-repeated formulation about the place, but in fact the more your visit approximates what it's like to live here, the better it will be. This book attempts to give the visitor some sense of what it's like to exist as that anomalous creature, the Manhattanite.

What we want to leave readers with is some echo of Walt Whitman, so they can say along with him, about this place of boiling energy, superb paradox, and staggering hubris, "My city!"

H I S T O R Y

"THAT'S WHY THEY CALL IT NEW YORK," the *New York Times* quoted a spectator, witnessing the demolition of the old Penn Station. "Nothing's allowed to grow old here."

That's not entirely true, of course. There are glorious pockets of Manhattan where the past is remarkably well preserved. But to a startling degree, much of the industry that built Manhattan was applied toward eradicating anything that came before. Here was a city where the mercantile urge was absolute, and all other values had to bow before it. If there was a choice between history and commerce, commerce won.

The Europeans arrived, they conquered, they erased. The city's topography—its watercourses, hills, and shorelines the product of eons of geologic activity—was leveled, drained, channeled, graded, and smoothed. A satisfactory tabula rasa was presented to the builder and the effects of millions of years of time were removed as if by scourge.

Equally extreme has been the obliteration of the island's aboriginal culture. In the face of the European's windy ambitions, the inhabitants of Manhattan for several thousand years previous vanished like smoke. Signs of their passing were discarded or crushed as worthless. But the good colonial burghers were equally cavalier about their own historical spoor. Thus we are left to reconstruct the early history of Manhattan from incomplete records and shreds of evidence.

The island's bedrock foundation has allowed the city's skyscrapers to tower into the sky.

■ MANHATTAN BEDROCK

In its original, unmodified state, the landscape of the island was rugged and relatively hilly, abounding in low, abrupt slopes of some 100-130 feet, higher at the northern end of the island. Geologists describe Manhattan as a gneissoid ridge, with underlying beds of schist.

The 450-million-year-old bedrock of schist and gneiss—and one is schist as gneiss as the other—would eventually be pressed into service to support the foundations of the greatest collection of tall buildings the world has ever known. The immediately recognizable skyline of Manhattan—with a vast aggregation of skyscrapers in its midsection, and another, smaller concentration at its southern tip—is not an accident of urban design, but a function of geology.

Like a breaching whale, the Manhattan bedrock rises near the surface in Midtown (outcroppings can clearly be seen in Central Park). Then it dips back down below the accumulation of sediment, only to rise briefly again at the lower end of the island. Skyscrapers are most easily built where bedrock is close to the surface, so the Manhattan skyline follows this subterranean contour: the mini-Alps of Midtown, another range of towers around Wall Street, and a low-profile saddle of smaller buildings slung in between.

At the end of the last Ice Age, around 10,000 years ago by the archaeological evidence, groups of Paleo-Indians, or Stone Age Indians, began arriving on the Eastern Seaboard and began summering in Manhattan.

■ ALGONQUIANS

The natives of Manhattan were members of several of the hundreds of autonomous bands that hunted and fished the area. To the Indians themselves the only distinction worth noting was their specific clan or family. Anthropologists, however, have determined that these particular people were of the Algonquian linguistic family.

The Algonquians were a large and multifarious people, living in a sprawling territory that stretched from Montana and Alberta, Canada, in the west, south to northern Tennessee, and east to New England. In the northeast, their territory was obtruded upon by the Iroquois, a fact which caused a great deal of boundary warfare and scalp-taking. The Algonquians of the eastern woodlands, however, were no strangers to internecine battles, and one of their primary characteristics seems to be that when they were not warring with their neighbors, they were fighting among themselves.

Along the Hudson and the Mohawk rivers, there was a constant seesawing pressure from the mighty Iroquois Confederacy of the northern interior. These were the most well-organized and socially developed tribes in the whole of the East, highly efficient as fighting groups, and adroit at maintaining a civilized peace also. Later on, some of the governing principles of the Iroquois would find their way into the United States Constitution.

Among the people whom the Iroquois bedeviled were the Mahicans, including the Wappingers Confederacy. A small clan of this tribe, part of the Wickquaeskeek band, removed themselves far away from the Iroquois threat to live in what is now Westchester County and the Bronx. They were called by the tongue-crunching name of Reckgawawancs, after one of their *sachems*, or chieftains. They worshipped Kickeron as their supreme god, and feared Manitou, the horned snake, as their devil.

They were not much struck by Manhattan. Its chilly rock shelves and open hillsides were too exposed to the elements, to the winds which blew off the sea or down Mohicanituck, the great river. For most of them, the island was of use simply as a summer resort.

In summer, they would repair to villages and encampments on the island's shoreline. They were great seafood eaters, and downed so many clams, mussels, and oysters that by the end of the summer great mounds of shells formed beside their encampments, memories of feasts past. They fished with seine and gill nets, took deer and rabbit from the copious supply the island provided, and ate from small plots of corn, squash, and beans.

Even though the coastal corridor from New York to Boston was the most densely populated area of eastern North America in aboriginal times, there were never more than 5,000 Indians living on Manhattan Island, usually far fewer. The names and sites of various towns have been recorded: Naigianac, which would have been located at Corlear's Hook, between where the Manhattan and Brooklyn bridges are now; Sapokanican, on the west side, near Gansevoort Market; and Shorakapok, "the resting place," on the northern tip of the island.

The Algonquians of Manhattan—the Wappingers and the other bands who occasionally estivated there, including the Canarsee of Long Island and the Delaware from the western side of the Hudson—were uniformly described in early European literature as "devils," and perhaps to Western European eyes, that is what they looked like.

They were tall, with black hair and black eyes. They sometimes stained their skin with a saffron color and tattooed their faces with scenes from their dreams. An Algonquian male usually wore a scalplock, a single roach of stiffened hair, sometimes dyed red, with a lock trailing down as a goad to the enemy — as if to say, "take it if you can!" They burned the rest of the hair off their heads with red-hot stones.

Algonquian women wore a single braid, sometimes with a square cap of beaded shells. Both sexes wore leggings, hemp or leather breechclouts, and robes. These last were sometimes marvelously worked, of wild turkey feathers for men, and of beaded shells for women. The houses—made of bark, and resembling overturned bowls—were owned by, or identified with, specific women of the tribe, with the men associated only by marriage.

Given the unbroken expanse of concrete and asphalt it has become, it is a fantastic game to imagine what Manhattan Island was like before the Europeans arrived. The closest approximation in existence today might be certain rocky promontory islands off the Maine coast. Though covered with beech, locust, lime, and elm trees, the island was known mostly for its many stands of birch, which must have whitened the light in the forest like so many daytime moons. A pure spring ran year-round from the bluff on the island's northern tip, making the area a favored resting spot for locals.

■ VIKINGS

The first trans-Atlantic settlers to live among these aboriginal inhabitants may not have been Dutch. Basing their conclusions on no small amount of conjecture and a little fanciful embroidering of old Norse sagas, some historians conclude that the Vikings preceded other Europeans to Manhattan Island by some 500 years.

In A.D. 1010, a Norseman from Greenland named Thorfinn Karlsefensi planted a rag-tag colony which he called "Streamfjord" on the coast of North America. By comparing landscapes and directions, scholars have identified the place as Manhattan.

About 130 people, including Karlsefensi's new bride Gudrid, lived on the island for three years. The explorer himself continued down the Eastern Seaboard as far as Albemarle Sound in North Carolina, briefly setting up a colony at Powell Point. But Indians drove them away, and Karlsefensi returned to Streamfjord where he found a disgruntled male citizenry fighting over Gudrid and the few other women. Disgusted himself, Karlsefensi decamped for Greenland, and the Viking sojourn on Manhattan was over.

Norse settlers left behind no artifact, were reflected in no legend, and seemed to leave no impression at all upon the original inhabitants of the island. Indeed their presence is highly conjectural, and when they left it was if they had never been there. For half a millennium afterwards, no other foreign intrusion disturbed the suzerainty of the people who lived in the area.

■ EUROPEAN EXPLORATION

That the official European "discoverer" of Manhattan was later eaten by cannibals may be considered simply the first note in a history of high irony that has kept New York entertained through much of its existence. Giovanni da Verrazano was a Florentine-born noble in the service of the French king and the silk merchants of Lyons, who were eager to find passage to the fabled riches of Asia. Or, as Verrazano put it, to "the happy shores of Cathay."

Here is how he describes his brief but memorable brush with primeval Manhattan:

> *We* found a very good piece of land situated within two small prominent hills, in the midst of which flowed to the sea a very great river which was deep at the mouth . . . . We went with the small boat, entering the said river to the land, which we found much peopled. The people . . . clothed with

the feathers of various colors, came toward us joyfully, shouting with admiration, showing us where we could land the boat more safely. We entered the river, within the land, about half a league, where we saw it formed a very beautiful lake with a circuit of about three leagues. They [the Indians] went across, going from one part to another, in as many as thirty of their little barges. Innumerable people passed from one shore to the other in order to see us. In an instant, as is wont to happen in navigation, a gale of unfavorable wind blew in from the sea. We were forced to return to the ship, and left the said land with much regret because of its commodiousness and beauty, thinking it was not without some properties of value, for all its hills showed indications of minerals.

And that was that. The river was, of course, the Hudson, the place "within two small prominent hills" was the Narrows, now named after Verrazano, and the "very beautiful lake" was Upper New York Bay (a French nautical league equals about 2.2 miles, and the Upper Bay is indeed about five miles across). He christened the place Angoulême, after the given name of the French king, Henri Angoulême.

This fully documented European visit was a decided anti-climax, not only for Verrazano but for the inhabitants of the area, who no doubt would have wished for a closer commune with their visitors. *La Dauphine,* a 100-ton ship of the royal French navy, which Verrazano borrowed courtesy of the French king, François I, was the largest vessel that had ever appeared in those waters. It must have appeared to the natives as something from a dream.

That the *Dauphine* appeared at all was almost a miracle. Verrazano's 1524 voyage was not only a wonderful feat of seamanship, it was a marvel of good luck. Departing from Dieppe, France, on the English Channel, he crossed the Atlantic smoothly, sticking as far north as he could to avoid France's enemy, the Spanish. He made landfall at Cape Fear, North Carolina, and sailed up the coast to Newfoundland in a little over three and a half months, with favorable winds and without serious bad weather.

The caution Verrazano displayed in New York, when he turned tail at the slightest hint of ill wind, continued to make his journey a catalog of missed opportunities, including his missing the Chesapeake and Delaware bays altogether. As it was, Samuel Eliot Morison, the Harvard historian of the European discovery of America, calls Verrazano's failure to explore the Hudson "the greatest opportunity missed by any North American explorer."

■ HISTORY TIMELINE ■

1524   Italian explorer Giovanni da Verrazano is the first European to make documented journey to New York Harbor.

1525   Esteban Gomez, a black Portuguese mariner employed by Spain, sails into New York's harbor in search of gold and silver.

1609   Henry Hudson, sailing for the Dutch, enters what is now the Hudson River.

1624   Belgian and then Dutch settlers arrive in New York City.

1625   The Dutch West India Company erects the city's first office building on Whitehall Street. The following year Peter Minuit, first director general of New Amsterdam, purchases Manhattan from local Indian tribe for knives, tools, and cloth.

1647   Peter Stuyvesant, known for his wooden leg and despotic rule, becomes governor of the Dutch colony.

1654   First Jewish settlers arrive after being expelled from Portuguese Brazil.

1674   England trades Holland the South American colony of Surinam for Manhattan and names the territory New York.

1702   Queen Anne of England appoints her cousin, Lord Cornbury—who enjoys dressing as a woman—governor of New York.

1754   King's College founded (now Columbia University).

1770   First blood shed in the War of Independence at Battle of Golden Hill.

1776   New York City falls to British, who torch Manhattan.

1789   George Washington takes presidential oath on balcony of the Federal Hall and New York City becomes the nation's first capital.

1792   Two dozen traders sitting beneath a buttonwood tree on what is now Wall Street make a pact setting forth rules for trade in securities.

1801   *New York Post* founded by Alexander Hamilton.

1835   Great Fire: Almost all of Lower Manhattan is destroyed.

1851   *New York Times* first published.

1853   New York City hosts the Crystal Palace Exposition, America's first world's fair.

1857   First elevator installed in New York City. Work begins on Central Park.

1859 Cooper Union, founded as the country's first coeducational college, open to all races and creeds. The following year presidential candidate Abraham Lincoln, a dark horse, delivers a pivotal speech at the college.

1863 In response to Civil War draft, riots rage throughout the city.

1870 First subway constructed by Alfred Ely Beach, inventor of the typewriter.

1873 Boss Tweed is convicted after years of corruption in Tammany Hall.

1877 Alexander Graham Bell demonstrates the telephone.

1883 Brooklyn Bridge opens, connecting Brooklyn to Manhattan.

1886 Statue of Liberty erected in New York Harbor.

1896 First bagel sold in New York City.

1911 Fire at Triangle Shirtwaist Company kills hundreds of workers, mostly young Jewish and Italian women. The tragedy sparks labor reform.

1920 Babe Ruth joins the New York Yankees.

1923 Jack Dempsey defends his title against Argentinean fighter Luis Angel Firpo.

1929 Stock market crashes; Great Depression begins.

1931 Completion of Empire State Building, then the world's tallest at 102 stories.

1933 Reformer Fiorello La Guardia begins three terms as mayor; Prohibition ends.

1935 The first public housing project in the United States erected on the Lower East Side.

1947 Jackie Robinson, the major leagues' first black baseball player, signs with the Brooklyn Dodgers.

1969 Police raid Stonewall Inn for violating state liquor law banning sale of alcohol to homosexuals—and the patrons fight back.

1970 In the first New York City marathon, 127 runners circle Central Park four times.

1975 New York City hits hard times; bailed out by Felix Rohatyn's plan that saves the city from defaulting on $13 billion in bonds.

1990 Census records 1,488,000 residents in Manhattan; over 90 languages spoken.

If Verrazano did not pursue his opportunity upon entering New York Harbor, his French patrons squandered the chance for imperial expansion he presented them. François I was soon distracted by a disastrous war against Charles II in Italy, and the silk merchants of Lyons were not impressed with the samples of tobacco and other New World artifacts that Verrazano brought back.

Four years later, in 1528, off the Caribbean island of Guadeloupe, Verrazano's caution deserted him, and he waded ashore into the arms of a tribe of ferocious Caribs. While his brother and partner Girolamo watched in horror from a long boat offshore, the Indians killed the European discoverer of Manhattan and ate him on the spot, "down to the tiniest bone."

New York Harbor did receive some desultory French visitors including Jehan Cossin, notable for having first mapped Manhattan. But generally, the French allowed the legacy of Verrazano (whom they called "Jean Verason") to lapse into obscurity. It took the large Italian-American community in New York to resurrect this native son, put up a statue of him (in Battery Park, facing his eponymous Narrows) and celebrate his discoveries. A year after Verrazano's brief visit, another European, Esteban Gomez, a Portuguese Moor sailing for Spain, also sighted the magnificent bay and the little island floating therein.

Then, for a long time, nothing.

Wars in Europe, the vagaries of navigation, the immense logistical effort required for any colonial enterprise kept the Europeans from Manhattan for most of the sixteenth century. For all the scarcity of the newcomers, the Algonquians at this time were like swimmers in a pool in which the plug has been pulled. They might have felt the faint tug of the sea change coming.

It was not until September 2, 1609, that it arrived, in the form of a tiny, 74-foot sailing brig called the *Half Moon*. It was piloted by an Englishman, Henry Hudson, in service to a Dutch master. He came to the area, like Verrazano and most early explorers before him, looking for something else. (The similarities between Verrazano and Hudson are striking: they both sought passage to Asia, were employed by foreign governments, and came to violent ends—Hudson during his exploration of the bay named in his honor, when he was set adrift by a mutinous crew.) The Dutch East India Company, chartered in 1602 by the Dutch government, had hired "Hendrick Hudson" to search for the Northwest Passage to the Spice Islands of the Orient.

According to a contemporary history, Hudson "entered into as fine a river as can be found, wide and deep, with good anchorages on both sides." He laid in on the west side of the harbor, in Hoboken Bay, amid marshes thick with waterfowl. There he was visited by friendly Raritan Indians from a Delaware tribe of Algonquians.

Looking through his spyglass across the expanse of river, he could see other aboriginals, Mahicans, standing in canoes among the reeds at the northern end of Manhattan Island, in what the Dutch would call Spuyten Duyvil Creek. A few days later, in an encounter with this group, he kidnapped two Indians, intending to take them back to Holland for display.

The *Half Moon* was no more than a yacht, really, shallow-drafted and smaller than the *Mayflower.* Hudson was able to use it to explore the Hudson as far as Albany. On his way upriver, one of his Mahican captives drowned, and the other escaped and made his way back to Manhattan. When Hudson decided the river

A painting by Frederic A. Chapman depicts the arrival of Hudson's ship, the Half Moon, *in the bay of New York in September of 1609. (Library of Congress)*

could not be the fabled Northwest Passage after all, he turned back to the sea, finding an unfriendly reception when he retraced his route.

His Indian captive had raised the alarm about the aggressive tendencies of the visitors. On October 6, as the *Half Moon* hove into view in the river above Manhattan, a half-dozen canoe-loads of Mahicans shot out from the reeds at Spuyten Duyvil. Hudson had to use his cannon to fight them off.

Thus the battle was joined, which would be taken up intermittently over the next half century, until the end of Indian hostilities in the New York area. Indeed, the local Wappingers (of which the Mahicans were a tribe) still recalled Hudson and his perfidy some 15 years later, when they met with colonists who'd come to settle New Amsterdam.

■ COLONIAL ERA

Unlike the French with Verrazano, the Dutch immediately followed up on the possibilities associated with Hudson's 1609 visit to New York. The next year and

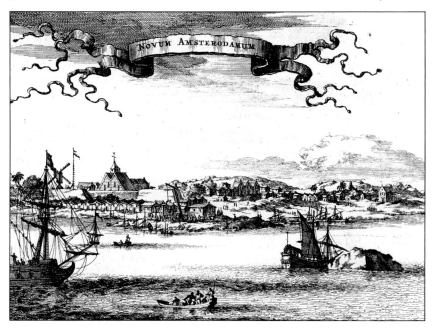

An early engraving shows the Dutch colony of New Amsterdam. (Library of Congress)

for almost every succeeding year until a permanent settlement was established, the New Netherlands Company sent vessels to trade for furs with the Indians. Adrian Block, the Dutch captain of the *Tyger*, navigated the East River—which he named "Hell Gate" for its treacherous currents—and was the first to chart Manhattan as a separate island. When the *Tyger* burned, Block spent the winter of 1613 on the island and built another ship with which to sail back to Holland.

In 1624, another government-chartered trading cartel, the Dutch West Indies Company, established the first permanent European presence on Manhattan. Yet the original settlers on the island were not Dutch

Peter Minuit, Dutch director general of the colony of New Amsterdam. (Library of Congress)

at all, but Belgians. Fleeing religious persecution, about a hundred French-speaking Protestant Walloons came to the New World and headed for Fort Orange, at the present-day site of Albany. Eight families stayed behind on Governor's Island, and in the next year, 30 Dutch families arrived. Subsequently they all moved to lower Manhattan and the colonial experiment of New Amsterdam began in earnest.

The Dutch director general of the colony, Peter Minuit ("Peter Midnight"), liked to do things by the book, so he formalized the colony's possession of Manhattan by purchasing it from the Indians. In trade he gave them knives, beads, and ceramics, cloth, and tools—not the "trinkets" that are generally reported. The transaction had other aspects enshrined in pseudo-history which bear re-examining.

Take the oft-quoted price that Minuit paid for Manhattan, for example. The goods he gave the Canarsees were said to be worth 60 guilders, translated into the "$24" that endures to this day. By what mysterious method of monetary conversion was this number calculated? Yet it has taken a solemn place in the lexicon of history, and is offered up as evidence of either aboriginal naiveté or imperialist exploitation. (In the 1970s, when New York City was on the verge of bankruptcy, representatives of the Algonquians wryly offered to buy Manhattan back—for $24. "Guilt feelings have plagued us all," the Algonquians professed. "We knew it was a bad investment when we sold it.") To the original Indians, however, metal blades and tools and ceramic pots were priceless. Furthermore, to Indians, what could be traded was not the plot of earth, but temporary use of its resources. The Canarsees understood the deal as an agreement not to interfere with the Dutch colonials' fishing and hunting. The two peoples were trading apples and oranges.

At any rate, the joke was on the Dutch. The Indians they were dealing with, most likely Canarsees from Long Island, did not even "own" Manhattan. The Wickquaeskeek band had control of the northern two-thirds of the island, but Minuit was ignorant of such subtle gradations of Indian clan ties. Indeed, much to the consternation of the Europeans, the Native Americans of the area often would end up "selling" the same turf over and over again.

Land grab or no land grab, the little colony hung on. Its timber resources were prodigious, and Minuit built what was at the time the world's largest vessel, the 800-ton *New Netherland.* It evoked wonder in European ports when it arrived there. Minuit, though, had a run-in with the home office and was fired, and like Henry Hudson before him, disappeared at sea.

A succession of incompetent or corrupt governors followed. One of them, the bellicose Willem van Kieft, arranged for a massacre of the local Algonquians at Corlear's Hook, touching off a five-year-long war with the Indians. The superior firepower of the Dutch soon prevailed. Except for intermittent rebellions, such as the massacres of 1655 and the Peach Tree War (when a colonist killed an Indian he thought was stealing peaches), indigenous resistance to the colony ended by the end of the seventeenth century. Remnants of the clan that held the island upon the European arrival faded into the populations of the north, effectively eliminated as a human community.

It was under Kieft, however, that black slaves, first brought to the island in 1625, began to be manumitted in 1644. In general, New Amsterdam had a fairly enlightened policy toward slavery—"comparatively mild" was the gently ironic phrase that James Weldon Johnson used. One rather twisted example of the Dutch colony's relative kindness was the tradition of an annual "free day": on Pinkster Fete, celebrated the third week of Easter, slaves were freed for the day.

Peter Stuyvesant, who arrived to take control of a shabby, struggling, miserable town in 1647, gave it over to the British 17 years later as a thriving, well-

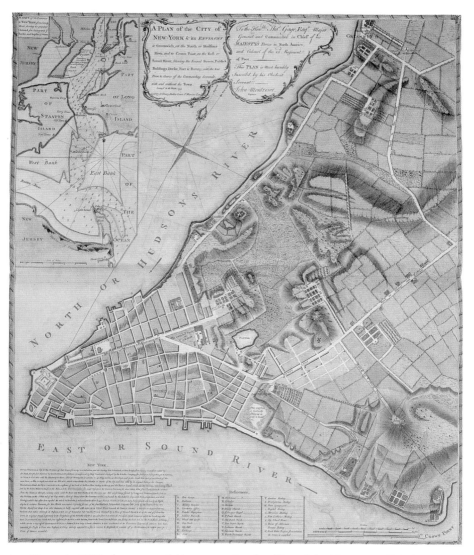

Drawn in 1765, the purpose of this map was largely military. John Montresor, a British army engineer, made it hastily in order to help the royal troops keep control over the city's riotous population which opposed the stamp tax.

Peter Stuyvesant, the last Dutch governor of New Amsterdam. (Library of Congress)

established community. Irascible, authoritarian, misanthropic Stuyvesant hobbled about his domain on a wooden leg, organizing improvements including a paid police force, a street plan, and a reorganized civic apparatus. But his iron hand was more a handicap than his wooden leg, and when English warships appeared in the harbor in 1664, the colonists were so sick of the dictatorial Stuyvesant that they surrendered to the British without a fight.

Control of Manhattan seesawed back and forth between England and Holland during the Anglo-Dutch Sea Wars of the midseventeenth century. The Dutch retook the colony in 1672, and renamed it New Orange. In 1674, however, the British traded its claims to Surinam in South America for Manhattan, one colony for another. Conventional wisdom of the time was that the Dutch got much the better deal, since the rich forests of Surinam would be forever worth more than a hardscrabble colony numbering less than 2,000 souls, whether it was called New Amsterdam or New Orange.

Charles II of England wanted to call it New York, after his brother the Duke of York (later James II). Under the English, the colony found itself in a similar predicament as with the Dutch, increasingly dissatisfied with the colonial yoke. An abortive move against British rule in 1691, called Leisler's Rebellion after the hapless Capt. Jacob Leisler who led it, was less a measure of the urge toward independence than of intrigue between the Catholic upper classes and the Protestant plebes. Leisler wound up hanged for his trouble.

The English governors were an uneven lot, some of them decidedly eccentric. Witness Lord Cornbury, who enjoyed riding his horse into taverns and ordering a drink for himself and water for his steed. At a party he extolled the virtues of his wife's earlobes, demanding that every man present feel for himself. He liked to dress in women's clothes, explaining that since he was cousin and representative of Queen Anne, it was proper that he show the colonials what their sovereign might look like. All this might have been forgiven, were it not for Lord Cornbury's proclivity for debt. He was tossed into prison and shipped back to England.

■ INDEPENDENCE

It was corrupt and despotic rulers like Lord Cornbury who fed colonial unrest and contributed to a growing anti-British sentiment that swelled to climax in the Revolutionary War. Although New York was the most pro-British of the thirteen colonies, rebellious fervor in Manhattan was potent, and when the Declaration of Independence was read on the steps of the old city hall on July 9, 1776, the crowd reacted violently, pulling down a statue of King George. The fledgling nation had declared itself, and the British were not about to wish it Godspeed. War began almost immediately, with Lord Cornwallis commanding British troops and a relatively unknown Virginia planter, George Washington, leading the Americans. Control of the Hudson River was deemed essential by the British, and England's General Howe concentrated all his efforts on securing Manhattan, approaching the island via Brooklyn in the hot summer of 1776.

The somewhat beleaguered position of the American forces can be deduced from the tone of a dispatch from Gen. George Washington on the eve of the conflict:

At the present time my forces consist entirely of Delaware militia and smallwoods Marylanders—a total of 5,000 troops to stand against 25,000 of the enemy, and I begin to notice that many of us are lads under 15 and old men, none of whom could truly be called soldiers . . . . As I write these words, the enemy is plainly in sight beyond the river. How it will end only Providence can direct, but dear God, what brave men I shall lose before this business ends.

The British landed at Kip's Bay on September 15, and Washington's rag-tag army ran like rabbits. Pursued westward across the island by the more formidable redcoats, they could do no more than fight courageous but doomed delaying actions, one of them at McGowan's Pass in what is today Central Park. By fall, Washington was in retreat, his army surviving only because of heroic measures taken in the Battle of Harlem Heights. The American army abandoned the island to the British, retreating north to West Point.

In New York, life during wartime took on an insular opulence in an otherwise threadbare world. As with many popular revolts, the empire held the cities, but the countryside was in the hands of the American irregulars—whom today we would call guerrillas. Manhattan became an island in more senses than one, a doomed outpost surrounded by a hostile sea of revolution. British officers could hold gala balls and great feasts, but nothing could entirely obscure the pervading siege mentality.

Manhattan—already more pro-British than not—became a haven for Tory Loyalists, mostly wealthy merchants and shippers, who prospered as suppliers to the British army. Those insurrectionists unable or unwilling to flee suffered the indignities of occupation, including the forced quartering of British troops in their homes. The occupiers put the torch to Manhattan anyway, burning a quarter of it, including Trinity Church. Meanwhile, the colonial forces stood their ground, defeating the enemy in battle and on the guerrilla front. With the help of the French, the Americans delivered the final blow at Yorktown in 1782.

By the time the Loyalists and British surrendered Manhattan to the Americans on November 25, 1783—eight months after the end of the war—Manhattan was at half its pre-war population of 25,000, ravaged and decimated, its economy in ruins. From Trinity Church to the Battery, the city was nothing more than a charred swath. Its northern limit effectively ended at the old city hall (today the Federal Hall National Memorial at Nassau and Wall streets), although there were a few scattered outposts farther up the island.

Two years later, New York City had recovered enough of its grandeur to become the capital of the United States. Meanwhile, New York delegates, led by Alexander Hamilton, participated vigorously in the Constitutional Convention of 1787, arguing for a stronger centralized government; Hamilton's Federalist views ultimately carried the day. On April 23, 1789, George Washington returned to the city in triumph to take an oath as the country's first President. New York City would retain the title of capital only five years, from 1785 to 1790. Despite the ceremonial honor, there was a clear sense that New York's destiny lay elsewhere.

Washington takes the oath of office as first President of the United States on the balcony of Federal Hall (the old city hall) on April 23, 1789. (Library of Congress)

ALEXANDER HAMILTON

Alexander Hamilton may have been the quintessential eighteenth-century New Yorker, the kind of restless, questing man drawn to the energy and political excitement of Manhattan, elevated by the city, and elevating it in the process.

A brilliant orator and essayist, ceaseless promulgator of a strong central government, he performed Herculean duties to assure the creation of the United States of America out of what was then a loose coterie of territorial fiefdoms. When he was cut down at age 49 by political rival Aaron Burr in a duel, New York was robbed of its first citizen, and the new country lost a founding father and perhaps a future President.

Hamilton typified the Manhattan experience in that he came here from somewhere else. He was born in West Indies, on the island of Nevis, in 1755, an illegitimate son of a Scottish aristocrat. At that point in time, some of the old Dutch "triangle trade"—rum to the colonies, cotton to England, slaves to the West Indies—still survived, and Hamilton hitched a ride on it to arrive in Boston in 1773.

New York was a not a natural choice for a young man on the make—Boston and Philadelphia were much higher profile cities then—but somehow Hamilton understood its fundamental importance to colonial America. Enrolled in King's College (the present-day Columbia University), he became a student leader, a veritable rabble-rouser for independence from England. One of Hamilton's fiery speeches to the student body forced the school's Tory dean to flee, fearing for his life.

During the Revolutionary War, Hamilton proved a brilliant military leader, contributing most notably to victories at Monmouth and Yorktown. As Gen. George Washington's aide-de-camp and eventual amanuensis, Hamilton shaped the thinking (and many of the speeches) of the nation's first President.

His true provenance was not guns but words and ideas. All his life, Hamilton would demonstrate the ability to sway people with oratory and carefully reasoned essays. His contribution to the *Federalist Papers* (written with James Madison and John Jay) was fundamental in changing the course of the young republic, unifying it into a more cohesive whole.

As Secretary of the Treasury, it was Hamilton who first put the fledgling country on a firm financial footing, chartering the Bank of New York on the model of the Bank of England. Even Thomas Jefferson, long Hamilton's political foe, characterized him as "really a colossus" of the opposition. Hamilton almost single-handedly carried the day on a number of important issues, from ratification of the U.S. Constitution to neutrality in the war between France and England.

Thus it was a tantamount to a national tragedy when, on July 11, 1804, Hamilton met with Aaron Burr in Weehawken, New Jersey, in a duel that would cost him his life. Hamilton was opposed to dueling (partly because his son had been killed in a duel previously), and shot his pistol harmlessly into the air. His arch-rival Burr, however, demonstrated no such moral nicety, and Hamilton died the next day from a mortal wound. Following are sites associated with Hamilton's life:

Site of King's College (later Columbia University), Murray, Church, Barclay, and Greenwich streets. Hamilton graduated here in 1778, after a high-profile student career that featured membership in several pro-independence groups.

Site of Hamilton's house, Wall Street at Broad. Hamilton lived here on the south side of Wall Street during the post Revolutionary War years; his rival Burr lived a half block away.

Museum of the City of New York, 1220 Fifth Avenue (between 104th and 105th streets). A second-floor room exhibits memorabilia of the intense father-son political relationship between Hamilton and George Washington.

Statue of Hamilton, NW of the Metropolitan Museum of Art, Central Park. Carl Conrad's granite rendering is of a dynamic, youthful Hamilton.

Bank of New York and Trust Company, 48 Wall Street, a graceful Georgian edifice (the interior space is superb) that represents one of the many headquarters buildings erected over the years by the bank Hamilton chartered.

The *New York Post,* 210 South Street (between Catherine and Market streets). The tabloid makes much of its founding by Hamilton in 1801, even sporting a medallion-sized portrait of him in its logo.

Hamilton Square, Hamilton Place and West 140th Street. Marking the beginning of Hamilton Heights. The nomenclature of the Heights of Manhattan reflects a political reality, with Hamilton just below Washington.

Hamilton Grange, 287 Convent Avenue at 141st Street. Hamilton's summer residence, where he was living when he was killed by Burr. The National Park Service, which maintains the home, operates a small museum inside it. A statue of Hamilton is in front.

Trinity Churchyard, Rector and Broadway. The grave of Hamilton is in the southern sector, 40 feet from Broadway and clearly visible through the iron railing along Rector Street.

The city began to grow. It did so with a rapidity that was in those days unheard of—adding to itself as a magnet does when iron filings attach themselves to it. At the time of Washington's inauguration, 33,216 people lived in New York City (and thus in Manhattan, for until 1898 Manhattan and New York City were coterminous). Fifteen years later, at the turn of the century, the population would be twice that, and the old northern boundary line of City Hall long since roared past. Growth begat more growth. The magnet was money.

Manhattan's true ideal, tied to its great harbor, its trading history, and its flinty bedrock soul, would always be the commercial imperative.

In one sense business was a great leveler. In another it was social Darwinism at its worst. In post-Revolution New York City, those who were industrious or clever enough made great fortunes. Cornelius Vanderbilt began with a single ferryboat on Staten Island, transporting passengers to Manhattan for 10 cents. By the time he was 17, he owned a fleet of ferryboats and was well on his way to being a millionaire. On the other side of the coin were the wretched of Manhattan, who lived miserable existences in the shadow of great wealth.

Devotion to trade determined how New York City would grow for the next hundred years. More than any other great city in the world (London is a distant second, or perhaps today's Bangkok), here was a place where the urbanizing impulse could grow unchecked by any coherent program of restraint. The island was built close and narrow, its streets squeezed small to make more room for real estate.

From its beginnings New York was a utilitarian city, a no-nonsense commercial zone devoted to capitalist practice above all others. Comparable cities on the Continent might have broad avenues or generous plazas, pleasant prospects giving out to wide, engaging vistas. None of that for Manhattan. Civic amenities were wrung from an obdurate ruling class, which viewed any departure from strict practicality—and any check on its commercial impulses—with almost hysterical suspicion.

Even the city's 1811 grid plan, its major claim to urban design, was adopted primarily as a way to render money-making more efficient. There were more east-west streets included in the plan, for example, than north-south avenues, because commercial traffic ran river to river. The squares which punctuate Broadway are not so much concessions to the public need for open space as design imperatives when one broad thoroughfare crosses another. Only Central Park can be seen as a major departure from the idea of the city as a tool rather than an environment.

The towers of the World Trade Center rise above the graveyard of St. Paul's Chapel in testimony to two centuries of urban development.

Oddly enough, all this nineteenth-century utilitarianism produced a city which had more romance, more dreams, more spirit attached to it than almost any other. Almost in spite of itself, Manhattan stumbled into a golden age.

■ THE MAGNET OF MONEY

By the middle of the nineteenth century, many of the developments which were to make New York a world-class city were already in place. In 1801, Alexander Hamilton founded the *New York Post*—not the city's first newspaper, but the oldest one still publishing. The New York Stock Exchange began in 1792 as traders gathered under a buttonwood tree near its present-day site of business. In the first decades of the century, the Erie Canal opened and Robert Fulton pioneered steam power, both improvements immeasurably increasing transportation opportunities and the reach of New York's commercial power.

European immigrants continued to pour in: an average of 4,000 a year during the 1820s, a total of 14,000 in 1830 alone. The German revolutions of the 1840s, the Irish Potato Famine of 1846–51, and other political upheavals on the Continent served to spur emigration to America. From 1840 to 1856, three million immigrants arrived, representing a never-again-equaled ratio of newcomers to the existing population.

With new political realities came grudging social reform and cultural opportunities. Full suffrage for white males was granted in 1826, and slavery in New York State was outlawed a year later. The New York Philharmonic and the Metropolitan Opera were formed, and a nascent literary scene developed, spurred by Washington Irving, Edgar Allan Poe, Herman Melville, and James Fenimore Cooper.

It would be hard to underestimate the galloping vitality of Manhattan as it prepared to enter its golden age, but it would be just as hard for modern sensibilities to comprehend the squalor and misery that were the flip side of growth. The Five Points area (the intersection of Baxter, Worth, and Mulberry streets, near present-day Foley Square) developed into an incredible morass of poverty, crime, and disease. Charles Dickens, a chronicler of the slums of London and the Continent, said on his visit to America that Five Points compared in misery to anything he had ever seen:

> *What* place is this, to which the squalid street conducts us? A kind of square of leprous houses, some of which are attainable only by crazy

wooden steps without . . . . These narrow ways diverging right and left, and reeking everywhere with dirt and filth. Such lives as are led here, bear the same fruit here as elsewhere. The coarse and bloated faces at the doors have counterparts at home [in England] and all the world over. Debauchery has made the very houses prematurely old. See how the rotten beams are tumbling down, and the patched and broken windows seem to scowl dimly, like eyes that have been hurt in drunken frays. Many of these pigs live here. Do they ever wonder why their masters walk up right instead of going on all-fours, and why they talk instead of grunting?

Those pigs Dickens was talking about were the city's quasi-official street cleaners, and in 1817 there were 20,000 roaming the city, scarfing down the litter and offal they found on the pavements. All this crowding and inattention to public hygiene

This photograph of a Salvation Army lodging house in 1897 illustrates how poverty and homelessness have long been an ugly facet of Manhattan life. (Museum of the City of New York)

unleashed a series of cholera and yellow fever epidemics that decimated the city. But it was not until 1896, due to the crusading efforts of photographer-activist Jacob Riis, that Five Points was leveled.

As the mid-century rolled around, Manhattan's urban sprawl had reached 23rd Street, with farflung outposts to the north. Although high society in New York had started to solidify into the kind of elaborate caste system portrayed in Edith Wharton's *The Age of Innocence,* New York was still comparatively a wide-open town. In 1854 a Rosa Parks–style civil suit, brought by Elizabeth Jennings against a streetcar company, opened public transportation to blacks.

It's not surprising that the booming city attracted its share of predators. The most notorious one was born in 1823 on Cherry Street, and rose through the ranks of the Democratic party to head one of the most corrupt and long-running political machines of all times. This was William Marcy "Boss" Tweed, the head of Tammany Hall. An erstwhile fraternal organization (devoted to "St. Tammany," a bogus Iroquois chieftain, in rude parody of upper-class organizations named after saints), Tammany Hall devolved into a graft-generating machine par excellence.

A Thomas Nast cartoon from Harper's Weekly *in 1871 depicts figures from the Tammany Hall scandal passing the blame. "Boss" Tweed is pictured on the left. (New-York Historical Society)*

Wall Street, Half Past Two O'clock, Oct. 13, 1857, *painted by James H. Cafferty and Charles G. Rosenberg, depicts one of the city's early financial panics. (Museum of the City of New York)*

Tweed and his cronies looted the city of $160 million over the years, spending $10,000 of the city's money on $75 worth of pencils, for example, and inflating the bill on the courthouse north of City Hall (derisively known as "Tweed Courthouse" to this day) to $12 million. Tweed's reign did have salutary side effects perhaps unintended by him, and quite apart from his wide-ranging contributions to charities. Because its power base comprised the teeming wards of the Lower East Side, Tammany Hall busily registered to vote thousands of newly arrived immigrants, involving them, however shadily, in the political process.

Reformers repeatedly assailed Tammany and Tweed, to which he would disdainfully sneer, "Well, what are you going to do about it?" Tweed's grip was finally broken by the combined efforts of reformers like Henry Ward Beecher, political cartoonist Thomas Nast, and the *New York Times*, which was founded in 1851 and cut its teeth on the Tweed scandals. Boss Tweed fled the country to avoid prosecution, but astoundingly was recognized by police in Spain from his portrayal in Thomas Nast's cartoons. He died in debtor's prison.

■ CIVIL WAR TO THE GAY NINETIES

In the years immediately preceding the Civil War, New York City was prime battleground for the Great Debate over slavery. From his pulpit at Plymouth Church in Brooklyn, Henry Ward Beecher led a fiery abolitionist charge. A tall, awkward political newcomer, Abraham Lincoln, wearing a tight black frock coat and a new pair of boots, made the speech of his political life at Manhattan's Cooper Union early in 1860. The words of his famed "right makes might" speech were printed by five newspapers the next day, sending Lincoln further along the path to the Presidency.

For all that, Tammany Hall and the Democratic leadership of New York City resisted Republican inroads. The shippers and exporters of Manhattan feared a war would disrupt the flow of cotton from the South. "The City of New York," read an editorial in the *Evening Post* the same month as Lincoln's Cooper Union speech, "belongs almost as much to the South as to the North."

New York is traditionally portrayed as a stronghold of copperheads (Confederate sympathizers) during the Civil War, and it is true that there was strong sentiment on both sides. The horrendous draft riots that gripped Manhattan during the conflict, however, were not so much pro-South as a reaction against the iniquities of the conscription law. Poor Irish laborers, who could not afford

ABRAHAM LINCOLN AT COOPER UNION

In February 1860, Illinois representative Abraham Lincoln was invited to speak at Cooper Union. Running against Stephen Douglas, Lincoln was the dark horse in the Presidential campaign but his address, an analysis of the anti-slavery movement, was a staggering success. By the time Lincoln had delivered his concluding remarks (printed below) he had captivated his audience. Abraham Lincoln won New York, and nine months later, the Presidency.

Neither let us be slandered from our duty by false accusations against us, nor frightened from it by menaces of destruction to the government, nor of dungeons to ourselves. Let us have faith that right makes might and in that faith let us, to the end, dare to do our duty, as we understand it.

The following day, Tribune *editor Horace Greeley printed his response to the event:*

The speech of Abraham Lincoln at the Cooper Institute last evening was one of the happiest and most convincing political arguments ever made in this City, and was addressed to a crowded and most appreciating audience. Since the days of Clay and Webster, no man has spoken to a larger assemblage of the intellect and mental culture of our City. Mr. Lincoln is one of Nature's orators, using his rare powers solely and effectively to elucidate and to convince, though their inevitable effect is to delight and electrify as well. We present herewith a very full and accurate report of this Speech; yet the tones, the gestures, the kindling eye and mirth-provoking look, defy the reporter's skill. The vast assemblage frequently rang with cheers and shouts of applause, which were prolonged and intensified at the close. No man ever before made such an impression on his first appeal to a New York audience . . . .

the $300 to buy their way out of the draft, burned and looted for a four-day stretch.

Despite Tammany's plunderings and the disruptions of the Civil War, New York City continued to prosper and grow. The face of the city was changing quickly. The firm of McKim, Mead & White, the greatest architectural concern in the country, formed in 1879 and would transform Manhattan with Beaux Arts masterpieces. Thomas Edison began supplying electricity to homes in 1882, and a decade later the first great blazing advertising displays of Times Square were erected. The Brooklyn Bridge connected the country's most populous cities—Brooklyn and Manhattan—in 1883.

Two developments that made Manhattan what it is today occurred with relatively little fanfare. In 1857, Elisha Graves Otis installed the first elevator, or "vertical railroad" as it was originally called. And in 1888, the world's first steel-framed skyscraper, the Tower Building, gave Otis's railroad the "track" to run on. It was erected by architect Bradford Gilbert on Exchange Place near Broadway. Together, the elevator and skyscraper allowed the vast warrens of Midtown and the Financial District, concentrations of offices which let Manhattan become "headquarter city."

By the last quarter of the century elevated trains were running on Third, Sixth, and Ninth avenues, bringing the masses to the Financial District in the morning and carting them home again at night: the commuting society was born. Life in New York began to achieve some of the pace and velocity for which it would become famous. As the transportation system began to reach into the surrounding cities, the map of New York City was summarily redrawn.

Many factors contributed to the creation of Greater New York City in 1898, but once again, the commercial imperative was overarching. The city's monied classes wanted the tax base that the densely populated cities of Brooklyn, Queens, the Bronx, and Staten Island could give them. They did not want workers taking their paychecks out of the city to pay taxes somewhere else. It was a case of unite and conquer.

The completion of the Brooklyn Bridge in 1883 marked the beginning of an era of extraordinary engineering feats. (Library of Congress)

GOLDEN AGE SNOB

*D*uring this summer, a young friend of mine was so charmed with the attorney general that he advised with me about giving him an exceptionally handsome entertainment. This idea took shape the following winter, when he came and asked me to assist him in getting up for him a superb banquet at Delmonico's. He wanted the brilliant people of society to be invited to it and no pains or expense to be spared to make it the affair of the winter . . . .

Great care was taken in the selection of the guests. New York sent to this feast the brilliant men and women of that day, and the feast was worthy of them. The "I" table (shape of letter I) was literally a garden of superb roses; a border of heartsease, the width of one's hand, encircled it, and was most artistic. Delmonico's ballroom, where we dined, had never been so elaborately decorated. The mural decorations were superb; plaques of lilies of the valley, of tulips, and of azaleas adorned the walls; and the dinner itself was pronounced the best effort of Delmonico's chefs. What added much to the general effect was, on leaving the table for a short half hour, to find the same dining room, in that short space of time, converted into a brilliant ballroom, all full of the guests of the patriarchs, and a ball under full headway.

We here reach a period when New York society turned over a new leaf. Up to this time, for one to be worth $1 million was to be rated as a man of fortune, but now, bygones must be bygones. New York's ideas as to values, when fortune was named, leaped boldly up to $10 million, $50 million, $100 million, and the necessities and luxuries followed suit. One was no longer content with a dinner of a dozen or more to be served by a couple of servants. Fashion demanded that you be received in the hall of the house in which you were to dine by from five to six servants, who, with the butler, were to serve the repast . . . . Soft strains of music were introduced between the courses, and in some houses gold replaced silver in the way of plate, and everything that skill and art could suggest was added to make the dinners not a vulgar display but a great gastronomic effort, evidencing the possession by the host of both money and taste.

—Ward McAllister, *Society As I Have Found It,* 1890

For the upper classes, the last decade of the century was indeed the "Gay Nineties," a period of fancy dress balls and social snobbery. The "400," defined by social sycophant Ward McAllister as the number of people who could fit into Caroline Schermerhorn Astor's ballroom, were anointed as the new Manhattan royalty. The number was more symbolic than literal, as Mrs. Astor's ballroom could easily accommodate more than 400 people.

Yet the world of the "400" was doomed even as it was celebrated. Vast socioeconomic changes were underway, fueled by one of the most astonishing population shifts the world has ever seen. In the first two decades of the new century, a third of Eastern Europe's Jews emigrated, most to New York City and environs, over 1.5 million people in all. They joined peasants and laborers from the south of Italy, and continuing influxes from Ireland, Germany, and Russia. In Ellis Island's peak year as an immigrant receiving station, 1,285,349 people passed through it, sometimes at the astonishing rate of 5,000 a day.

By sheer weight of numbers, the new European immigrants tipped the political

The first performance of the Floradora Sextette on November 10, 1900. Supposedly, all the girls went on to marry millionaires. (Museum of the City of New York)

scales of New York to the left. Many of them, indeed, were socialists and communists fleeing from the oppressive regimes of Europe. They began to agitate for social and workplace reforms. At first, these rumblings were dismissed or brutally suppressed, but the 1911 Triangle Shirtwaist Fire, in which 146 sweatshop workers—mostly women—died, coalesced public opinion in favor of reform. Soon afterward the state legislature passed a battery of laws to protect factory workers from dangerous conditions and unreasonable hours and wages.

■ JAZZ AGE MANHATTAN

The coming of Prohibition in 1920 transformed social habits in an odd and paradoxical way: by making alcohol forbidden, Prohibition managed to make it respectable. Imposed by rural Protestants upon urban Catholics, the measure was largely ignored on the island of Manhattan, as the speakeasy became a new kind of social nexus. Often called the Jazz Age for the new form of music played in

A Jacob Riis photo shows immigrant children pledging allegiance to their new country. (Library of Congress)

nightclubs, the '20s were chronicled by writers as diverse as Langston Hughes, F. Scott Fitzgerald, and Damon Runyon. The irrepressible Jimmy Walker, mayor of New York, who used to arrive for work at one o'clock and leave by three, symbolized the charismatic, hard-partying atmosphere of New York during this period.

The Jazz Age was a decade-long party from which the city awoke, depressed and chagrined, with the Wall Street crash of 1929. Walker was turned out of office in a wave of scandals, and a Jewish-Italian bulldog named Fiorello La Guardia took over the mayor's office. La Guardia was the living symbol of New York all through the hard times of the Depression. He was always perceived as taking the part of the little guy—perhaps because he was one himself. When thousands of unemployed workers camped out in Central Park, they joined their disgruntled counterparts across the country in calling their collection of shanties a "Hooverville" after the Republican President—but they never blamed their mayor.

NEWS ITEM:
March 5, 1928

"Heiress Hears Broadway's Call" Lisbeth Higgins, only child of a wealthy ink manufacturer, who is the latest deb to go Broadway, and her dancing partner, George Clifford. They are seen here executing the "Dance Militaire."

(Underwood Photo Archives)

Manhattan

Mayor La Guardia reads the comics over the radio during a strike of newspaper delivery men. (Museum of the City of New York)

One art that La Guardia perfected was going hat in hand to the Democratic President (and ex-governor of New York State) who replaced Hoover, Franklin Delano Roosevelt. Again and again, La Guardia would journey to Washington, D.C., repeatedly coming back with a New Deal public works trophy that employed thousands of people. The impact on Manhattan's skyline was noticeable: the Triborough Bridge, the Henry Hudson Bridge, the Battery Park Tunnel, numerous highways, and other projects were all constructed through this partnership of city and federal governments.

Overseeing much of the construction was Robert Moses, officially Parks Commissioner, but a holder of numerous other governmental titles as well. A master builder and a monstrous ego, Moses ruthlessly imposed his vision of New York City on Manhattan and the other boroughs. Generally, that vision was monumental in scope, and while the grand achievement of Moses is undeniable (and everywhere to be seen), it was gained at great cost to the community. His roads bisected whole neighborhoods with little regard for social repercussions. Moses imagined a Manhattan ringed with superhighways and slashed through with elevated thoroughfares. Perhaps blessedly, that vision was only partially realized.

Manhattan entered World War II on the brink of another population shift that would change its fortunes forever. Only dimly perceived in the tumult of the war years, suburbia was growing even during the Depression. But the burgeoning satellite communities of New Jersey, Connecticut, and upstate New York spelled doom for the urban way of life that Manhattan had symbolized for a century.

At the end of World War II, the island lent its name to the government program for the making of the nuclear bomb: The Manhattan Project. It was perhaps the last great gasp of the science-and-technology revolution which had helped make mid-century New York into the world's greatest urban center.

■ POST-WAR TO PRESENT

The pattern that developed in Manhattan during the '50s was being duplicated in large urban centers throughout the country. The automobile and the superhighway were making commuting long distances cheap and easy, and suddenly America saw itself changing from an urban society to a suburban one.

The depredations that this change visited upon Manhattan, and upon other cities across America, were devastating. New York City's tax base was hemorrhaging at an alarming rate. In the two decades following World War II, over one million families left New York. Corporate headquarters, which used to be located in Manhattan as a matter of course, now decamped to exurban ring cities, lured by lower taxes and rents.

In simple terms, everyone prosperous enough to leave the city seemed to be doing so, until Manhattan was left with a brutally segregated, two-tier society: the rich, who could afford the high cost of living and the higher taxes, and the poor, who drained the coffers of social welfare funds.

By 1975, the chickens had come home to roost, and New York City teetered on the edge of bankruptcy. Only a vigorous state bail-out plan, engineered by investment banker Felix Rohatyn, saved the city from defaulting on $13 billion in bonds: the Municipal Assistance Corporation was formed, to borrow money when the city's credit turned sour.

Commuters from New Jersey stream toward Manhattan on a hot summer morning.

It turned out that the investment the state made in the city was sound, since during the boom decade of the 1980s, Manhattan in particular and New York City in general was reborn. Corporate takeovers and a surging bull market anchored a new prosperity that seemed to extend to the arts, to the rebuilding of the Manhattan infrastructure, and to the spirit of the city as a whole. The propulsive mayoralty of Ed Koch mirrored and epitomized the street attitude of the time: Manhattan was reveling in the tough, exuberant pride of the survivor.

It is clear now that the crest of the 1980s, like the trough of the 1970s, was nothing more than an example of the periodic swings in Manhattan's fortunes. In 1993, the city's first black mayor, David Dinkins, gave way to an ex-D.A. named Rudolph Giuliani, its first Republican mayor in decades, a famed racketbuster voted in at a time when fear of crime—if not crime itself—was on the rise. The population of New York City—unlike the dwindling populations of other major centers across America—remains stable. But there is as of yet no permanent solution to the problem of a city that fails to raise enough revenue to cover the cost of its services.

New York remains an incredible magnet for immigration. A vaunted "third wave" of newcomers swelled during the last few decades, coming not primarily from Europe, but from Asia. They add to a mix in a city that has always been fueled by heterogeneity. According to the last census, the ethnic origins of New Yorkers still span an amazing spectrum. The top 10, from last to first: English, Chinese, Polish, Russian, Dominican, West Indian, German, Irish, Italian, and Puerto Rican.

It is ironic, but walking above this Babel of Manhattan—in fact, having a strong hand in building the Towers of Babel all over the city—are living symbols of New York's most ancient people. A healthy majority of ironworkers on all city skyscrapers are Native Americans, widely employed due to their uncanny sense of balance. History has come full circle, and the first Manhattanites continue to erect the towers that represent its future.

One version of the future has Manhattan going it alone, the product of a civic divorce of massive proportions. This speculative scenario has Staten Island seceding from Greater New York City to incorporate on its own—not at all impossible, since secessionist spirit is strong in the borough. A Staten Island referendum in spring of 1993 on the issue of whether or not to secede from the city was approved by a two-to-one margin. If Staten Island succeeds in leaving, it would make secession easier for Queens (where there is also strong secessionist sentiment). Manhattan would be left with the Bronx and Brooklyn, an alliance that would probably fly apart quickly.

Manhattan as a city unto itself? Unlikely, but not unimaginable. New York City *was* Manhattan for the first two centuries of its existence, and some see poetic justice in a return to that state of affairs. In a sense, it would recognize what all those who love Manhattan know to be true—that here is an island which stands on its own.

Manhattan of the 1980s as imagined in the 1930s would have "aero-rooming places atop 200-story buildings and penthouses amid stars and clouds." (Underwood Photo Archives)

LOWER MANHATTAN

LIKE THE BOW AND FORECASTLE OF SOME PROUD SHIP, the towers and skyscrapers of Lower Manhattan present a thrusting, arrogant profile to the world. It's a sight that can still make your heart catch in your throat, as you clear the Narrows and approach New York City by sea.

Clustered at the island's southern tip are the steel-and-concrete thickets of the Financial District. Flanking it on the southeastern shore of Manhattan are South Street Seaport and the clot of government bureaucracy around City Hall; on the west are the suave, intricately planned precincts of Battery Park City and the World Financial Center. Looming over all, of course, the World Trade Center defines the skyline.

The northern border of the area is generally construed as Chambers Street and City Hall Park. As a vertical ghetto of finance and government, Lower Manhattan is one of the least residential neighborhoods on the island. The colossal weight of history and high finance have so compressed this turf that a visitor can easily take in many of its salient attractions in a single walking tour.

Just don't go at night—unless you want to have the city to yourself. **Wall Street** at night is one of the eeriest places imaginable, not in any high-crime sense, but just because it has been so thoroughly emptied of human life. It calls to mind some monstrous marionette whose puppeteer has dropped the strings. It's been that way for quite some time. Wall Street, wrote Herman Melville in 1853, " . . . Of weekdays hums with industry and life, at nightfall echoes with sheer vacancy, and all through Sunday is forlorn."

Contrast this with the frenzied rush and swirl on days when the markets are running, and it almost seems as if two separate neighborhoods are manifest. Drawn by the sharp scent of money, three million people invade Lower Manhattan each workday. They come by subway, by commuter PATH train, by taxi and car and bus, by helicopter and ferry. At lunchtime, the streets bulge with humanity.

Then, at around three o'clock, the exodus begins, to the Upper East and West sides, to Jersey and Connecticut and to the outer boroughs. By seven, the hectic daytime scurry has quieted. It is this vast systolic movement, this ebb and flow of workers, that gives Lower Manhattan its life.

"Sometimes, from beyond the skyscrapers, the cry of a tugboat finds you in your insomnia, and you remember that this desert of iron and cement is an island ." —Albert Camus

There are a few exceptions proving the rule, at the same time providing delightful pockets of neighborhood life in a place generally assumed bereft of it. On the East River waterfront, South Street Seaport, thronged with people after work and on weekends, and the neighboring **Fulton Street Fish Market,** which cranks up around midnight, represent two such Lower Manhattan exceptions. Battery Park City, along the Hudson waterfront, is another. It's a designed city of 25,000, with an anomalous, almost suburban feel, sited on the edge of some of the priciest real estate on Earth.

■ BATTERY PARK

The original warehouses and mercantile buildings of Lower Manhattan were built right to the shoreline, but over the years the wonders of landfill have provided the Financial District with a fringe of green. This is Battery Park, the site of the **Castle Clinton National Monument,** departure point for **ferries to Ellis Island and the Statue of Liberty.**

The park is as fine a place to view New York Harbor as there is on the island. The lines of people waiting for the ferries draw pushcarts, acrobats, and street musicians to the **Admiral George Dewey Promenade,** and the resulting mummery is a great way for tourists to receive a jolt of Manhattan energy.

Battery Park has long been a place for New Yorkers to strut their stuff: in 1705, Edward Hyde, Lord Cornbury, the transvestite lord governor who was cousin to Queen Anne, was stopped by a constable here for parading in ladies' regalia. His defense was that he was emulating the Queen, but surveying the crowd on the promenade today, you may speculate that he was simply marooned in the wrong century.

Inside the landscaped confines of the park itself, you'll find a **memorial to explorer Giovanni da Verrazano,** erected in 1909, as an Italian-American contribution to the hoopla surrounding the tercentennial of Henry Hudson's visit. Appropriately, Verrazano gazes out toward his eponymous narrows and the bridge which spans it. A **memorial flagpole,** given to the city by the Dutch government, commemorates Peter Minuit's 1626 "purchase" of Manhattan Island from the Canarsees. **Hope Garden** memorializes the thousands who have died of AIDS. Finally, a **World War II monument** features a huge sculpture of a fierce, soaring raptor, set amid granite cenotaphs listing the names of all soldiers and sailors who died in the Atlantic.

Castle Clinton sat 300 feet offshore when it was built in 1811, which gives you some idea of the recent vintage of the Battery Park turf. The Indians called the rocks on which the fort was built "Kapsee," where they landed when they came from Brooklyn. Castle Clinton was originally called West Battery (its twin was East Battery, or Fort William, on Governor's Island), and it was erected to face off the British threat in the War of 1812. The "battery" after which Battery Park is named never fired a shot in wartime.

Castle Clinton afterwards wore many hats. As "Castle Garden" it was roofed over for a concert hall, and it was there that in 1850 huckster-showman P. T. Barnum presented his much-hyped discovery, the "Swedish Nightingale," Jenny Lind. Later it became a receiving hall for immigrants, but some contemporary New Yorkers remember it as the site (until 1941) of the New York Aquarium.

All this history is covered in a small, tidy museum near the east gate of the castle. The dioramas located there are graphic representations of the changeable Manhattan shoreline, and the changeable nature of the fort itself. Squat against the soaring towers of the Financial District, Castle Clinton is worth examining if you're stopping there a moment to pick up tickets for the Statue of Liberty and Ellis Island ferries.

A garland of superb architecture rings Battery Park. **Pier A,** with its distinctive clocktower, once was graced with lyrical Beaux Arts tinplate siding, but time and weather forced it to be sheathed in bland aluminum. To the north, there is the superbly situated **Whitehall Building** at 17 Battery Place, the Moorish-accented Art Deco masterpiece of the **Downtown Athletic Club** at 19 West Street, and the 1905 **entry kiosk for the Bowling Green IRT Subway Station,** one of the oldest in the system.

Just south of the Customs House at 7 State Street is a 1793 Federal townhouse that is now the **Shrine of Saint Mother Elizabeth Ann Seton.** Mother Seton founded the Sisters of Charity, the country's first order of nuns in 1809. In 1975, she became the first native-born American to be canonized. Her shrine is located in the oldest surviving residential building in Lower Manhattan, one of what was originally a row of townhouses, built back in the days when harbor merchants liked to live right on the water. Nearby, at the back of the plaza at 17 State Street, is the site of **Herman Melville's birthplace,** now the home of **New York Unearthed,** a wonderful archaeological museum administered by the South Street Museum.

Nathaniel Currier's lithograph of the Battery by moonlight in 1850.
(Museum of the City of New York)

At the southeast corner of Battery Park, across State Street, is **Peter Minuit Plaza,** named after the Dutch director general of New Amsterdam. Located here is a memorial to New York's first Jewish immigrants, refugees expelled from Portugal's Brazilian colony, who arrived in 1654 in what was then New Amsterdam. Beleaguered by pirates, turned away from other ports, they found a home here in an early demonstration of the Dutch colony's tolerant and ecumenical attitude. The 23 Sephardic newcomers eventually founded a synagogue (Shearith Israel, or "Remnant of Israel") and formed the core of New York's soon-to-burgeon Jewish community.

On the southeastern edge of Battery Park is the **Staten Island Ferry Building,** a '50s-vintage hodgepodge recently damaged by fire and soon to be replaced. The prize-winning new design: a postmodernist structure sporting a huge clockface—the better to speed time-obsessed New Yorkers on their way. Next door is the **Battery Maritime Building,** its aluminum siding painted green to resemble weathered copper, where the ferries to Governor's Island embark. Plans are to house arts organizations in the cavernous interior.

The **Staten Island Ferry** itself, at 50 cents a round trip (about a half hour each way), is still one of the best deals for natives and tourists alike. The view on the return from Staten Island, as Lower Manhattan looms like a capitalist fairyland, is one awe-inspiring sight. "We were very tired, we were very merry," quoth Edna St. Vincent Millay, "We had gone back and forth all night on the ferry." Many people still take the ferry not for transport, but just for the joy of the ride.

■ BOWLING GREEN

Reach Bowling Green from the northeast corner of Battery Park, where State Street debouches into Broadway. Yes, it originally was just that, a bowling green, rented by area property owners from the Crown at the rate of one peppercorn per annum.

Here once stood the famous statue of England's King George III, torn down on July 9, 1776, by a mob inspired by that rabble-rousing document, the Declaration of Independence. In a fine ironic turn, the lead in the gold-leafed, larger-than-life statue was melted down to make bullets—42,000 of them—for use against the British (the final toll, according to legend, was 400 redcoats killed). Only the tail of the statue's horse survives, in the collection of the New-York Historical Society.

A view looking towards the Battery at night in the 1990s contrasts nicely with the image of over a century ago on the previous page.

*Patriots pull down the statue of King George III at Bowling Green in July of
1776. (Museum of the City of New York)*

Today, Bowling Green is marked by glories of the past and present, including its
colonial-era iron fence, likewise attacked by the 1776 mob and stripped of its
royal golden finials. The ancient, tiny green seems somehow a fitting launching
pad for Broadway, which dissects Manhattan to the north. Sea breezes gust around
the landscaped fountain, and flocks of harbor gulls compete with city pigeons, as
if this were the isobar of maritime and urban environments.

Facing the Green on the south side, anchoring the whole space, is the splen-
didly recherché **U.S. Customs House,** built in 1907 and recently renamed the
Alexander Hamilton Customs House. The statues of its façade—and there are
quite a host of them, in keeping with the Beaux Arts style—gaze up Broadway as
if expecting what? A blast of wind? Deliverance? A bus? The four large allegorical
groups out front represent (from east to west) Asia, America, Europe, and Africa.

In 1994, the **George Gustav Heye Center of the National Museum of the
American Indian** opened its exhibit space here. The Heye Center, removed from
its longtime Harlem home in Audubon Terrace, is now run by the Smithsonian
Institution, and the move was intended to increase visibility of this collection.

For an anachronistic comment on the new tenant, note the figure of the Indian in Daniel Chester French's allegorical *America* sculpture at the Customs House entrance: in classic feather headdress, behind a torch-bearing figure of Liberty. Whatever way the architecture interacts with the museum's contents (the collection contains an amazing 1.3 million artifacts, some to be diverted to a new Smithsonian exhibit in Washington, D.C.), the building is there to be appreciated in its own right—including, inside, the great **rotunda murals by Reginald Marsh.**

On the west side of the Green, at 25 Broadway, is the elaborate daydream of the **Cunard Building,** a throwback to the time when the firm's great liners traversed the Atlantic, and now a U.S. post office. Opposite, at **26 Broadway,** is a quirky building that was the former headquarters of Standard Oil—note the humongous rooftop ornament, shaped like an oil lamp. Suitably enough, what was once the center of John D. Rockefeller's web now hosts the **Museum of American Financial History,** "dedicated to the U.S. capital markets and the people who made them famous."

SELLING MONEY

One day earlier in his career Dall was in the market to buy (borrow) fifty million dollars. He checked around and found the money market was 4 to 4.25 percent, which meant he could buy (borrow) at 4.25 percent or sell (lend) at 4 percent. When he actually tried to buy fifty million dollars at 4.25 percent, however, the market moved to 4.25 to 4.5 percent. The sellers were scared off by a large buyer. Dall bid 4.5. The market moved again, to 4.5 to 4.75 percent. He raised his bid several more times with the same result, then went to Bill Simon's office to tell him he couldn't buy money. All the sellers were running like chickens.

"Then you be the seller," said Simon.

So Dall became the seller, although he actually needed to buy. He sold fifty million dollars at 5.5 percent. He sold another fifty million dollars at 5.5 percent. Then, as Simon had guessed, the market collapsed. Everyone wanted to sell. There were no buyers. "Buy them back now," said Simon when the market reached 4 percent. So Dall not only got his fifty million dollars at 4 percent but took a profit on the money he had sold at higher rates.

—Michael Lewis, *Liar's Poker,* 1989

On the north side of Bowling Green, facing toward Wall Street, is Arturo DiModica's sculpture *Charging Bull.* DiModica had the admirable chutzpah to erect his massive 3.5-ton bronze bull just after the October 1987 stock market crash, in the middle of the night, without getting city permission. He has since been battling for donations to keep it there.

■ STATUE OF LIBERTY AND ELLIS ISLAND

The irony is that in the beginning, the American people didn't even want the Statue of Liberty: we had to be virtually flogged into accepting the colossal statue as a gift from France. Eventually, though, we adopted her as our own, and *Liberty Enlightening the World* (as she is formally called) has become a treasured symbol, perhaps the most successful and celebrated public sculpture ever erected.

The Algonquians called the 12-acre, oval island she stands upon *Minissais,* or

The Statue of Liberty under construction in the 1880s. (Library of Congress)

"Littlest Island." It later became Bedloe Island, after Isaac Bedloe or Bedlow, an early landowner; in 1952, it was rechristened Liberty Island. The star-shaped ramparts upon which the pedestal rests date from 1811 when they comprised Fort Wood, named in honor of the hero of the Battle of Fort Erie.

That pedestal was problematic back in the 1880s, when *Liberty* was in the process of being erected. The statue's genesis involved three Frenchmen: the French historian Edouard-René de Laboulaye, who first proposed it; Frédéric-Auguste

*"A big girl who is obviously going to have a baby. The Birth of a Nation,
I suppose." —James Agate, on the Statue of Liberty*

Bartholdi, the sculptor who worked indefatigably to build it and get it placed; and Alexandre-Gustave Eiffel, the famous engineer who designed its superstructure. The French people, motivated partly by a desire to embarrass their own repressive government, paid for the statue themselves, raising one million francs by subscription. The statue was a gift from the French to the American people, who only had to pay for the cost of the pedestal.

The citizenry of nineteenth-century America weren't up for it. The pedestal got to only 15 feet (out of the 142-foot total) when work stopped for lack of money. Liberty's arm toured America for fund-raising purposes, being most prominently displayed in Madison Square Park. Finally, under the prodding of daily editorials by Joseph Pulitzer in his *New York World* newspaper, enough subscription money was raised—some of it coming in by the nickel and penny, with Pulitzer running the names of all contributors in the *World*. The statue was shipped over in crates from Bartholdi's workshop in Paris and dedicated on October 28, 1886.

Liberty stands 151 feet tall, with a massive 42-foot arm, and eyes that are 10 feet across. (Bartholdi's mother was the model, a fact which places the statue in a whole new Oedipal light.) Even given the massive dimensions (30 feet higher than the Colossus of Rhodes, one of the Seven Wonders of the Ancient World), it is dwarfed in the expanse of New York Harbor. But to a generation of immigrants, the slowly shifting view of the Statue of Liberty as they steamed by it on the approach to nearby Ellis Island must have been emotionally overpowering.

Due to a centennial refurbishing, Liberty shines literally brighter than ever, since her torch was retooled according to Bartholdi's original gold-leafed design (the old torch was removed to the museum lobby). The tablet she holds in her hands does not, as many people believe, contain the lines of the famous Emma Lazarus poem, "The New Colossus":

> *G*ive me your tired, your poor,
> Your huddled masses yearning to breathe free,
> The wretched refuse of your teeming shore.
> Send these, the homeless, tempest-tossed to me,
> I lift my lamp beside the golden door.

Instead, the tablet is meant to symbolize the American Declaration of Independence, and is inscribed with the date of that document: July IV MDCCLXXVI. The poem is engraved on the statue's base.

"The last time I was inside a woman was when I took a tour of the Statue of Liberty," Woody Allen joked, but the line to tour the statue is sometimes impossibly long. On summer weekends, the only way to get into the statue for the elevator ride and the 171-step climb to the top is to go early in the day, since the National Park Service, which has jurisdiction here, cuts the line off as early as two o'clock.

Visiting **Ellis Island and the Museum of Immigration** is another style of experience, necessarily less monumental, more informational, but in a way just as impressive. The two-island trip represents a physical and emotional commitment and winds up being a draining but immensely satisfying day. The Park Service recommends Liberty Island first and then Ellis; but ferries run both ways, the New Jersey ferry going first to Ellis, and the Manhattan ferry going first to Liberty.

Actually two small islands joined and enlarged by landfill, Ellis Island is named after Samuel Ellis, the New Jersey farmer who owned it. The Indians called it Oyster Island, and the British, who used it for hangings, named it Gibbet Isle. The Federal government made it into a military outpost and munitions dump until the end of the nineteenth century. When it became obvious that Castle Clinton in Battery Park was being overwhelmed as an immigrant-receiving station, that operation was transferred here.

The first Ellis Island immigrant stepped ashore in 1892, and over 12 million people followed, sometimes as many as 5,000 a day. These were Emma Lazarus's poor, almost all making the trans-Atlantic crossing in steerage class, since first-class passengers were allowed to proceed directly to the Manhattan docks. Ellis Island processed the immigrants cattle-style, with medical checkups and legal tests designed to ferret out "any convict, lunatic, idiot or any person unable to take care of himself or herself without becoming a public charge." Only about two percent of applicants were turned away. Among those who came through Ellis were songwriter Irving Berlin, director Frank Capra, jurist Felix Frankfurter, poet Kahlil Gibran, and actors Bela Lugosi and Rudolph Valentino.

The present-day museum memorializing the immigrant experience was the work of a centennial committee headed by Lee Iacocca, the Chrysler chairman and son of immigrants who came through Ellis Island. It is centered in the odd, turreted, Byzantine-flavored Reception Hall, but there is a Wall of Honor outside, inscribed with the names of 250,000 immigrants. (Names are still being added, with a $100 donation per name.)

The experience of following the footsteps of immigrants, guided through the process by accessible and compelling exhibits, can be extremely moving. On the first floor are rooms devoted to immigration in general, including a "Peopling of America" exhibit that shows just who came (and is coming) and from where. The second floor includes the Great Hall (officially called the Registry Room), which many immigrants cite as their clearest memory of Ellis Island. Exhibit rooms off this impressive space lead the visitor through the check-in and vetting procedure that all new immigrants went through.

The third floor has some of the most dramatic exhibits of the museum: "Treasures from Home," which displays clothing, photos, and artifacts that the immigrants brought with them; "Silent Voices," a record of the spooky time that Ellis Island was abandoned, and a recreated dorm room that shows just how quasi-military was the immigrant experience there. Also on this floor is "Ellis Island Chronicles," with dioramas showing how the island grew via landfill (much of it dug from subway excavation in Manhattan) and development.

Immigrants arriving at Ellis Island around 1910. (Culver Pictures NYC)

The Great Hall where immigrants were first processed upon arrival at Ellis Island. (National Park Service)

An interesting Ellis Island historical footnote is in the process of being decided by the U.S. Supreme Court. The states of New York and New Jersey are squabbling over what amounts to boasting rights to Ellis Island, since formal jurisdiction has long been given over to the Federal government. New York's claim is based on a 160-year-old interstate compact. New Jersey argues that this should be restricted only to the island's original three acres, not the present-day 27.5 acres.

Although much of the argument is moot, there are some real issues. The scheduled addition of a footbridge might funnel more visitors (and their dollars) through New Jersey. Concession dollars are split by New Jersey and New York. Whatever the outcome of that issue, the experience is a heady one, and the two island-sized monuments in New York Harbor represent a superb way to familiarize oneself with its historic dimensions.

A few pointers: to do both islands, the best way is to make a day of it, and pack a picnic lunch. A repast taken on the lawns of either island is a delightful way to break up the day, and spellbinding views of Manhattan are thrown in for free.

Although hordes of screeching schoolchildren might accurately recall the clamor of immigration, perhaps the best time to hit Ellis Island is after 2:30 in the afternoon, when the school excursions have cleared out. Evening hours in summer can also be superbly meditative.

Tickets for the Liberty and Ellis Island ferryboats are purchased at Castle Clinton in Battery Park. Running usually on the half hour, depending on the season, the boats usually go to each island in turn, and one ticket buys you passage to both.

■ WALL STREET

Gothic **Trinity Church** stands at the west end of Wall Street like a Biblical admonition against the temptations of the materialist life. It used to look a lot sterner and blacker, until a recent restoration brought its sandstone back to the original rose-hued shade. This is the third Trinity Church on the site—the first was built in 1698. Among the 1,186 New Yorkers interred in its pretty, moss-grown cemetery are founding fathers Alexander Hamilton and Francis Lewis, Captain James "Don't Give Up the Ship" Lawrence, and steamship inventor Robert Fulton (his memorial is outside, but his remains are in the Livingston family crypt inside the church property).

Ground zero for American capitalism is the **New York Stock Exchange** at Wall and Broad streets, founded in 1792 under a buttonwood tree. Best way to glimpse the frenzied workings of the place is to show up at the visitors entrance at 20 Broad Street, between 9:15 A.M. and 4:00 P.M. on trading days, with last entry at 2:45 P.M. (656-5168). Free tickets, passed out while the supply lasts, afford entry into an exhibit and screening room, where a short film on the Exchange goes a long way in explaining what you are about to see. Then on to the gallery above the floor itself, whence visitors watch the hectic rush of 200 million shares a day being traded.

What you'll see below you is an array of "trading posts"—computerized command centers that bristle with video monitors and spindly brackets holding CRTs. Each stock is assigned to a specific "section" of the trading post, with a small army of clerks, runners, brokers, and pages assigned to each section. The frenetic action on the floor consists of buy and sell orders being funneled through this electronically sophisticated but still curiously anachronistic system of exchange.

In essence, the New York Stock Exchange is a raucous, roiling, free-running auction, one which sets the stock price for many of America's largest companies. The rule of the market is inexorable: if more people want to buy a stock than want to sell it, the price goes up; conversely, if more people want to sell than buy, the price goes down. Careers, fortunes, and lives have been wrecked on the shoals of this simple but capricious dictum.

For an interesting counterpoint, exit the Exchange and check out the façade of the **Morgan Guaranty and Trust Company** at 23 Wall Street, still marked by the 1920 explosion of an anti-capitalist anarchist's bomb—look under the second window from the east on the building's north side. This was long the headquarters of J. P. Morgan, financier extraordinaire and architect of the U.S. Steel conglomerate—and one of nineteenth-century New York's notorious robber barons. Morgan was the most respectable of these powerful industrialists, whose motto was once pronounced by railroad buccaneer Jay Gould: "If it's not nailed down, it's mine. If I can pry it up, it's not nailed down."

J. Pierpont Morgan in 1902. (The Pierpont Morgan Library, NYC)

At Wall and Broad streets is also the stolid Greek Revival **Federal Hall,** an 1842 Parthenon that stands on the site—marked by a statue of the man himself—where George Washington was inaugurated as the first President of the United States in 1789. Inside is a mini-museum and self-guided tour. Federal Hall is a good place to pick up the **Heritage Trail,** a self-guided walking tour of Lower Manhattan, punctuated by informative markers.

A worthy side trip from Wall Street is to dip south on Broad to **Fraunces Tavern** at 54 Pearl Street, billed as the oldest tavern in New York City. The truth is more complicated than that, but the site does have history, even though the present building was erected in 1907—a reconstruction, not a recreation.

Traders take a break (above) from the frenzy of the Stock Exchange floor (top). Japanese influence is reflected in the design of Chase Plaza (left) as well as in the markets of Wall Street.

The **Fraunces Tavern Museum** (inside the restaurant) is a quaint, surprisingly effective look at the colonial and early federal history of the place. The original tavern on the site did host George Washington as he bade farewell to his troops on December 4, 1783, and it was noteworthy for being the hostelry of Samuel Fraunces, George Washington's steward and one of the most prominent black New Yorkers of the period. Across the street from Fraunces Tavern, in the plaza at 85 Broad Street, are three Plexiglas cases displaying Dutch and English archeological artifacts.

FAREWELL AT FRAUNCES' TAVERN

*T*he Long Room of Fraunces' Tavern had recently been used for the dinner given by Governor Clinton on the day the American army entered the city . . . . On the morning of December 4, 1783, Washington and his officers met here for the last time as soldiers of the Revolutionary Army . . . . His emotion was too strong to be concealed, and was evidently reciprocated by all present. After partaking of a slight refreshment, and after a few moments of silence, the General filled his glass with wine, and turning to his officers said: "With a heart full of love and gratitude, I now take leave of you. I most devoutly wish your latter days may be as prosperous and happy as your former ones have been glorious and honorable." After the officers had responded in a glass of wine, he requested that each one of them should come and take him by the hand. General Knox, who was nearest him, turned and grasped his hand and they embraced each other in silence. In the same affectionate manner every officer parted from the Commander-in-Chief, who then left the room without a word, and passing through lines of infantry drawn up to receive him, walked silently to Whitehall, where a barge was waiting to carry him to Paulus Hook. He was on his way to Annapolis, to surrender his commission to the Continental Congress, and then to his beloved Mount Vernon.

—W. Garrison Bayles, *Old Taverns of New York*, 1915

■ SOUTH STREET SEAPORT

Although widely decried by some snobby Manhattanites as "a playground for yuppies," the South Street Seaport (Fulton Street at the East River) complex of shops, museums, and markets has some marvelous things to recommend it. Yes, its bars and restaurants do get invaded after every workday by hordes of hungry and thirsty (mostly just thirsty) workers from Wall Street, but if this phenomenon bothers you, go before five o'clock.

Although it appears to be a worthy preservation of a waterfront parcel of real estate, the Seaport's genesis reveals more complicated politics. A small group of preservationists began a campaign to save some of the last eighteenth-century waterfront buildings left in Manhattan. To their surprise, they received financial support from real estate interests desperately seeking a way to limit the sprawl of the Financial District—and thus increase the value of existing downtown office space. The creation of the South Street Seaport answered needs of both the real estate moguls and the preservationists in one bold stroke.

Luckily, a ready antidote to the cloying flavor of pre-packaged development (much of Seaport is leased by the Rouse Company, developers of similar harborfront projects, Faneuil Hall in Boston and Harbor Place Baltimore) is available immediately at hand. The Fulton Fish Market at South and Fulton streets is much smaller than it was in its glory days, but is still a sprawling, messy, smelly, old-fashioned ichthyic bazaar.

The market is a weird throwback of a place, named after Robert Fulton—inventor of the submarine, the torpedo, and the steamship, as well as pioneer and sometime monopolist of Hudson River transportation. It remains thick with the polyglot cries of fishmongers and longshoremen, though only a tiny percentage of its flounder, tuna, oysters, and crabs still come directly into the market by boat (most come in by truck). Together with the Hunts Point Market in the Bronx and the Wholesale Meat District on the West Side, Fulton Street provides the fare for the city's tables.

Tours are available April through September under the aegis of the South Street Seaport Museum, but it's worth a quick visit even without a guide. Get there early —5 or 6 A.M. is best—to see the sidewalks still covered with spilled diamonds of crushed ice, glittering with fish scales, slimy with discarded entrails. Those blocky paving stones, by the way, are actually bricks recycled from eighteenth- and nineteenth-century ship ballast. Styrofoam crates of iced shrimp, huge bloodied carcasses of tuna and shark, and bushels of shellfish are sold from booths which spread from the "Tin Building" to the cavernous space beneath East River Drive. You can see the city's top restaurateurs—and best home cooks—haggling with the countermen, pressing the fish-flesh to gauge its freshness.

The rest of the Seaport is given over to stores and restaurants, its commerce anchored by a dollop of history. The **Titanic Memorial,** once located near Battery Park, was moved here in 1976. It was funded by subscription to commemorate the 1912 super-liner disaster. The "**Museum Block**" (Front, Water, Fulton, and Beekman streets) includes a **visitors center** at 207 Front, an old-style printer, a charts-and-maps store, and a gallery, with the **Trans-Lux Seaport Theater** (133 Beekman) providing an audio-visual presentation on the area, "The Seaport Experience."

Schermerhorn Row is a charming block of restored Federal warehouses (Fulton, Front, John, and South streets) that were originally built on a wharf 600 feet from the shoreline. Part of the block faces the **Fulton Market Building** at 11 Fulton Street, a scrupulous reconstruction of the 1883 original. Finally, there is the **Pier 17 Pavilion,** a massive emporium of fast food, restaurants, T-shirts, and tourist baubles built out over an East River pier.

South of this, on Piers 15 and 16, are the Seaport's **floating exhibits.** Some are berthed here permanently: the *Peking,* the second-largest sailing ship in the world; the lighthouse ship the *Ambrose,* once anchored in the harbor; the three-masted

Caroling at South Street Seaport at Christmastime (above). Miss Liberty takes a coffee break from entertaining the Wall Street crowd. (photo by Katsuyoshi Tanaka)

Wavetree; and the century-old schooner *Pioneer.* Entry to all is included with museum admission. From Pier 16, the Seaport Line offers rides on the *Andrew Fletcher,* an old-style sidewheeler, and the *DeWitt Clinton,* a steamship.

Bruce Weber wrote in the *New York Times* in June of 1994 about a boat tour on Seaport Liberty Cruises around the southern tip of Manhattan:

> On a sunny morning, with the wind spilling your hair in your eyes and the air as balmy as bath water, you look at the vertical spires of lower Manhattan, as tightly packed as porcupine quills, not to mention the Statue of Liberty, Ellis Island and the Verrazano-Narrows Bridge in the distance, and you understand why people want to come here and maybe even remember why you moved here yourself.

■ BROOKLYN BRIDGE AND CITY HALL

One of the prime virtues of the South Street Seaport is the superb view it affords of one of the great architectural masterworks of all time, the **Brooklyn Bridge** (Manhattan terminus at Park Row). The bridge was begun in 1869 by John Roebling, who died before construction started: a ferry crushed his foot as he was surveying the site and the master engineer died of complications. His son Washington Roebling completed the bridge in 1883. Over the course of its construction, the bridge claimed 20 lives and another dozen died in a stampede of panicked pedestrians a week after the span opened.

Originally called the New York and Brooklyn Bridge, the completed span linked what were then separate cities, and was hailed as a modern miracle. The magnificent Gothic towers anchoring each end were meant to be gateways to their respective cities. Walt Whitman and Hart Crane memorialized it, Le Corbusier praised it as "full of native sap," and today architectural historians place it on par with the Eiffel Tower as one of the great engineering and aesthetic achievements of the nineteenth century. There were a few doubters: vaudeville comedian Eddie Foy was supposed to have cracked: "All that trouble just to get to Brooklyn."

Although a long central pedestrian ramp has replaced the graceful original walkways, crossing over the Brooklyn Bridge on foot remains one of the most exhilarating experiences anywhere in the city, with great views of Lower Manhattan and access to attractive Brooklyn Heights at the other end.

BLIND AMBITION

I think of all the powerful or semi-powerful men and women throughout the world, toiling at one task or another—a store, a mine, a bank, a profession—somewhere outside of New York, whose one ambition is to reach the place where their wealth will permit them to enter and remain in New York, dominant above the mass, luxuriating in what they consider luxury.

The illusion of it, the hypnosis deep and moving that it is! How the strong and the weak, the wise and the fools, the greedy of heart and of eye, seek the nepenthe, the Lethe, of its something hugeness. I always marvel at those who are willing, seemingly, to pay any price—*the* price, whatever it may be—for one sip of this poison cup. What a stinging, quivering zest they display. How beauty is willing to sell its bloom, virtue its last rag, strength an almost usurious portion of that which it controls, youth its very best years, its hope or dream of fame, fame and power their dignity and presence, age its weary hours, to secure but a minor part of all this, a taste of its vibrating presence and the picture that it makes. Can you not hear them almost, singing its praises?

—Theodore Dreiser, *The Color of a Great City,* 1923

*A*s the Mercedes ascended the bridge's great arc, he could see the island of Manhattan off to the left. The towers were jammed together so tightly, he could feel the mass and stupendous weight. Just think of the millions, from all over the globe, who yearned to be on that island, in those towers, in those narrow streets! There it was, the Rome, the Paris, the London of the twentieth century, the city of ambition, the dense magnetic rock, the irresistible destination of all those who insist on being *where things are happening*—and he was among the victors! He lived on Park Avenue, the street of dreams! He worked on Wall Street, fifty floors up, for the legendary Pierce & Pierce, overlooking the world! He was at the wheel of a $48,000 roadster with one of the most beautiful women in New York—no Comp. Lit. scholar, perhaps, but gorgeous—beside him! A frisky young animal! He was of that breed whose natural destiny it was . . . to have what they wanted!

—Tom Wolfe, *Bonfire of the Vanities,* 1987

The Manhattan terminus of the Brooklyn Bridge gives out onto a thick cluster of government buildings. Its locus is **City Hall Park** (Broadway and Park Row), site of the charming, diminutive **City Hall**. The French Renaissance–Federal hybrid was once sided with cheap brownstone on its northern side, since its designers never expected the city to grow past it. (The brownstone was replaced with limestone during a 1959 restoration). The building to the north, now municipal offices, is familiarly known as **Tweed Courthouse,** in honor of the political boss who funneled into his own pockets $10 million of the $14 million spent on building it.

To the south of City Hall Park is **Park Row,** once nicknamed "Newspaper Row" because the *Sun,* the *World,* and the *Tribune,* among other papers, were headquartered there. In 1893, New York City had 19 daily papers, and this street—now known mostly for its computer and electronic stores—was the hub.

Across the park, at 233 Broadway, is the **Woolworth Building,** a giant Gothic confection that was, from 1913 until the Bank of Manhattan overtook it in 1929, the world's tallest building. For his ornate office, F. W. Woolworth, a farmer's son from upstate New York, replicated Napoleon's audience room at Compiègne. The

The Brooklyn Bridge on a moody day (above). The ornate lobby of the Woolworth Building (right).

equally ornate lobby features a wry bas-relief of Woolworth counting—yes!—nickels and dimes. Nicknamed "the Cathedral of Commerce," the Woolworth Building was long a goading vision which could be seen from all over Lower Manhattan—including the slums of the Lower East Side.

■ WORLD TRADE CENTER

"They look like the boxes that the Empire State Building came in." Thus runs the typical man-in-the-street sneer at the chilly International style of the World Trade Center. The quarter-mile-tall, 110-story diplopic towers transformed the skyline of Lower Manhattan.

Begun in 1962, completed a decade and a half later, the WTC looked like what it was—a building complex underwritten by a government agency (Port Authority of New York and New Jersey). The whole structure is a hi-tech beehive, with 50,000 worker bees, and another 80,000 visitors buzzing in and out daily. Designed by Minoru Yamasaki and executed by a dozen engineering firms, the World Trade Center houses the myriad exchanges, companies, and agencies involved in world trade under one—or maybe two—roofs.

The World Trade Center was slow to shake off the effects of a bomb blast in February of 1993, with the Vista Hotel and the rooftop restaurants within the complex especially slow to reopen. Cellar in the Sky, a windowless aerie for oenophiles atop the north tower, lost over $2 million worth of wine, and walls ran red two stories down. Increased security measures and a lingering sense of vulnerability and paranoia are the other legacies of the bombers, but no substantial structural damage to the buildings was incurred.

There are seven buildings in the World Trade Center complex, plus the **Austin J. Tobin Plaza,** a five-acre concrete expanse with the same frigid feel as the towers themselves. The Plaza is closed in winter due to killer ice hurtling down from above, but it plays host in summer to greenmarkets (Tuesdays and Thursdays) and concerts. The scattering of sculptures—a 25-foot bronze sphere by Fritz Koenig, a pyramid by Masayuki Nagare, *Ideogram* (a letter from a forgotten alphabet?) by James Rosati, and a mobile by Alexander Calder—can't do much to humanize the surroundings. A recently announced redesign effort is aimed at luring more people to the space.

No matter what you think of the Trade Center's final form, however, there is no

WORLD TRADE CENTER ANTICS

Name: Philippe Petit　　　　　　　　　　　**Date:** August 7, 1974
Feat: Walking from the north to south tower on a high wire
Duration: One hour
Description: Petit and his accomplices planned for almost a decade and then worked stealthily to set up the stunt. Disguised as workmen, they climbed to the north tower and used a crossbow to shoot a guy-wire over to the south tower, where two other men waited. Using the wire, they eventually strung a cable between the two buildings. With a 35-foot balancing pole, the aerialist stepped out on the wire at 7:15 A.M.—just at the morning rush hour. Traffic stalled and crowds gathered as Petit leisurely strolled the 164-foot wire, doing deep knee bends and one-legged stands. After planning for it for nine years, Petit was not about to rush his moment of glory.
Legal File: Agreed to do community service (performing as an aerialist for children in Central Park) in lieu of jail time.

❖

Name: Owen Quinn　　　　　　　　　　　　**Date:** July 1975
Feat: Parachuted from the top of the north tower
Duration: Under two minutes
Description: Quinn was a construction worker involved in the building of the World Trade Center. After clambering over the side of the roof, he tumbled in free-fall, building up speed, until he was halfway down. Then he floated to the bottom, landing in the still-unfinished Tobin Plaza.
Legal File: Charged with disorderly conduct, trespassing, and reckless endangerment; all charges dropped.

❖

Name: George Willig　　　　　　　　　　　**Date:** May 26, 1977
Feat: Scaling the south tower of the World Trade Center
Duration: Three-and-a-half hours
Description: Willig designed and engineered his own climbing devices, which he fitted into the tracks for the automatic window washers on the exterior of the building. Two cops on a window-washing scaffold joined him at the 55th floor and, failing to talk him out of his climb, accompanied him to the top.
Legal File: The city sued him for $250,000, but settled for $1.10: a penny a floor.

way to diminish the astonishingly complex procedure it took to erect the place. Part of it had to be built below the waterline, so a giant concrete "bathtub" was first built to keep the sea out. From inside the bathtub 1.2 million cubic yards of dirt were removed. Finally, upon the foundation of Manhattan mica schist bedrock, 100 million tons of steel (a dozen different grades), glass, concrete, and other materials were built into the twin towers.

Some term it one of the most ambitious engineering feats of all time, so the least one can do is volunteer to be jerked to the roof by high-speed express elevator and have a look down. The World Trade Center **Observation Deck** is a glass-enclosed space on the 107th floor of the south tower (WTC 2 to bureaucrats and aficionados).

From 1,350 feet in the air, all of greater New York City, the lower Hudson Valley, and the Eastern Seaboard from northern New Jersey to southern Connecticut are potentially within view—the window-glass is etched with silhouettes for easy identification. "Potentially" is the operative word here, since the deck is sometimes socked in by clouds. To prevent high-altitude disappointment, it's best to pay attention to the visibility rating in the lobby before you go up. Ascending another 67 feet to the rooftop promenade above the 110th floor is a windier, more invigorating experience.

Across the street from the World Trade Center at Fulton and Broadway, and standing in thorough contrast to it, is **St. Paul's Chapel.** Built in 1766, this delightful Georgian edifice is the oldest building in Manhattan. Wags say George Washington slept here, a reference to the dull Episcopalian sermons, but the Father of Our Country did come by to worship, and his pew is thoughtfully pointed out by a plaque. The pink-and-green pastel interior, with Waterford chandeliers, is best enjoyed during the noonday chamber music concerts.

Stretched along the Hudson waterfront to the north and west of the World Trade Center, resting on landfill that is one-quarter made up of the earth dug for the WTC foundations, the **World Financial Center** and Battery Park City do their best to mitigate the awful dominating effect of the twin towers on lower Manhattan.

They are only partially successful. The World Financial Center is a complex of four office towers, ranging in height from 34 to 51 stories, each with a distinctive rooftop profile. A pedestrian walkway from the World Trade Center brings you directly into the **Winter Garden,** an airy public space with the only 90-foot palm trees on Manhattan. Expansive views of the harbor are the attraction here, as are

A bridge-painter's view of New York City Marathon runners traversing the Verrazano-Narrows Bridge. (photo by Katsuyoshi Tanaka)

the occasional concerts and other events held throughout the year. The shops are on the high end of the spectrum: Bally of Switzerland, Barney's, Rizzoli International Bookstore.

The World Financial Center divides Battery Park City, the 92-acre planned community that is a well-intended but slightly flavorless mix of pricey condos and apartments, parks, and cultural institutions. Its best features are not the rather pristine, antiseptic residential neighborhoods (there are four: Battery Place, Rector Place, Gateway Plaza, and the imaginatively named North Residential Neighborhood), but rather the river views and open spaces. **The South Gardens** are an intentionally wild bit of landscaped lagoon, while **Hudson River Park**, north of Vesey Street, features a fine playground and, at its north end, great bronze sculptures by Tom Otterness.

The denizens of Battery Park City—and their neighbors—have truly embraced the **Esplanade**, a walkway along the Harbor with wonderful prospects of the Statue of Liberty, Ellis Island, and the Narrows. Lower Manhattan in general is also the preferred venue for watching sunsets, since farther north the Palisades interfere. Here, though, with the New Jersey pollution throwing up a refracting haze, sunset can be a gorgeous, lingering lightshow.

Fanfare surrounding the inauguration of the Statue of Liberty in 1886. (Library of Congress)

LOWER EAST SIDE

IT IS SOMEHOW FITTING THAT immediately abutting City Hall is an ethnic sprawl that continues north for 25 blocks and embraces some of the most immigrant-hallowed turf in America. Bordered by City Hall, Broadway, the East River, and Houston Street, the area is like a giant slice of multi-cultural pie. If Manhattan was made by "huddled masses yearning to breathe free," these intensely parochial neighborhoods, dense and flavorful, are where they huddled.

And still huddle today. Chinatown is Manhattan's most vibrant ethnic enclave by far, a dynamic and amorphous presence that is still chewing up blocks of Little Italy and other neighborhoods on its fringes, growing, absorbing, co-opting. Contrast the vibrancy of Chinatown with the static, museum-piece aura of Little Italy. Once the proud home to a healthy chunk of New York's huge Italian immigrant population, it now lives largely off the reputation of the past, although the dwindling core of a neighborhood remains.

Most of Manhattan's Italian Americans have decamped for the boroughs, Long Island, or New Jersey, leaving behind the husk of a neighborhood—and some great restaurants. Every time a sign with Chinese ideograms goes up on the fringe of Little Italy—try strolling up Mott Street north of Canal, once solid Italian turf—the neighborhood dynamic is demonstrated anew. Which is not to say that Little Italy doesn't have things to recommend it. A great cannoli is a great cannoli, after all.

Back when Little Italy was truly Italian and Chinatown stayed within its borders, the teeming tenements and slums of the Lower East Side hosted a century-long ethnic jamboree that embraced generations of Jewish, Italian, Irish, Eastern European, German, and Puerto Rican immigrants—a mix of heritages and cultures that to this day remains unequaled anywhere on the globe.

■ CHINATOWN

It is the largest community of Chinese in the Western Hemisphere, home to 150,000 immigrants from all over Asia—ethnic Chinese from the Mainland, from Taiwan, Vietnam, Burma, Singapore—plus a smattering of Chinese from places like Cuba and South America, mixed with a few other, primarily Asian,

THE VILLAGES & DOWNTOWN

0   1000   2000

feet

Alexander Hamilton Customs House, 33
Alternative Museum, 4
Austin J. Tobin Plaza, 25
Bowling Green, 32
Christopher Park, 1
Civic Center, 16
Confucius Plaza, 12
Crosby St., 10
Duane Park, 17
Esplanade, 20
Federal Hall, 27
Guggenheim Museum Soho, 6
Hudson River Park, 12
Knickerbocker Village, 13
Lower East Side Tenement Museum, 11
Manhattan Community College, 18
Municipal Building, 14
Museum Block, 5
Museum of American Financial History, 31
National Museum of the American Indian, 33
New Museum of Contemporary Art, 7
New York City Fire Museum, 9
New York University, 3
Pier 17 Pavilion, 30
Schermerhorn Row, 28
Soho Cast-Iron Historic District, 8
South Street Seaport, 29
Staten Island Ferry Building, 34
Trinity Church, 26
Tweed Courthouse, 15
Washington Market Park, 19
Washington Square Park, 2
Woolworth Building, 23
World Financial Center, 22
World Trade Center, 24

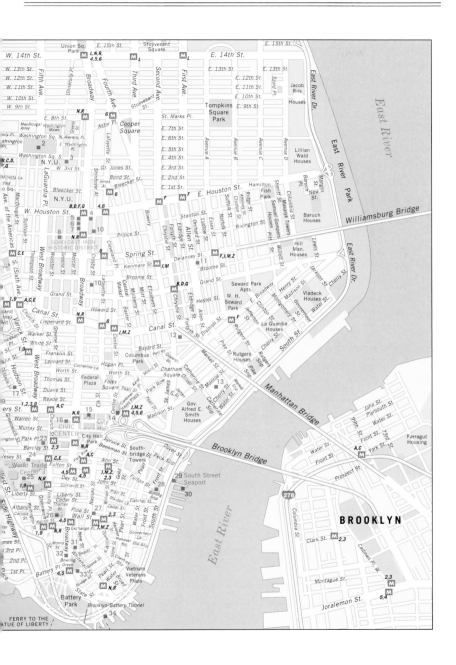

nationalities. Another 150,000 ethnic Chinese inhabit New York's other China-towns—Flushing in Queens, and Eighth Avenue in Brooklyn—but Manhattan's Chinatown is the central community.

Its surprising growth is of rather recent history. The first immigrants were primarily Cantonese railroad workers from the West, who during the 1870s settled in a fairly proscribed area of Manhattan—the 13 blocks bounded by Canal, Worth, and Baxter streets, and the Bowery, near the terminus of the Manhattan Bridge. The neighborhood endured for over a century without much change in its boundaries.

Not until 1965, when Congress increased Asian immigration quotas, did new-comers begin to flood in and Chinatown push north into Little Italy and the Lower East Side. Coincidentally, the 1970s witnessed an upsurge of interest in Chinese food, which all the newly arrived chefs were happy to provide. With Hong Kong facing the "big gong" of 1997—when the colony is slated to rejoin the Mainland—the Asian influx continues.

Chinatown is a noisy, garish, aromatic, jam-packed neighborhood, with crinkum-crankum streets and some of the oldest tenements extant on the island. Living quarters are handed down over generations, and it is nearly impossible for anyone outside the community to find a residence here. Many of the apartments are illegally subdivided into *gong si fong,* or "public rooms," crude flophouses that stack eight, ten, sometimes twenty people in what was originally a one-bedroom apartment.

For most *guey low faan*—"foreign devils"—Chinatown is primarily a place to eat and soak up atmosphere. But for the members of the hermetic Chinese community, some of whom might live here for years and never speak a word of English, China-town is a place of work. Over 600 piecework garment factories are located here—some no better than sweat shops. There are over 350 restaurants, and some 50 "spas" or *bagnios* as well—combination health spa and massage parlors which employ hordes of young Asian women. The standard for all these places is a six-day, 60- to 80-hour week.

Work, and saving. Chinatown has 27 banks, by far the highest bank-per-capita ratio in the city. The waiters in the restaurants and the workers in the sweat shops save for the "eight bigs" (a color television, a refrigerator, a washing machine, furniture, a camera, a VCR, a telephone, and a car), to send money back to their place of origin (80 percent of Chinatown residents are foreign born), or to buy a small business.

You may want to enter Chinatown through the "back door" of **Foley Square,** which represents the north end of the City Hall area and is surrounded by a hodgepodge of municipal offices and criminal justice buildings. Given the heavy civic activity in the area, it's ironic to remember that this turf was formerly one of the most murderous slums of Manhattan, the notorious **Five Corners** area, haunt of such nineteenth-century gangs as the Plug Uglies, the Dead Rabbits, and the Shirttails.

In back of the **Municipal Building** is the plaza where artist Richard Serra installed his controversial *Tilted Arc* sculpture, which gave rise to one of the more notorious battles over art in public spaces. The rusty metal monolith bisected the plaza, forcing hundreds of office workers to walk around it. The workers rebelled, and after a court battle the sculpture was yanked—a victory for the practical-minded or the Philistines, depending on your point of view.

Northwest of Foley Square, on the south side of Duane Street between Broadway and Lafayette, is the site of the **Negro Burial Ground,** an eighteenth-century grave site that was originally located just outside the borders of New Amsterdam. As many as 20,000 people were buried here, but the site was lost as the city grew northwards.

In 1990, when excavations for a government office building uncovered 39 graves, almost half of them children, community outcry forced the abandonment of construction. There is presently a design commission, formed under the auspices of the Urban Center, to determine how best to commemorate what would in effect be one of the oldest sites of the African-American community in Manhattan.

From "Law and Order" and "NYPD Blue" you'll recognize the **Criminal Courts Building** at 100 Centre Street. An Art Moderne rockpile, its ziggurat construction was designed by the same architect—Harvey Wiley Corbett—who did Rockefeller Center. Since metal detectors were installed here in the mid-1980s, cops routinely pick weapons out of the bushes out front—and these are ditched by people headed *into* court, folks.

The Criminal Courts Building is also called **"the Tombs,"** after a long-gone prison that used to be located just to the north. The **White Street Correctional Facility** that is there now, connected to the Tombs by a "bridge of sighs," was briefly the center of controversy when African Americans objected to the depiction of their community in one of the series of bas-relief panels on the building's east side.

Fresh flounder for sale at a Chinatown fishmonger's (top). Chinese New Year usually falls between late January and early March according to the lunar calendar (above). (photo by Katsuyoshi Tanaka)

Canal Street is Chinatown's traditional northern border, and the sidewalks are jammed with food shops of every flavor. The giant **Pearl River** department store at 277 Canal stocks a vast array of Asian consumer goods, and the neighborhood's many apothecaries offer ginseng, herbs, and potions, as well as such oddities as dried seal penises, deer gland oil, and elk antler.

The classic thoroughfare of Chinatown is **Mott Street,** a kaleidoscopic realm of sights, flavors, odors. Restaurants and markets display racks of barbecued ducks in their storefront windows, smoked in tea and glazed to caramel perfection. In **Chinatown Fair** (8 Mott Street), an arcade off **Chatham Square,** you'll find a tic-tac-toe-playing chicken, who makes her moves with grains of rice. Head east off Mott on Pell Street to find tiny, crooked Doyers Street, its **"bloody angle"** notorious during the turn-of-the-century wars between the Hip Sing and On Leong tongs. Today, though both tongs still survive, Doyers draws visitors as the site of some superb restaurants.

Doyers Street leads out directly upon Chatham Square, the eastern locus of Chinatown. At its center stands a memorial to Chinese Americans killed in combat. Off the square, at 55 James Street, is the **Shearith Israel Cemetery,** dating from 1683 and the oldest man-made relic on Manhattan. Also nearby is **Knickerbocker Village** (Catherine and Monroe streets), where in the summer of 1950 a squad of nine FBI men came and arrested Ethel Rosenberg (in apartment GE11) for the capital crime of treason. Three years later, Ethel and husband Julius were executed for selling nuclear secrets to the Soviet Union.

The bronze statue of Confucius (by the sculptor Tiu Shih) in front of Confucius Plaza, the residential high-rise just to the north of Chatham Square, did not come easy. It was supported by traditionalists from Taiwan, but opposed by leftist Mainland Chinese immigrants, who considered the sage a reactionary symbol of old China. That the statue is there tells you who won, and says something about the political makeup of Chinatown.

Confucius Plaza abuts the mangled terminus of the **Manhattan Bridge,** its once-grand triumphal arch modified beyond recognition over time by streetcar and subway approaches. The Daniel Chester French sculptures (he also did the ones on the U.S. Customs House façade) were transferred to the Brooklyn Museum to make way for roadway modifications. One of the more bizarre sculptural touches to remain is the rendering of a buffalo hunt, right between the allegorical figures of Commerce and Industry. This 1905 bridge, designed for lighter traffic than today's auto, truck, and train onslaught, has suffered for its reconfiguring, and pales in comparison with its mighty neighbor, the Brooklyn Bridge, to the south.

■ LITTLE ITALY

Little Italy is concentrated in the Mulberry-to-Mott corridor north of Canal, with most of the restaurants in the blocks around Grand and Hester. Wander too far off this axis and you'll encounter signs written in Chinese (they'd be on Mulberry Street, too, if the local neighborhood association hadn't requested otherwise), as the turf becomes increasingly Sinicized.

Even the **Festa di San Gennaro,** Little Italy's showcase street fair celebrated for the 10 days around September 19, has become diluted with non-Italian influences—the vendors sell egg rolls and tacos alongside the traditional sausage and peppers. Named after the patron saint of Naples (a reliquary of whose blood is supposed to liquefy each year on his feast day), the festival is either marvelously tacky, sentimentally moving, or obnoxiously raucous, depending on your mood. Still, to ride a miniature ferris wheel among nineteenth-century tenements is a surreal enough experience to warrant a try.

Traditional Italian sausage for sale during the San Gennaro Festival in Little Italy. (photo by Katsuyoshi Tanaka). San Gennaro is the patron saint of Naples. (right)

A relic of another kind, of Little Italy's Mafia-connected notoriety, stands on the corner of Mulberry and Hester: **Umberto's Clam House**, where on April 7, 1972, "Crazy" Joey Gallo got his. Gallo was a mob rub-out guy with pretensions: he used to quote Sartre and dabble in oil painting. He also kept a lion chained in the basement of his social club in Brooklyn, in case he wanted to bring somebody down there and make him an offer he couldn't refuse.

Gallo's assassination at Umberto's was payback for years of contract hits and high visibility. There's still a bullet hole in the rear kitchen door. Another legacy of the place's Mafia past has a certain delicious irony: for almost a decade, the federal government ran the place, taking it over after the bust of Matthew (Matty the Horse) Ianniello and eight other owners. They had skimmed $2 million off the take at Umberto's, and the unlikely result of their convictions was Feds "owning" a mob hang-out.

Bordering Little Italy, to the immediate west at 240 Centre Street, is the fabulously baroque **Old NYC Police Headquarters**, built in 1909 and converted to high-priced condos in 1988. Model Cindy Crawford, actress Winona Ryder, and tennis ace Steffi Graf are among the celebrities who have apartments here. At the far northern reaches of the area, on the corner of Lafayette and East Houston, is

An illustration from the Police Gazette, *circa 1890, shows "A party of New York girls enjoying a little after-dinner pistol practice at the trains that rush by the windows of their hotel." (Culver Pictures, NYC)*

Some of New York's finest display their motoring skills in this 1930s photograph.
(Underwood Photo Archives)

SELLING NUBBINS

I set my sights on the Feast of San Gennaro, the street fair that draws over three million New Yorkers and visitors to Little Italy each September. Knowing that I had neither the stamina nor the courage (nor, for that matter, the vendor's license) to have my own booth for the entire eleven-day run of the Feast, I decided instead that I would try to join forces with another vendor. I called the San Gennaro Society; a man with a hoarse, New Yorky rasp told me that all prospective vendors should report to the "trailer office" at 195 Hester Street between ten A.M. and five P.M. on September third, a few days before the Feast was to commence. Hying myself to this location on the appointed day, I climbed three wooden steps and knocked on the door of the trailer parked on the side of the street. A teenage boy opened the door for me, revealing a plump woman in her sixties adorned with a royal blue sweatshirt and with two pink hair curlers atop her head.

"Can I help you?" she asked, her voice a mixture of warmth and gravel.

"Yes. Is this the place where people who want to be vendors come?"

A wide variety of "fruit" magnets available here. No refrigerator is complete without them. (photo by Katsuyoshi Tanaka)

"What do you sell?"

"I've, unh…I've invented a new snack food."

"Oh, really?" she asked, not all that interested. "What is it?"

"They're called Nubbins. It's like French bread with melted chocolate inside it. I'm wondering if it'd be possible to supply it to someone who would sell it at his stand."

She looked concerned.

"It's French bread with chocolate?" she asked.

I nodded.

She visibly shuddered.

"Oooh," she said, grimacing, "you just sent *shivers* down my spine."

"Well, you've had croissants with chocolate inside them before, right?" I tried to reason. "It's like that." I described their appearance as "lovely."

She looked down at the floor as if averting the sight of blood. "That would be very difficult to get someone to resell."

—Henry Alford, *Municipal Bondage*, 1993

Gold Rolex watches only $25! Just one of the incredible bargains to be had along Canal Street.

the equally well-restored **Puck Building,** built by the founders of the *fin-de-siècle* humor magazine, *Puck,* and later home to the modern-day, similarly catty satire magazine, *Spy.*

■ LOWER EAST SIDE

"Everybody ought to have a Lower East Side in their life," said Irving Berlin, and it would take the composer of "God Bless America" to lay a sunny face on the vast conglomeration of slums, tenement dwellings, and historical misery to which the district played host.

In the nineteenth century, the miasmic living conditions in these tenement apartments, especially in hovel-like structures illegally slapped onto the rear of the buildings (reformer-photographer Jacob Riis called them "caves"), meant disease ran rampant. Families were packed in, and privacy was nonexistent. The whole seething mass of humanity was shorted on city services and quarantined from "respectable" people.

But Berlin had a point: hard times may take on a roseate glow in retrospect, especially when they are shared by such a vibrant community as the Jewish one which flourished here, a half-million strong, in the rough half-century after 1880. It's only part of the story on display in the **Lower East Side Tenement Museum** at 97 Orchard Street, which also includes the stories of other ethnic groups—most notably freed slaves—that are part of Lower East Side history. This is a "living history" museum, housed in one of the very tenements it seeks to memorialize.

The neighborhood today is primarily Puerto Rican and Hispanic ("**Loisada**" is Spanish street slang for the East Side south of 14th Street), but increasingly, Chinese and other Asian immigrants are settling the corridor of East Broadway. There are still remnants of the Yiddish Golden Age, like the **Eldridge Street Synagogue** (12 Eldridge Street), the first building in the New World erected by Eastern European Orthodox Jews. Comedian Eddie Cantor's boyhood home was across the street.

It is the shops and emporia of the neighborhood which afford the clearest glimpse into the past. Take **Hollander Pickle Products** (known as Guss's) at 35 Essex Street, a deliriously pungent shop where the pickles are displayed immersed in brine, still in their huge wooden barrels. **Russ & Daughters** at 179 East Houston Street sells smoked fish, but is really a purveyor of something far more ethereal— the authentic Lower East Side experience.

IMMIGRANT WORK

*A*t eight in the morning I put my left arm through the strap of the basket, lifting it and adjusting it on my back, the other arm through the strap of the boiler, over my neck, keeping the boiler on my chest. All you could see of me from a distance was my troublesome straw hat! My instructions were to walk up Elizabeth Street four blocks, turn east and cross the Bowery, which already had the elevated, then walk two blocks more. When I reached the blocks of private houses, I was to walk up the stoops, pull the bell, and when the door opened, to say, "Buy tinware."

At my first port of call my heart was in my mouth. I hesitated. Taking a long breath, I climbed up a stoop and yanked the bell. I was in suspense. The door opened. A redheaded young giant appeared. He looked at me and my outfit without a word. He was not a bit rough. He merely laid his hand very gently on the boiler in front of me and gave me a good shove. I descended backwards rapidly, finally landing in a sitting position in the middle of the street, my stock strewn about me in all directions. With great effort I managed to readjust my basket and wash boiler. Now what? I thought. I could not pull another bell if I tried. I turned back to Elizabeth Street. Entering a yard I saw an open door—a woman near it. I made my first sale—a cup for ten cents—the profit was not bad!

—Samuel Cohen, ca. 1900, as excerpted from *How We Lived: A Documentary History of Immigrant Jews In America 1880-1930,* 1979

Immigrant vendors of the Lower East Side, ca. 1910. (Underwood Photo Archives)

Economy Candy Market (108 Rivington Street), where the halvah is made on the premises, has an astounding, colorful, variegated, mouth-watering inventory for the bargain-minded. Finally, **Schapiro's Wine Co.** (124 Rivington) is Manhattan's only kosher winery, and offers free wine tastings and tours daily, on the hour, from 11 A.M. to 4 P.M.

Orchard Street, south of Houston, is another cultural survivor masked as a retail bazaar. The street may no longer be dense with pushcarts, but the bargains live on, in a riot of discount houses, cubbyhole shops, and spillover sidewalk sale racks. Name brands at a discount—the idea is commonplace today, but Orchard Street was the original. And even though the merchandise here may be infiltrated with cheap knock-offs, the sheer experience of retail frenzy (especially on Sunday, when the street is closed to cars) is hard to beat.

The **Williamsburg Bridge** (Manhattan terminus on Delancey Street) was the second span to cross the East River to Brooklyn, and is surely among the most uninspired bridges in the area. Until it was recently cleared out by bulldozer, a shantytown of homeless people was sheltered beneath the bridge. Nearby at 255 Grand Street is the pioneering **Henry Street Settlement,** a social-service organization that was among the first to reach out to the vast population of the Lower East Side with medical, cultural, educational, and housing aid. Today its three theaters and exhibit spaces offer a rich mix of Latino and multi-cultural exhibits and performances.

East River Park, a green crescent beneath the Williamsburg Bridge north from Corlear's Hook, is an exuberant (if overgrown) "front yard" of the neighboring housing projects. Especially in summer, it is alive with the sounds of impromptu crap games, boom boxes, and softball. Vendors hawk tropical-hued cones shaved off from solid blocks of ice, or barbecued shish kebab featuring meat of unknown provenance. The bridge booms with traffic up above, the East River tidal strait roils next door: one of the overlooked pleasures of Manhattan.

"The excitement of New York City is that you turn a corner and it's an entirely different set."
—Alan King

TRIBECA AND SOHO

"THE ROLE OF THE ARTIST IN NEW YORK," said former mayor Ed Koch, indulging in some fine Manhattan-style irony and at the same time formulating a real estate aphorism, "is to make a neighborhood so desirable that artists can't afford to live there anymore." He was talking about two neighborhoods in particular, **TriBeCa and SoHo,** which in the last few decades have grown and blossomed as residential districts after being "discovered" by a vanguard of artists in search of cheap studio space.

SoHo came first. It was named not after the London district (confusingly known as "the Greenwich Village of London") but as an acronym formed from "South of Houston Street." Its development into one of Manhattan's priciest neighborhoods followed a process that has since become formula in other neighborhoods (most notably TriBeCa).

It goes something like this: cheap commercial space attracts artists looking for studios, the artists exude a certain bohemian cachet, attracting trendoids with money but often little artistic cachet of their own, and the resulting competition for space forces out the artists, who move on to trigger the whole process elsewhere.

Besides their romantic genesis into modern-day Manhattan neighborhoods, one other thing SoHo and TriBeCa shared was great cast-iron architecture. The cast-iron façade, one of New York's gifts to the world, developed in the mid-nineteenth century as a cheap way to mimic fancy architectural detailing. Cast-iron façades were bolted onto the brick or stone masonry of the building, sheathing it in elaborate, often lyrical ornamentation.

The appeal of these façades is illustrated by the tragicomic story of one Manhattan warehouse, built in 1849 by ironmonger James Bogardus, the originator and acknowledged master of the process. In 1970, when the TriBeCa warehouse was demolished, the cast-iron was unbolted and slated for re-erection elsewhere. Somewhere along the way, this priceless urban artifact was stolen by "scrapnappers" and sold for junk.

■ TRIBECA

TriBeCa was once known as the Lower West Side, but savvy realtors in the mid-1970s knew the power of a catchy name—they had just witnessed the wonders it

BEFORE BIG ART

*U*p until a few years ago Soho was an obscure district of lofts used chiefly for storage and light manufacturing. It was, of course, a combination of many unattractive things that led to the Soho of today, but quite definitely the paramount factor was the advent of Big Art. Before Big Art came along, painters lived, as God undoubtedly intended them to, in garrets or remodeled carriage houses, and painted paintings of a reasonable size. A painting of a reasonable size is a painting that one can easily hang over a sofa. If a painting cannot be easily hung over a sofa it is obviously a painting painted by a painter who got too big for his brushes . . . .

One day a Big Artist realized that if he took all of the sewing machines and bales of rags out of a three-thousand-square-foot loft and put in a bathroom and kitchen he would be able to live and make Big Art in the same place. He was quickly followed by other Big Artists and they by Big Lawyers, Big Boutique Owners, and Big Rich Kids. Soon there was a Soho and it was positively awash in hardwood floors, talked-to plants, indoor swings, enormous record collections, hiking boots, Conceptual Artists, video communes, Art book stores, Art grocery stores, Art restaurants, Art bars, Art galleries, and boutiques selling tie-dyed raincoats, macramé flower pots, and Art Deco salad plates.

—Fran Lebowitz, *Metropolitan Life,* 1974

had done for SoHo. Thus the acronym "TriBeCa" (try-beck-ah) was born, an acronym of sorts for "the triangle below Canal." Within the boundaries of Canal Street, West Broadway, and the Hudson, there was much valuable turf waiting to be exploited.

It worked. TriBeCa today is a thriving commercial, residential, and artistic community. At the apex of its triangle is the World Trade Center, and to some extent the whole neighborhood is shadowed by this double vision of Big Brother, looming like madness overhead. Maybe that's why TriBeCa has retained—much more than SoHo—its urban frontier feel. Despite the spiraling real estate prices, there is something provisional and sparse about TriBeCa as a neighborhood—which, given the overdeveloped and overpopulated character of other parts of Manhattan, is exactly how some residents like it.

The area first bloomed as a commercial center with the age of the steamship, when the deep-water wharves along the Hudson took away shipping business from the older, shallow-draft piers of the East River. Washington Market, the island's first major fruit and vegetable market, became the impetus for much of the district's commercial development, as the Federal and Greek Revival residences in the area were converted to warehouses.

The eastern edge of the neighborhood is permeable, so we begin with an institution somewhat outside its purlieu, but somehow fitting in with TriBeCa's overall mood: **the Clocktower** at 108 Leonard Street and Broadway, a non-profit arm of the Institute of Contemporary Art, with a magnificent Beaux Arts exterior. The gallery itself seeks to strop the cutting edge of the avant-garde, but the Clocktower's best feature has nothing to do with art: climb the stairs to see the escapement of the actual clock, 14 stories above City Hall Park.

Closer to West Broadway, which functions as TriBeCa's main stem, is **Franklin Furnace** at 112 Franklin Street; part bookstore, part gallery, part theater, part "installation," it is all alternative. Nearby, at 38 White Street, is **Let There Be Neon,** a riotous emporium offering small- as well as large-scale expressions of what began as an advertising gimmick and wound up as an art form.

Nearer the water, at 375 Greenwich Street, is the **TriBeCa Film Center,** a professional building located in an old coffee warehouse, full of editing and screening

Free advice from a panel of experts.

rooms, production offices, and hot talent. The facility was developed by Robert De Niro, as a kind of love letter to his profession and his home town. De Niro keeps an office there, as do Stephen Spielberg, Ron Howard, and Quincy Jones.

Somehow the most endearing aspects of trendy TriBeCa are those that reveal its historic origins. **Harrison Street** between Greenwich and Hudson streets is a perfect museum of a block, its Federal row houses standing in mute reproach to the massive **Independence Plaza** housing complex and the huge **Manhattan Community College** nearby.

Duane Park, at Duane and Hudson, is another neighborhood area with anachronistic appeal to it. Or try the two-block-long **Staple Street,** a charming throwback to the days when this area supplied the island's "staples" of fruit, vegetables, dairy, and coffee. Nearby on Chambers Street between West and Greenwich is **Washington Market Park,** one of the island's best-designed small parks, on the site of the original eighteenth-century market.

At Pier 26 of the Hudson is the **River Project,** reaching even farther into the island's past to reclaim something that's almost totally disappeared: the littoral fringe of Manhattan. A park that restores this fragment of shoreline to its original

"In New York, people who thought they were alone find there are more people like themselves."
—*Chita Rivera*

state is proposed; for now, the River Project features an "estuarium," exhibits, and educational programs.

Canal Street, which forms TriBeCa's northern boundary and runs straight through to Chinatown, has become a vast casbah of electronic shops, hardware stores, and bargain retail outlets of every kind. In the nineteenth century, there actually was a canal on Canal Street, 40 feet wide and with a promenade on either side. It drained the Collect, a superb freshwater pond that gradually, over the colonial years, became unusable from pollution. The canal—a public works project meant to give employment to the restive unemployed—was later covered over.

Long known as a retail hardware mecca, in the last decade Canal Street has picked up a flea-market flavor. People knew something was up when East Village New Wavers began journeying downtown in the early '80s to buy their fashion accessories in Canal Street plumbing outlets. **Pearl Paint** (308 Canal), the best-stocked, best-priced art supply store in town, helped to draw the bohemian crowd. Today, beginning with the flavor and funk of Chinatown, the thoroughfare is an island-long celebration of bargain-bin retail.

■ SoHo

It began as "Hell's Hundred Acres," because the crowded slums were repeatedly beset by inferno-like fires, but SoHo boomed after the Civil War, when the neighborhood came to be known simply as the "Eighth Ward." Whole city blocks of large, multi-storied warehouse buildings became the norm. As late as the 1960s, SoHo was just one more fading Manhattan commercial district, filled with gorgeous but badly run-down architectural gems.

It is useful to remember, in order not to be taken for a total rube, that in Manhattan "Houston Street" is pronounced not like the city in Texas but as "HOUSE-ton." This is because the name came not from Sam Houston, nor yet from the Dutch words for "house" and "garden" (*huys* and *tuyn,* respectively), but from William Houstoun, a delegate to the Constitutional Convention from the state of Georgia. He married the daughter of the owner of the land tract that Houston Street originally cut through.

However you pronounce it, **Houston Street** is the northern boundary of one of Manhattan's major gallery districts. More than just the galleries and museums, however, art transformed this whole neighborhood in the space of two decades, changing it from a down-at-the-heels warehouse district to a shopping, dining, and cultural center par excellence. When the city legally blessed the previously commercially zoned loft spaces for residences in 1972, real estate values soared into the stratosphere, and a star was born.

All that money has had some salubrious effect on the streets. The **SoHo Cast-Iron Historic District** (roughly bounded by Houston, West Broadway, Crosby, and Canal streets) was created to preserve the exquisite façades, and the streets and curbs are being laboriously restored with their original "Belgian brick" cobblestones. The major street-level transformation has been the burgeoning presence of upscale stores and restaurants.

One of the great free shows in Manhattan is a leisurely tour of SoHo's art galleries, which offer a thick nest of color, lyricism, and pretension in a remarkably concentrated space. West Broadway (a separate street, two blocks west of Broadway) and Greene Street are SoHo's most prestigious addresses for galleries, but the whole neighborhood is rife with them, many warrened away on upper floors of the old warehouse buildings.

The cast-iron façades for which SoHo is famous. (photo by Katsuyoshi Tanaka)

This has advantages and disadvantages for the casual visitor, who may be overwhelmed by choice, but who will no doubt appreciate the proximity of one gallery to another. Almost all the galleries of SoHo maintain an open-door policy, and welcome browsers. The atmosphere—and the conduct expected of visitors—is similar to that of a small museum.

> For **information about particular SoHo galleries,** refer to "Visiting SoHo Galleries" opposite, to our map on p. 117, and to the *Gallery Guide* available in most SoHo kiosks and galleries.

The live arts are equally well represented in SoHo, beginning with the **Performing Garage** (33 Wooster Street), one of the oldest alternative theaters in America, and host to the resident **Wooster Group.** Monologist Spalding Gray got his start here. On the western fringe of SoHo at 209 West Houston is the venerable **Film Forum,** a three-theater complex that supports an ambitious slate of art and revival films.

Also to the west is the **New York City Fire Museum** at 278 Spring Street, which boasts that it's the largest museum of its kind in the country. It features old engines and equipment, and exhibits on fires, like the disastrous one in 1835, which destroyed much of the old Dutch part of Manhattan.

The block of Broadway south of Houston is beginning to be known as SoHo's "Museum Row," what with all the non-profit exhibition spaces opening in recent years. The **Guggenheim Museum SoHo** is at 575 Broadway, while across the street is the **New Museum of Contemporary Art** at 583 Broadway, which exhibits artists who no doubt consider the Guggenheim mummified. At the **Alternative Museum** (594 Broadway), there are Wednesday evening jazz and contemporary classical concerts, poetry readings, and dance recitals to go along with the art on the walls. Finally, at 593 Broadway, there is the **Museum for African Art,** with an exhibit space designed by Maya Lin, the same woman who designed the Vietnam Memorial in Washington, D.C.

VISITING SoHo GALLERIES

The SoHo gallery scene is decidedly low-key, so if you plan to spend a day there, dress down and relax. Before you set off to explore, drop by any gallery to pick up a *Gallery Guide*, then adjourn to Dean & DeLuca's at 560 Broadway to drink coffee and plot a strategy. Eight galleries is a reasonable goal for one day, but choose 12 on the assumption that a few will bomb. One might be inexplicably closed, and you might take an instant dislike to another.

Check each gallery's hours, as most are closed Sundays and Mondays, and many change their hours come summertime. Several large buildings on Broadway house from five to 18 galleries each—especially good to remember if it begins to rain or your shoes hurt. Keep in mind that many of the most well-respected galleries are tucked away on upper floors or behind spare façades: that showy storefront with a few big names on display may not be your best option.

A good introduction to SoHo might be **Quartet Editions** at 568 Broadway, which sells prints of works by artists such as Gregory Amenoff, Eric Fischle, Red Grooms, and Joan Snyder. At the **John Good Gallery,** 532 Broadway, you'll see contemporary painting and sculpture by respected new artists like Nancy Haynes, Greg Colson, and Britain's Fiona Ray. Next on your list might be the well-established **Holly Solomon Gallery** at 172 Mercer.

The Drawing Center at 35 Wooster hosts discussions and performances like "Cadavre Exquis," a revival of a Surrealist art-game in which each of three artists depicts one third of a human body on a piece of paper folded in thirds, none seeing what the other has drawn. If you go, chances are you'll find youngsters sprawled on the gallery floor working on projects related to the current show. Showing artists outside the art mainstream are **Ricco/Maresca** (152 Wooster), which represents artists with little or no formal training, and **Cavin-Morris Gallery** at 560 Broadway, which represents many self-taught black and Latin artists.

Vintage and contemporary photography is exhibited at 415 W. Broadway at **Witkin Gallery**—its 25th anniversary show featured photographers Edward Steichen, Berenice Abbott, Robert Doisneau, Manuel Bravo, and Edward Weston.

Ready for a break? Stop by the T Salon Restaurant at 142 Mercer for soup, sandwiches, or a salad, or have high tea there at 3:30. Refreshed, go on to **A/D** on the sixth floor at 560 Broadway, which specializes in usable objects by contemporary painters and sculptors. Perhaps that weimaraner-ornamented wallpaper border by

continues

William Wegman would work in your dining room, and Sol Lewitt's geometrically patterned table and Chuck Close's oversized photo portrait-cum-rug would spruce up the living room.

Of course, for a comparable price, you might decide to purchase a piece of art. Within the $500 to $1,500 range, works on paper (or sometimes photography) offer the broadest selection. A number of galleries exhibit works on paper exclusively; try **Castelli Graphics, Crown Point Press, Pelavin Editions, Petersburg Press, Vinalhaven Press,** or **Quartet Editions.** If you spy something slightly above your price range, it never hurts to ask for a discount. If you're seriously interested but not ready to leap, ask for a slide and biographical information.

—Marion Dillon, art consultant with Dillon Hardesty

The Leo Castelli gallery on Green Street.

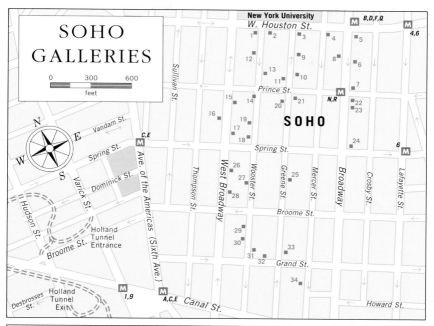

SOHO
GALLERIES

0   300   600
feet

A/D *966–5154* 22

Alternative Museum *966–4444* 5

American Fine Arts *941–0401* 31

Artists Space *226–3970* 33

Barbara Gladstone *431–3334* 20

Bess Cutler *219–1577* 28

Brooke Alexander *925–4338* 27

Cavin-Morris *226–3768* 22

Crown Point Press *226–5476* 7

Dia Center for the Arts
   473-8072 12

The Drawing Center *219–2166* 30

Fawbush *274–0660* 32

Feature *941–7077* 25

Gagosian *228–2878* 13

Holly Solomon *941–5777* 4

Jay Gorney *966–4480* 21

John Good *941–8066* 24

John Weber *966–6115* 9

Jose Freire Fine Art *941–8611* 14

Leo Castelli *431–5160* 16

Leo Castelli *431–6279* 6

Mary Boone *431–1818* 17

Max Protetch *966–5454* 22

Metro Pictures *925–8335* 3

Nancy Hoffman *966–6676* 15

New Museum of Contemporary Art
   219–1355 8

OK Harris *431–3600* 26

Pace *431–9224* 9

Pamela Auchincloss *966–7753* 23

Pat Hearn *941–7055* 29

Paula Cooper *674–0766* 1

Phyllis Kind *925–1200* 10

Quartet Editions *219–2819* 7

Ricco/Maresca *780–0071* 2

Ronald Feldman *226–3232* 34

Sonnabend *966–6160* 16

Sperone Westwater *460–5497* 11

Stephen Rosenberg *431–4838* 18

Tony Shafrazi *274–9300* 19

THE VILLAGES

"GREENWICH VILLAGE HAS NO BOUNDARIES," said Hippolyte Havel, anarchist, headwaiter, longtime confrère to the crusading communist "Red Emma" Goldman. "It is a state of mind."

It is true that Greenwich Village and its fellow traveler, the East Village, have a collective reputation which far outstrips their geography—and habitually attract such lofty pronouncements as Havel's. But it is equally true that we can delineate the turf with some precision. The Villages girdle Manhattan river to river, south of 14th Street and north of Houston Street. Broadway is the traditional boundary between the two, with the area between Hudson Street and the river sometimes informally known as the West Village.

■ GREENWICH VILLAGE

"Greenwich Village" is actually redundant, since "Greenwich" itself means "green village." The Mahicans called their settlement there Sapokanican. In the late seventeenth and early eighteenth centuries, Greenwich Village was a sleepy, farm-oriented suburb to the north of the clamorous urban mass of Lower Manhattan—a rural refuge of the wealthy, the Hamptons of its day. One of these arrivistes, Brooklyn farmer Yellis Mandeville, named the place "Greenwyck" after a village in Brooklyn.

Disease is what made the Village boom, what transformed it from a rich man's playground to an integral part of the urban metropolis. When a series of contagions hit Lower Manhattan, beginning with an epidemic of smallpox in 1739, western Greenwich Village was the refuge of choice for those rich enough to flee. (Disease did find some of these refugees, but the Village's sparser population seemed at least to promise less contact with the infected.) Subsequent scourges of cholera and yellow fever prompted new stampedes north, culminating in the great yellow fever plague of 1822. This last caused such a population shift that ferries from Brooklyn were rerouted to land at the Village instead of Wall Street.

When the fevers subsided, many of those displaced returned to their old haunts in Lower Manhattan, but others liked the pastoral precincts of the Village so much that they stayed on. Its population quadrupled in the second quarter of the nineteenth century, but as Manhattan charged north, Greenwich Village remained a charming enclave, exempting itself from the grid plan that was imposing utilitarian order upon the island. Its crazy-quilt lanes and streets, many of them following old Indian paths and colonial property lines, set it apart from other, newer neighborhoods.

The quirky nature of the surroundings attracted an equally quirky population. A burgeoning French presence in the Village, plus a subsequent influx of artists, political radicals, and bohemians, lent the place an air of the foreign, the free, and the licentious. In the years before and after World War I, the Village peaked as a hotbed of free love and socialism, free verse and abstract art. The 1950s and '60s saw a resurgence in the area's reputation for the unorthodox, with Abstract Expressionists, beatniks, and folkies taking up residence. Today, that reputation is only a faint ghost haunting a still picturesque, but determinedly upper-middle-class neighborhood.

Like a solar system with twin suns, Greenwich Village revolves around two squares. **Washington Square** is the largest and oldest public space in the neighborhood. From **Sheridan Square** west to the river runs yet another important axis of Village life, **Christopher Street**, symbolic and geographic center of gay and lesbian New York.

■ CHRISTOPHER STREET AND SHERIDAN SQUARE

Sheridan Square is more a confluence of streets than a true square, a quadruple intersection where the traffic runs in at crazy and sometimes terrifying angles. As a neighborhood, Sheridan Square is in many ways the heart of the Village, a heart which beats faster than a pedestrian's in a mad dash across Seventh Avenue.

Seventh Avenue is, indeed, the reason for the truncated nature of streets in the area. During World War I, the IRT subway—then held by a private company—wanted to extend its line south, and it preferred to build under an established street. Such was the sway the IRT had with city government that a thoroughfare —Seventh Avenue South—was promptly cut through the Village.

Seen on a map, Seventh Avenue can be identified as the interloper it is. Longtime Villagers still refer to the swath it bulldozed as "**the Cut.**" The Cut brought even more traffic and noise to the neighborhood once Seventh Avenue was connected with the **Holland Tunnel**.

Sheridan Square (bounded by West Fourth and Barrow streets, Washington Place, and Seventh Avenue South) is sometimes confused with another, adjacent

After seven years of construction, the Holland Tunnel opened to traffic in 1927. (Underwood Photo Archives)

green space. The leafy park near Sheridan Square is actually **Christopher Park** (Grove and Christopher streets, Seventh Avenue South). One reason for the confusion just might be the statue of Civil War general Philip Sheridan, standing not in Sheridan Square but in Christopher Park.

Among other things, the Sheridan Square area is the "Times Square of Off-Broadway," with an unrivaled concentration of popular, small, or experimental theaters. **Circle in the Square,** the original Off-Broadway company, started out as the Loft Players at 5 Sheridan Square: their first hit, and the production that more or less created the phenomenon of Off-Broadway, was Tennessee Williams's *Summer and Smoke* in 1952. Circle in the Square moved to Bleecker Street in 1960, then to Times Square in 1972.

Just south of Sheridan Square, at 99 Seventh Avenue South, is **Circle Repertory Company,** home to Lanford Wilson, among other playwrights. At One Sheridan Square is the **Charles Ludlum Theater,** where the **Ridiculous Theater Company** stages its hilarious (and stinging) parodies. The site was once the home of **Cafe Society** (one of New York's first non-segregated nightclubs), where Billie Holiday burst forth upon the world in 1938.

Matching the theater on the stage is the theater of the streets—especially Christopher Street. While the homosexual community has become more politically active throughout the city and country, it was here that the first blow was struck for gay rights. On the night of June 28, 1969, police raided the **Stonewall Inn** (then located at 51 Christopher Street), because back then it was a violation of state liquor law to sell a homosexual a drink. While the arrested patrons were at first docile, harsh police action created something previously unthinkable: a gay crowd that fought back.

The Gay Pride movement dates from this event, with end-of-June marches all over the country celebrating the community and the victory over prejudice that the incident at the Stonewall signified. Though the inn has gone through a few incarnations since then (there is now a bar next door that calls itself Stonewall), Christopher Street retains its status as the gay community's main drag—sometimes literally, as during the annual Halloween Parade.

There are charming remnants of historical Greenwich Village tucked away just off Christopher on its march west to the river. **Grove Court** (entrance between 10 and 12 Grove Street) is a gorgeous little cul-de-sac, originally built for the families

The Stonewall Gay/Lesbian Parade has become an annual event marking the police raid and subsequent riot at the Stonewall Inn in June of 1969.

of tradesmen, but now the domain of the wealthy. **St. Luke's Chapel** (St. Luke's-in-the-Fields), at 487 Hudson Street, had a complete square of row-houses surrounding it when it was built, in the year of the yellow fever epidemic, 1822. Its parish house, still standing, was the boyhood home of writer Bret Harte.

Farther east on Bedford Street near Sixth Avenue is the oldest house in the Village (1799) at 77 Bedford. The 9$^{1}/_{2}$-foot-wide house next door was home to both Edna St. Vincent Millay and John Barrymore (at different times). Where Christopher Street hits Sixth Avenue, there is a small, crooked street that would seem to be an emblem of the homosexual community, but isn't. **Gay Street** is almost an alley, named after an early Greenwich Village farm family. From the mid-nineteenth century to the 1920s, Gay Street was an incredibly overpopulated black ghetto. But in the 1950s it became famous as the site of the apartment (at 14 Gay Street) in Ruth McKenney's long-running Broadway play *My Sister Eileen,* starring Shirley Booth, and later made into the musical *Wonderful Town,* with Rosalind Russell.

North on Sixth Avenue from the Christopher Street intersection is the **Jefferson Market Library,** a mock-Bavarian assemblage that appears to be a hallucination in orange brick. Built on the site of the old Jefferson produce market, the building was originally a district courthouse (the first night court in the country convened there). By 1945 it had fallen into disuse, its clocks forever stalled at 3:20. Only a vigorous preservation effort prevented it from being replaced by an apartment building; it reopened as a public library in 1967.

Near Jefferson Market, on West 10th Street, is **Patchin Place** and its Sixth Avenue twin, **Milligan Place,** hideaway residential courts that, like Grove Court, were originally built as working-class housing. The poet e.e. cummings was a longtime resident of Patchin Place, as was the novelist Djuna Barnes. Today, upscale groceries like the marvelously fragrant, jam-packed **Balducci's** (424 Sixth Avenue) and nearby **Jefferson Market** carry on the area's comestible tradition.

■ WASHINGTON SQUARE

The area now called Washington Square once drained a creek the Indians called Manata—"Devil Water." Minetta Creek, now channeled and controlled, still flows underneath the park. It's a reminder of the time when the area was a miasmic marsh, used as a communal burial plot. The bodies of cholera victims from all over the city were dumped into the swamp, still wrapped in their yellow shrouds. Some were later moved, but there are still an estimated 10,000 to 20,000 bodies buried beneath Washington Square—testimony to the lethal epidemics that hit Manhattan in the eighteenth and early nineteenth centuries.

From a cemetery and potter's field it was only a short step down to a hanging ground, which the site became in the eighteenth century. Like the subterranean Minetta Creek, there is a *memento mori* of this period, too: the celebrated "hanging

GENTEEL WASHINGTON SQUARE

*T*he ideal of quiet and of genteel retirement, in 1835, was found in Washington Square, where the Doctor built himself a handsome, modern, wide-fronted house, with a big balcony before the drawing-room windows, and a flight of white marble steps ascending to a portal which was also faced with white marble. This structure, and many of its neighbors, which it exactly resembled, were supposed, forty years ago, to embody the last results of architectural science, and they remain to this day very solid and honorable dwellings. In front of them was the square, containing a considerable quantity of inexpensive vegetation, enclosed by a wooden paling, which increased its rural and accessible appearance; and round the corner was the more august precinct of the Fifth Avenue, taking its origin at this point with a spacious and confident air which already marked it for high destinies. I know not whether it is owing to the tenderness of early associations, but this portion of New York appears to many persons the most delectable. It has a kind of established repose which is not of frequent occurrence in other quarters of the long, shrill city; it has a riper, richer more honorable look than any of the upper ramifications of the great longitudinal thoroughfare—the look of having had something of a social history. It was here, as you might have been informed on good authority, that you had come into a world which appeared to offer a variety of sources of interest; it was here that your grandmother lived, in venerable solitude, and dispensed a hospitality which commended itself alike to the infant imagination and the infant palate; it was here that you took your first walks abroad, following the nursery-maid with unequal step, and sniffing up the strange odor of the ailanthus-trees which at that time formed the principal umbrage of the Square, and diffused an aroma that you were not yet critical enough to dislike as it deserved; it was here, finally, that your first school, kept by a broad-bosomed, broad-based old lady with a ferule, who was always having tea in a blue cup, with a saucer that didn't match, enlarged the circle both of your observations and your sensations.

—Henry James, *Washington Square,* 1881

Washington Square is alive with music from the first warm day of spring to the last of autumn.

tree," the large elm in the northwestern quadrant of the park. It is believed to be the oldest tree in Manhattan, and criminals were hung from its boughs as late as 1819.

It wasn't until July 4, 1828, that Washington Square opened as a public space—a military parade ground. The **triumphal arch** that is the Square's most recognizable feature had its first incarnation in 1889. The original arch was wooden, and commemorated the centennial of George Washington's inauguration as U.S. President. It proved so popular it was replaced with a permanent marble version in 1895, courtesy of funds raised from the public, partially through a benefit concert given by Polish patriot and pianist Jan Paderewski.

In a stroke of performance art that claimed the arch for informed Village madness, a half-dozen co-conspirators—the painter Marcel Duchamp among them—climbed to its top in January 1917 to declare "the Free and Independent Republic of Washington Square." They read a proclamation—consisting of the word "whereas," repeated ad infinitum—got drunk and toasted the New Bohemia. Later on, during World War II, the hollow interior of the arch was rumored to be the adopted digs of an ingenious—but homeless—draft-dodger.

Washington Square today represents the benign tension between anarchy and order that occurs when the Village's old reputation for free-living clashes with its new reality as a solidly middle-class haven. The unruliness of the park crowd—which has at times included more than its share of marijuana peddlers and pickpockets—occasionally upsets the upscale neighborhood residents, but police seem to have struck a compromise between carnival craziness and public order. Most times, on a summer weekend, say, Washington Square still presents a superb *tableau vivant* of Village life, with street performers drawing huge crowds.

The institutional presence of **New York University** lies rather heavily upon the neighborhood surrounding Washington Square. **Bobst Library** (70 Washington Square South) is an especially oppressive presence, one of three "redskins" (buildings with red-stone façades) built when architect Philip Johnson proposed a comprehensive "look" for the whole university. Luckily, the plan was later abandoned. For a more graceful NYU presence, there's the **Judson Hall belltower** at 51 Washington Square South, which now serves as a dormitory—although there's plumbing only on the lower floors.

Balancing out the institutional architecture on the south side of the square are the restored properties to the north. Again, NYU owns or leases most of "The Row" of charming Federal or Greek Revival townhouses, some of them only the façades and shells of the originals. This is the Washington Square of the nineteenth century, when it was a residential haven for the wealthy, recognizable from the eponymous Henry James novel.

James's grandmother had a townhouse on the corner of Fifth at the square, now the site of **2 Fifth Avenue.** In the lobby here is an odd little reminder of the area's swampy roots: a clear pipe, where the waters of Minetta Brook may be seen bubbling from underground.

From the southwest corner of the park—where there are fierce street chess tournaments, similar to those portrayed in the movie *Searching for Bobby Fischer*—**MacDougal Street** provides an entry point into a "Positively Fourth Street" Dylanesque district of coffee houses, jazz clubs, and restaurants. This was originally one of Manhattan's many "Little Italy" neighborhoods, and the trattorias are still there, as well as the flavorful feel of the narrow, busy streets.

Off MacDougal, on tiny Minetta Lane, is **Minetta Lane Theatre,** an Off-Broadway venue, and Minetta Tavern, where a locked door off the basement leads to an open channel of—yes, once again—Minetta Creek. Another hidden treasure is the **MacDougal-Sullivan Gardens,** a private enclave mid-block, north of Houston Street. Also north of Houston one block over is **Sullivan Street Playhouse** (181 Sullivan Street), where the longest-running show in American history, *The Fantasticks,* continues its marathon dance on the boards.

North of Washington Square, Fifth Avenue begins its long run on a graceful note at **Washington Mews.** Like most Manhattan residential courts (and like its sister mews, **MacDougal Alley,** one block west), this one became a prestige address only in the twentieth century. It was originally a back street for tradespeople.

The long block of **Eighth Street** between Fifth and Sixth avenues has become enshrined in the shoppers' Hall of Fame as a sort of wannabe jamboree. Shoe and accessory stores lining the street dispense an instant East Village look that has itself become a fashion, after a sort. At least one address here is the real thing: **Electric Lady Studios,** downstairs from the Eighth Street Playhouse at 52 West Eighth Street, was founded by the late, great guitarist Jimi Hendrix in the '60s.

To get a glimpse of what Fifth Avenue was like in its glory days of huge residential mansions, check out the **Salmagundi Club** at 47 Fifth Avenue. Originally the Irad Hawley residence, after 1917 it became the new home to the oldest artists' club in the country, itself founded in 1870. The ground floor, maintained in its original nineteenth-century elegance, is sometimes open during exhibitions and is well worth a look.

ARTISTS IN THE '40S

In the 1920s and 1930s the New York art scene was small and artists were few, but in the 1940s it began to change. American artists began to know what was going on in Europe from reproductions; then in the late '30s impending war brought some of these painters to America. It was the beginning of the so-called New York School and the emergence of the abstract art movement, in particular, Abstract Expressionism.

I remember it well as I met my husband Fritz Bultman in 1942, and he was part of that group. Fritz was the son of an old New Orleans family, and he felt as if he'd "escaped" when he went to Europe at age 16 for three years, then returned to paint in New York. Manhattan was exhilarating, filled with other young artists and writers who crowded together in small apartments in the Village.

Some of these artists came from the WPA program and a good many from the Hans Hofmann School. Before that, the only places to study were the Art Students League and the National Academy, both of which taught traditional art. Hofmann was a big, jovial man with a heavy accent and a wonderful sense of humor who had come from Germany in 1931, taught at Berkeley, then started his own school in New York in 1933. Because he knew the work of Picasso, Braque, and Matisse, he was able to impart new ideas to the artists in New York, who only knew this new direction in painting from reproductions.

By the early '40s, abstract artists in New York began to come together, visit each others' studios, talk endlessly, and finally to show in the handful of galleries interested in their work. Short, elegant Gorky, gentle Pollock (when he was sober), temperamental Rothko, and de Kooning (the handsome Dutchman) were all there at the same time and began to exhibit at Julian Levy, Sidney Janis, Betty Parsons, and a bit later at Charlie Egan, Sam Kootz, and Peggy Guggenheim galleries. All together there were only about 50 artists and they all knew each other. Every gallery opening brought them together to celebrate and criticize each other's work and talk about it. After the openings, we would go out together for hamburgers and beer and talk late into the night—comparing Picasso to Matisse, classical and modern art.

All the artists believed intensely in what they were doing, and while they had some encouragement from the critics, they had few, if any, sales. The galleries were in the 57th Street area. There were few if any in the Village where many artists lived and worked, and there was no such thing as SoHo.

In the '50s the scene changed as artists began to sell modestly and more galleries opened. The Whitney Museum and the Stable Gallery had their "Annuals," so many artists could be shown together, and this was like an intense celebration. Since then, the growth of the art scene in New York City has been constant.

—Jeanne Bultman

"I guess I'm still here because everywhere else I go I feel like a misfit. Here, everyone's a misfit."
—*Joe Jackson*

Also warranting a quick visit are the **Forbes Magazine Galleries** at 62 Fifth Avenue, interesting for their insight into what a millionaire does with his spare time. This one, the flamboyant publisher of *Forbes* magazine, collected Fabergé eggs, toy soldiers, and yachts—all of which are represented here (the boats as models). Forbes enjoyed tweaking noses, and he located his headquarters not far from the offices of the American Communist Party.

■ EAST VILLAGE

When the Third Avenue El was pulled down in 1955, a longtime psychological boundary line went with it, allowing that Greenwich Village "state of mind" to migrate east. Today, it is the East Village which carries the bohemian torch of poverty, vanguard artistic movements, and social advocacy. The name is of fairly recent vintage: the East Village was once only the northern part of the Lower East Side—and is still called "Loisada" by its Latino inhabitants. In the 1950s, real estate

Greenwich Village has often served as the meeting place for political activists, as this 1930 rally demonstrates. (Underwood Photo Archives)

developers borrowed the cachet of its western neighbor when they wanted to upgrade the area's image. They first tried "Village East," then, after 1961, the East Village.

The results of all this image-buffing have been decidedly mixed. The East Village remains largely scruffy and neo-bohemian, featuring a vibrant mix of artists, students, Ukrainian immigrants, and social dropouts. St. Mark's Place remains one of the world's great street carnivals. The eastern fringe of the East Village is called **Alphabet City** (after the neighborhood's Avenues A through D), and has pretty much resisted the blandishments of development. East of the "DMZ"—the sardonic *nom de pave* for Avenue A—a close-knit Puerto Rican community and a fiercely political squatters' rights movement battle to keep out predatory outsiders.

Yet for all its low-rent reputation today, the East Village began its life as part of the vast estate of the Stuyvesant family, heirs to Director General Peter Stuyvesant's original land grant from the Dutch West India Company. The Bowery, the neighborhood's great historical thoroughfare and its working-class answer to Broadway, was once the road to Stuyvesant's farm, or "bouwerie."

Stuyvesant is still there, his bones resting beneath a children's playground near St. Mark's Church. But the East Village has undergone successive transformations

New Yorkers dress their car for the annual Puerto Rican Day parade.
(photo by Katsuyoshi Tanaka)

Who says there's no greenery in Manhattan?

from a rich man's turf to immigrant haven to hipster's paradise. Today, it is one of the most animated and compelling neighborhoods in Manhattan.

The best route to enter the neighborhood is via Eighth Street, which actually represents a little piece of the East Village that strayed west. Eighth Street gives out onto **Astor Place**, an abbreviated public space behind Cooper Union that sometimes serves as an informal flea market. **Astor Place Hair Designers,** located at 2 Astor Place, is famed for its radical haircuts and long lines that often spill out onto the sidewalk and add to the festival atmosphere of the area.

The Astor Place subway stop features a beaver motif on its decorative wall tiles. This is a reference to the fur-based fortune of John Jacob Astor, who lived on Lafayette Street south of Astor Place in the early nineteenth century. The stretch, known as **Colonnade Row,** was once lined with mansions, and some of their palatial façades still remain.

What is now the **Public Theater** (425 Lafayette) was the original Astor Library, founded after John Jacob's death in 1854, and moved uptown in 1895. The Public Theater is itself the legacy of impresario Joseph Papp, who in the mid-'60s almost single-handedly saved the beautiful Romanesque Revival building from demolition and installed a theatrical complex that proved ragingly successful.

Underwritten by such Public-produced Broadway hits as *A Chorus Line,* five playhouses and one cinema here put up a compelling list of drama and film each year, including the annual Festival Latino. The Public, together with Ellen Stewart's avant-garde **La Mama** E.T.C. at 74 East Fourth Street, are the twin gems of the East Village theater scene.

North and east of the Public, facing Astor Place with its huge, cube-like Tony Rosenthal sculpture *The Alamo* (push it—it weighs 3,000 pounds, but it turns!), is **Cooper Union** (7 East Seventh Street), one of the most remarkable colleges in the world. For one thing, in an age of spiraling educational costs, the school remains tuition-free—as intended by its idealistic founder, the remarkable inventor and self-made man, Peter Cooper.

Beginning with a grocery store, Cooper built a foundry and real estate empire that is the base of Cooper Union's extensive endowment (for example, Cooper Union owns the land upon which the Chrysler Building is sited). When Cooper Union opened in 1859, it was first in many fields: first coed, non-sectarian, non-segregated, and tuition-free college. All founded and funded by a man who could neither read nor write—but felt others should—and all located across the street from his original grocery store.

The building itself is remarkable in a couple of ways. A renovation in the mid-'70s confirmed that Cooper had used railroad rails as a structural device, making it the first steel-frame building and precursor to the modern skyscraper. Cooper also had the incredible prescience to include an elevator shaft in the original design, even though the elevator was not yet invented. Cooper Union's historic Great Hall hosted such luminaries as Susan B. Anthony and Mark Twain, as well as Abraham Lincoln, who gave a speech there that may have won him the presidency. A statue of Peter Cooper, by Augustus St. Gaudens (a Cooper Union graduate), sits in the square to the south of the building.

North of Cooper Union, running diagonally off Third Avenue, is Stuyvesant Street, which follows an old colonial pathway to the site of Peter Stuyvesant's country farmhouse. Located there now is **St.-Mark's-in-the-Bouwerie** at 131 East 10th Street, an Episcopal church that also serves the neighborhood as a community playhouse, public meeting hall, and cultural free-fire zone. The St. Mark's Poetry Project, founded by neighbor Allen Ginsberg (among others), is just one of the programs this remarkable landmark hosts and supports.

The area around Ninth Street and Stuyvesant is beginning to make a name for itself as a sort of Little Japan, hosting a collection of sake bars, restaurants, and Japanese language video stores. Even more concentrated along Sixth Street between First and Second avenues is a row of Indian restaurants so chock-a-block that some diners speculate they share one giant kitchen. The dominant immigrant culture of this lively neighborhood, however, is that of Eastern Europe: step into one of the many sausage-festooned butcher shops here to be transported instantly to the Ukraine.

St. Mark's Church also lent its name to **St. Mark's Place,** the three-block section of Eighth Street between Third Avenue and Avenue A. Here is a street-fair midway of edgy club-crawlers, disillusioned revolutionaries, and assorted fringe elements, a natural marshaling point for the armies of the twilight, a boulevard of broken flashbacks. St. Mark's is anchored—if that's the word—by **Tompkins Square Park** (bordered by Avenues A and B, Seventh and 10th streets), site of an infamous police riot in the summer of 1991, when the city tried to evict squatters from the area.

Tensions in the neighborhood have cooled since then, but there is a sense of the frontiers being pushed back by gentrification—the influx of upscale outsiders—and the real bohemia retreating to Alphabet City. One outpost there is the **Nuyorican Poetry Cafe** (236 East Third Street), a bar and performance space that features hilarious "poetry slams," readings of unproduced screenplays, and other spoken-word performances.

MANHATTAN JAZZ

New York City—and in this case we're talking Manhattan—remains *the* jazz mecca. Few other cities can boast the confluence of resident masters, journeymen/women, and emerging jazz artists, coupled with nightclubs, restaurants, bistros, pubs, barrooms, and in some cases outright holes-in-the-wall dedicated to jazz performance.

Although today the great majority of the most vital jazz clubs is below 14th Street downtown, Midtown's famed 52nd Street strip of jazz habitats and Uptown's Clark Monroe's Uptown House, Small's Paradise, Savoy Ballroom, The Cotton Club, and Minton's Playhouse, all have been history-making jazz haunts.

The last 40 years have changed that, however, and Downtown, especially Greenwich Village, is now the place for jazz. Take the **Village Vanguard** for instance, at 178 Seventh Avenue South (225-4037). Descending its narrow flight of stairs to the small, unassuming basement, a newcomer gets few clues that this is the most historic of all current Manhattan jazz clubs. Stay there long enough and gaze at the wall posters of the giants who've made history there, and you'll be quickly enchanted by the jazz truth of the place. Currently, the live sounds heard there can range from the mainstream to the cutting edge. Come on Monday nights to hear The Vanguard Jazz Orchestra, now in its third swinging decade.

Over at 131 West Third Street at the **Blue Note** (475-8592), the music is often pricey, but it's made by some of the giants—especially the great singers—of the idiom. Meanwhile, just up the street from the Blue Note, your pocketbook won't have to swing open so wide to get you into **Visiones** at 125 MacDougal Street in the Village (673-5576), which offers a tasty menu of emerging and slightly lesser known, but no less swinging, jazz bands.

Drifting uptown from the Village a bit, you might wander three blocks past 14th Street to 190 Third Avenue at 17th for **Fat Tuesday's** (533-7902), which bills itself as "The Mecca of Jazz." Its low-ceilinged room hosts a variety of good sounds, and you can catch the legendary guitarist Les Paul every Monday night. In TriBeCa is **The Knitting Factory** (transplanted from its original home in the East Village). It is New York's club home of the cutting edge, and of the most uncompromising music, jazz and otherwise—and there's no drink minimum. Located at 75 Leonard Street.

But maybe it's a quieter time you seek. Head back to Greenwich Village. Like a little jazz with your dinner? Try **Zinno** for superb Northern Italian cuisine and top-notch jazz/bass duos (126 West 13th Street, 924-5182). Out for a late aperitif after your evening on the town? **Bradley's** at 70 University Place (228-6440) is one of the great NYC jazz clubs, open a bit later than other clubs, and as great as the music usually is there, it's often just as fascinating to see what jazz greats are sitting at the bar and tables checking out the sounds.

The most complete guide to New York metro area jazz happenings is the free monthly, *Hot House,* readily obtainable at any of the jazz clubs.

—Willard Jenkins, National Jazz Service Organization

Jamming at the Village Vanguard.

CHELSEA, GRAMERCY PARK,
A N D   M U R R A Y   H I L L

THE AREA OF MANHATTAN BETWEEN THE VILLAGES AND MIDTOWN is something of a *quartier perdu*—a lost neighborhood—without the coherence of those districts above and below it. Within this sprawling heterogeneous belt, however, there are several celebrated neighborhoods that are among the most distinctive in New York. Not for ethnic rivalries, but for its patchwork nature, could the region from 14th Street to 42nd Street be characterized as the Balkans of Manhattan.

The Balkans as if designed by a mathematician, that is. For north of 14th Street, the city's grid system, implemented in 1811, kicked in in earnest. The plan lent the streets and neighborhoods a linear, calibrated atmosphere that seemed, in the eyes of the early nineteenth-century Americans at least, ultimately modern.

This area became densely settled at an incredibly rapid pace, during a time when Manhattan's settlement was quickly outstripping whatever boundaries were laid upon it. For a time, 14th Street was the town's northern limit, and whatever lay beyond was *ultima thule*. But the explosive population growth of the nineteenth century and the influx of immigrants pouring into the Lower East Side successively filled neighborhoods to the north.

Chief among these is Chelsea, which Capt. Thomas Clarke, owner of a farm in the area, named after the London neighborhood. A neighborhood that has consistently held an attraction for Manhattan's elite is Gramercy Park, centered around the only private park in the city. Cheek by jowl with the elegant aristocratic flavor of the park proper is the vast residential development of Stuyvesant Town, vertical village or human warehouse, depending on your point of view, but resolutely middle class. Nearby is Union Square, a revitalized neighborhood traditionally identified—for the rabble-rousing pro-labor speeches which used to be delivered within its precincts—with the proletariat.

Between the Union Square area and Chelsea is a district which has recently been going under the name of SoFi (**So**uth of the **Fi**atiron Building), a real estate developers' coinage with only mild currency. The Garment District, north of SoFi, has a much more secure identity, based in the intensive design, manufacturing, and wholesaling of much of the nation's clothing. East of the Garment District is an area with an aristocratic past and fairly mundane present: Murray Hill, once the chosen turf of the city's upper-class "Knickerbocracy." Today the neighborhood is famous as the site of the **Empire State Building.**

■ 14TH STREET

Fourteenth Street is a slack wire strung through the gut of Manhattan, thrummed upon by a strange assortment of street singers, bargain-bin shills, three-card-monte dealers, and meat-carcass teamsters. It's a place where dream books—those demotic pamphlets linking oneiric images with winning lottery numbers—are sold in vast quantities. When Tom Waits, that poet of the dispossessed, moved to Manhattan to oversee his Broadway show *Frank's Wild Years,* the place he chose to land was 14th Street. Say no more.

Stretching from river to river, the first great cross-town artery to announce the grid pattern to the north, 14th Street has for much of its existence served as a demarcation line. Even today, it is the traditional boundary which separates the leftish, arty districts of Greenwich Village, East Village, TriBeCa, and SoHo from the no-nonsense economic pursuits of Midtown.

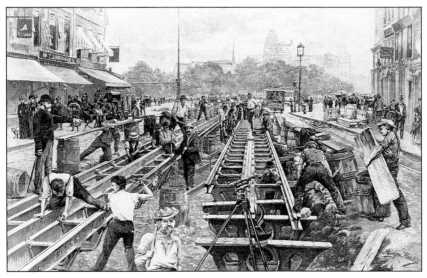

Laying the cable for the Broadway streetcars at Union Square in the 1870s. (Library of Congress)

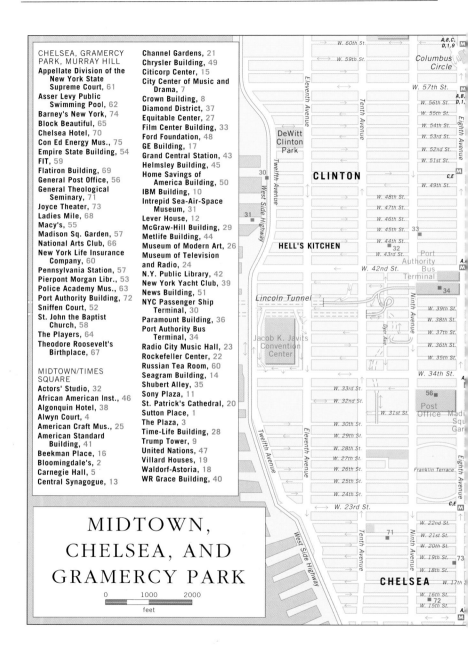

CHELSEA, GRAMERCY PARK, MURRAY HILL
Appellate Division of the New York State Supreme Court, 61
Asser Levy Public Swimming Pool, 62
Barney's New York, 74
Block Beautiful, 65
Chelsea Hotel, 70
Con Ed Energy Mus., 75
Empire State Building, 54
FIT, 59
Flatiron Building, 69
General Post Office, 56
General Theological Seminary, 71
Joyce Theater, 73
Ladies Mile, 68
Macy's, 55
Madison Sq. Garden, 57
National Arts Club, 66
New York Life Insurance Company, 60
Pennsylvania Station, 57
Pierpont Morgan Libr., 53
Police Academy Mus., 63
Port Authority Building, 72
Sniffen Court, 52
St. John the Baptist Church, 58
The Players, 64
Theodore Roosevelt's Birthplace, 67

MIDTOWN/TIMES SQUARE
Actors' Studio, 32
African American Inst., 46
Algonquin Hotel, 38
Alwyn Court, 4
American Craft Mus., 25
American Standard Building, 41
Beekman Place, 16
Bloomingdale's, 2
Carnegie Hall, 5
Central Synagogue, 13

Channel Gardens, 21
Chrysler Building, 49
Citicorp Center, 15
City Center of Music and Drama, 7
Crown Building, 8
Diamond District, 37
Equitable Center, 27
Film Center Building, 33
Ford Foundation, 48
GE Building, 17
Grand Central Station, 43
Helmsley Building, 45
Home Savings of America Building, 50
IBM Building, 10
Intrepid Sea-Air-Space Museum, 31
Lever House, 12
McGraw-Hill Building, 29
Metlife Building, 44
Museum of Modern Art, 26
Museum of Television and Radio, 24
N.Y. Public Library, 42
New York Yacht Club, 39
News Building, 51
NYC Passenger Ship Terminal, 30
Paramount Building, 36
Port Authority Bus Terminal, 34
Radio City Music Hall, 23
Rockefeller Center, 22
Russian Tea Room, 60
Seagram Building, 14
Shubert Alley, 35
Sony Plaza, 11
St. Patrick's Cathedral, 20
Sutton Place, 1
The Plaza, 3
Time-Life Building, 28
Trump Tower, 9
United Nations, 47
Villard Houses, 19
Waldorf-Astoria, 18
WR Grace Building, 40

MIDTOWN, CHELSEA, AND GRAMERCY PARK

0   1000   2000

feet

But to walk 14th Street from the East River to the Hudson is like plunging into a living diorama of Manhattan, one which measures the rich diversity of the place. Begin in Project-Land, with the Jacob Riis Houses on your left as you head west, and Stuyvesant Town looming on the right. You'll soon work into the nexus of history and present-day reality at Union Square, then immediately plunge into a three-block-long street bazaar that is a sort of Third World K-Mart. "Inside! Inside! Sta-yep inside!" implore the street shills, an unnecessary invitation, since the wares are spilling out onto the sidewalk.

If you survive that gauntlet of nickel-and-dime capitalism, you'll wind up in what was once called Little Spain—the block of 14th between Seventh and Eighth avenues—one of those Manhattan neighborhoods that host festivals for ethnic populations no longer living there. Then into the bizarre, lard-scummed streets of the Gansevoort wholesale meat market, an odoriferous place where packing crates are burned in 50-gallon drums all night long, and you are as likely to get knocked upside the head by 100-pound slabs of beef as to be propositioned by transvestite streetwalkers.

It's a strange-flavored trip, river to river on 14th Street: imagine a J. R. R. Tolkien–William S. Burroughs collaboration with a dash of Mexican soap opera. It's the kind of journey that can be accomplished nowhere but in Manhattan.

■ CHELSEA

Always a bridesmaid, Chelsea never reached really fashionable status in the nineteenth century, maintaining a slightly louche flavor that made it the natural landing place for Edith Wharton's Baroness Ellen Olenska in *The Age of Innocence.* It was not until well into the 1960s, however, that it recovered from its leapfrogged status to become a dynamic residential area with stores, theaters, and great restaurants.

Chelsea flirted with greatness before, when in the late nineteenth century Sixth Avenue between Eighth and 23rd streets featured such a concentration of clothiers and dry goods outlets that it was called **Ladies Mile.** It has also seen periods of notoriety. During the same period, and lasting until Prohibition, Sixth and Seventh avenues north from 23rd Street were part of the famed "Tenderloin," Manhattan's teeming, no-hold's-barred vice district.

An apocryphal story tells us the Tenderloin was so named by a corrupt police official, Alexander S. "Clubber" Williams, who earned his nickname from his famous quote: "There is more law in the end of a policeman's nightstick than in a decision of the Supreme Court." Williams was supposedly so gratified by the possibilities for graft in his newly assigned beat that he commented to a reporter: "I was living on rump steak in the Fourth District, but I will be having some tenderloin now." Alas, the story does not survive careful etymological scrutiny, but the character of the neighborhood, called "Satan's Circus" by reformers, was real enough. Dope, gambling, and prostitution flourished, eventually even ghettoized by street: 29th for whorehouses, 28th for high-stakes gambling, 27th for low-stakes games of chance.

Manhattan vice has since accomplished a diaspora to points elsewhere, and the kind of Ladies Mile shopping is represented in Chelsea only by such meccas as **Barney's New York** at 106 Seventh Avenue, the landmark men's (and more recently, women's) clothing outlet, and of course **Macy's** at 151 West 34th Street, celebrated as "the largest store in the world."

Near Barney's, and an unavoidable dominating presence in lower Chelsea, is the gargantuan **Port Authority Building** at 111 Eighth Avenue, precursor to the World Trade Center and featuring elevators big enough for full-size trucks. But the neighborhood's most famous landmark is the **Chelsea Hotel** at 22 West 23rd Street, host to successive generations of bohemians and more famous for its literary guests than for its rather seedy accommodations.

The list of Chelsea Hotel luminaries is endless: Mark Twain, William Dean Howells, and O. Henry all put in time here; both Thomas Wolfe and Tennessee Williams briefly lived and wrote at the hotel; Brendan Behan spent his New York sojourn based here; and Dylan Thomas was spending nights in the Chelsea when he drank himself to death at Greenwich Village's White Horse Tavern.

A new generation discovered the Chelsea Hotel in the '50s and '60s: Jack Kerouac made it a frequent haunt, Bob Dylan wrote about it, and Andy Warhol centered his film *Chelsea Girls* around it. Most infamously, it was here that punk rocker Sid Vicious stabbed girlfriend Nancy Spungen to death in 1978, an event chronicled in the film *Sid and Nancy.* The artistic history is just as rich as the literary, and the lobby walls are covered with a constantly changing exhibition of paintings proffered by guests in lieu of rent. Brass plaques on the front of the hotel memorialize many of the famous guests.

West of the Chelsea Hotel is the hulking **London Terrace,** a block-sized realm of 1,670 apartments located on the site of the house of Clement Clarke Moore, the grandson of Captain Clarke. A classics professor, Moore founded the **General Theological Seminary** (to the south at 175 Ninth Avenue) which survives to this day as a religious oasis; he also laid out many of the streets in the district. Moore is probably more famous as the author of "A Visit from St. Nicholas," a.k.a. "The Night Before Christmas."

If the somewhat embattled **Flower District,** centered at Sixth Avenue and 27th Street, currently faces increased competition from out-of-town wholesalers, it nonetheless presents a superb middle-of-the-night tableau for the insomniac visitor: orchids from Colombia are hawked alongside tulips from Holland, while riotous arrays of scents, colors, and foliage overwhelm the senses.

The north end of Chelsea is marked by the entertainment and transportation locus of **Madison Square Garden** and **Pennsylvania Station,** stretching from Seventh to Eighth avenues and 31st to 33rd streets. Penn Station, as it's usually called, represents one of the bitterest defeats for preservation forces in the history of Manhattan. In the 1960s, the soaring Beaux Arts majesty of McKim, Mead & White's original Pennsylvania Station was destroyed to erect the unabashedly ugly conglomeration that is on the site today. There is some talk of transforming the **General Post**

Pennsylvania Station before being replaced by what is now one of the ugliest, most difficult to navigate rail terminals in America. (New-York Historical Society)

A stately home fronting Gramercy Park.

Office, across Eighth Avenue from the Garden, into a new rail terminal; it was built by the same architects, and its resurrection as the new Penn Station would do much to assuage an old wound.

▪ GRAMERCY PARK

Although geographically well defined, Gramercy Park as a neighborhood is an amorphous thing, typical of Manhattan between 14th and 34th streets. The Dutch word *Crommessie,* meaning "crooked dagger" (for the shape of an area brook), was close in pronunciation to the archaic English exclamation, "gramercy!"—so the two words conflated. "Gramercy Park" as an address is a distinctive label claimed by far more area residents than perhaps warrant it, all wanting to cash in on its upscale cachet.

Taken together, **Stuyvesant Town** and **Peter Cooper Village** constitute the most salient feature of the area. Extending from 14th to 23rd streets and East River Drive to First Avenue, they comprise almost 9,000 apartments and house 25,000 residents with an air of tidiness and middle-class quietude that remind one of Akron, not Manhattan. Both developments are owned and managed by Metropolitan Life Insurance Company.

Stuyvesant Town (south of 20th Street) and Peter Cooper Village (north of 20th Street) are sited on the old Gashouse District. One of the most raucous and bloodthirsty neighborhoods in New York lore, the Gashouse District and its historical juxtaposition with Stuyvesant Town is fraught with irony, given the leafy, kid-heavy, auto-free environment of the development today. Just north of Peter Cooper Village at East 23rd and Asser Levy Place is the **Asser Levy Public Swimming Pool,** a throwback to the time when public works were thought to solve public problems. It has recently been restored to its original form.

Gramercy Park itself is a charming quadrant at the south end of Lexington Avenue, from East 20th to 21st streets. The park's loveliness is diminished only by the fact that it is closed to all but residents of the surrounding buildings—locks are changed twice a year, and a key to Gramercy is a Manhattan plum to be plucked only by those with luck or money. Every so often, there are "Free Gramercy Park" rumblings, but the movement's momentum is diminished by fear of just what the city might manage to do to a place that has remained so peaceful and pristine under private ownership.

Surrounding the park's southern perimeter are elegant townhouses, some now turned into clubs or museums: The **Players Club** at 16 Gramercy Park South, founded by Edwin Booth in 1888 and now a private library; the **National Arts Club** at 15 Gramercy Park South; and **Theodore Roosevelt's Birthplace** at 28 East 20th Street, a restored memorial museum to the twenty-sixth President. Nearby at 235 East 20th Street is the **Police Academy Museum,** a small but interesting collection celebrating New York's finest. South of the park, on 19th Street between Irving Place and Third Avenue, is the celebrated **"block beautiful,"** an elegantly quaint grouping of restored townhouses.

■ UNION SQUARE, SOFI, AND GARMENT DISTRICT

Most Manhattanites blithely enjoy the rather prosaic nature of today's Union Square Park and ignore its past. But it was here that Eugene Debs rallied the workers to the socialist cause, and the offices of numerous labor unions still surround the park. On the south side of the park stands the statue of Lafayette by Frédéric-Auguste Bartholdi, sculptor of the Statue of Liberty. The huge Independence Flagpole in the park's center was given to the city by the Tammany Hall political machine, whose headquarters was once nearby on 14th Street.

Union Square has recently been revitalized by a **Greenmarket,** which sprouts on its north side every Wednesday, Friday, and Saturday, a popular and crowded bazaar devoted to fruits, vegetables, and other comestibles. On the east side of the park, now obscured by the pyramid-topped **Zeckendorf Towers** apartment complex, is the **Con Edison clocktower** at the corner of Irving Place and 14th Street. In the headquarters below, the **Con Edison Energy Museum** (145 East 14th Street) displays lots of kid-friendly interactive exhibits.

Although the name "SoFi" is often derided, the area south of the Flatiron Building is booming, with publishing offices, shops, and cafes lending the area a vibrant street life. The **Flatiron Building** itself, at 175 Fifth Avenue, would, of course, be a superb centerpiece for any neighborhood. Originally called the Fuller Building, the Flatiron was later nicknamed by New Yorkers for its skinny, triangular, iron-like shape. The Flatiron was not, as is widely believed, the world's first skyscraper, but it *is* an important example of that era's style of steel-frame building.

Another stubborn myth swirling about the site is that here was coined the flapper phrase **"23 skiddoo,"** supposedly what cops said to male gawkers assembled to watch the winds around the building raise women's skirts. Interesting story, but ersatz etymology: the phrase was popular in the 1890s, long before the building went up in 1902.

The farmers market at Union Square brings a bit of the country into the city thrice weekly.

*The Flatiron Building, completed in 1903, was one of the city's first skyscrapers.
(Library of Congress)*

North of the Flatiron (NoFi?) is Madison Square, the original site of Madison Square Garden, which has had a peripatetic history in Manhattan. It moved to Eighth Avenue and 50th Street in 1925, then wound up at its present location above Pennsylvania Station in 1966. Its first site, at the corner of Fifth Avenue and 23rd Street, had an older show-biz lineage, being the locale of the **Hippodrome,** Manhattan's first "arena"-sized show palace. The canvas-topped coliseum opened May 2, 1853, with a show consisting of buxom, toga-clad female chariot drivers, an ostrich obstacle course, camels, elephants, and a pack of monkeys. Evidently, that wasn't enough, and the Hippodrome closed two years after it opened.

Today, the Madison Square area is known for the wholesale **Toy District,** concentrated on its west side, and for the superb architecture of two insurance buildings and a courthouse on its eastern perimeter: the **Metropolitan Life Insurance Company** at One Madison Avenue; the diminutive **Appellate Division of the New York State Supreme Court** at 27 Madison Avenue, called the "busiest courthouse in the nation"; and the gilt-topped towers of the **New York Life Insurance Company** at 51 Madison Avenue. On the northwest side of the park, at 24th Street, an obelisk marks the grave of the only man to be officially buried under a New York City street, Mexican War hero William J. Worth, eponym of Fort Worth, Texas.

The **Garment District,** which kicks in north of Madison Square and extends west to Seventh Avenue (renamed by city boosters as "Fashion Avenue"), is a dense hive of offices, showrooms, workshops, and factory lofts. Workers trundle huge racks of clothes on casters from one address to the other. This archaic form of transport helps set the tone for the whole Garment District, which with its obscure rules and narrow monopolies has something of the air of a medieval guild about it. Within the district itself arcane sub-divisions like the Fur District, the Fabric District, and the Millinery District prevail. Storefront wholesalers devote themselves only to snaps or hook-and-eyes and a jobber here might specialize in a single type of button. It seems like something from another age. According to *Cigar Aficionado* magazine, there are more cigars sold in the Garment District than any other area of the city: the people who work here still actually smoke them.

If the Garment District has a central focus, it's at 27th Street and Seventh Avenue, the campus of the **Fashion Institute of Technology** (FIT). This is the rag trade's flagship educational institution, and the school often features shows and exhibits which are open to the public.

■ MURRAY HILL

A residential area that used to boast some of the wealthiest New Yorkers' estates, Murray Hill has suffered from a lack of definition since the aristocrats moved up Fifth Avenue. No discernible distinctive neighborhood characteristic rose to replace them. There are other historical resonances—the English landed at **Kip's Bay** (East 34th Street and the East River) in the campaign against Washington in the Revolutionary War—but primarily the area has settled down into a comfortable, not-quite-Midtown blandness.

A survivor of the nineteenth-century period of great houses is perfectly preserved in the **Pierpont Morgan Library**, 29 East 36th Street. Built by financier J. P. Morgan across from his original mansion, this small, perfect museum is devoted to one of the world's most glorious collections of illuminated books, manuscripts, and drawings. But another real draw here is to see how the other half lived: Morgan's library and office are maintained just as he left them upon his death in 1913. At nearby **Sniffen Court** (150-158 East 36th Street) you can see how the horses of the other half lived—the lovely mews consists entirely of carriage houses from the mid-nineteenth century.

The area from **Beth Israel Medical Center** at 16th Street and First Avenue northward used to be called "Bedpan Alley," so great was its concentration of hospitals, and **Veterans Administration Hospital, Bellevue Hospital Center,** and **New York University Medical Center** (First Avenue, 23rd to 34th streets) still dominate this southeastern tier of Murray Hill. Bellevue, established in 1736, is one of the oldest hospitals in the country, a municipal institution serving all illnesses, but somehow unable to shake its reputation for being synonymous with the nuthouse.

■ EMPIRE STATE BUILDING

> *It's the nearest thing to heaven we have in New York.*
> —Deborah Kerr to Cary Grant in *An Affair to Remember*

If you count the twin towers of the World Trade Center as two, there are now actually three structures in the country that are nearer to heaven (Chicago's Sears Tower makes three).

But that's not the point. It may have been eclipsed as the world's tallest building, but the Empire State Building is still a little bit of paradise in Manhattan. At

"Gives the impression of height, doesn't it?" —*anonymous English visitor to the Empire State Building.*

the 102nd floor observatory snow sometimes falls up (due to crossdrafts), rain appears pink (a trick of the city's light), and Manhattan resembles what architect Philip Johnson called the giant "asparagus patch."

"Beauty killed the beast," said a policeman in the 1933 movie *King Kong* when the great ape toppled from it, two years after it was built. Actually, it wasn't beauty but gravity that killed the beast, and in its elegant defiance of same the Empire State Building endures as the central beacon of Manhattan, part Midtown fertility symbol, part communal widow's walk.

The story of the Empire State Building begins with a black man named Francisco Bastian, who in 1638 took ownership of the site on which it was built. It was part swamp then, fed by Sunfish Creek, with a good fishing hole for eels. In 1799, a farmer named John Thomson bought the site, and then it changed hands several times in the go-go years of the mid-nineteenth century, finally winding up the property of the first family of Manhattan, the Astors.

EIGHTH WONDER OF THE WORLD

*A*nd in the middle of Manhattan there stood the ultimate monument of technological achievement, the Empire State Building, the Eighth Wonder of the World. It was less than fifteen years old, and had been put into full use only during the war (in the slump it had been dubbed the Empty State Building), but it had already attained mythical status. It was the city's crown. It was the building that King Kong had stood upon. Legends of many kinds were told of it—how Henry Ford, learning of the immense excavations required to build it, thought it might have a disastrous effect upon the rotation of the earth—how, when a B-25 bomber flew into its eightieth floor, Betty Lou Oliver a stenographer fell seventy-six floors in an elevator—how a sandwich man climbed thirty-one floors with sustenance for businessmen during the elevator strike—how when a strong wind blew the building swayed several feet in each direction. Everybody went up the Empire State Building, every visiting film star, everybody's aunt, every serviceman on leave, every child on a school outing. . . . There was nothing like the Empire State Building, in all its glamor, its grandeur and its 1265 feet. Even Englishmen, in those days given to attitudes of general disdain, were impelled into admiration. "Gives quite an impression of height, doesn't it?" said one of them when asked for his reactions.

—Jan Morris, *Manhattan '45,* 1986

EMPIRE STATE BUILDING FACTS

SITE: 83,860 square feet

INTERIOR: 37 million cubic feet

STEEL: 60,000 tons

BRICKS: 10 million

STONE: 200,000 cubic feet

HEIGHT: 1,250 feet

FLOORS: 102

STEPS: 1,860

RADIATORS: 6,700

TENANTS: 25,000, with 40,000 visitors daily

ELEVATOR SHAFTS: 73, almost 7 miles total

LIGHTNING STRIKES: An average of 500 per year

LIVES LOST DURING CONSTRUCTION: 14

WEIGHT: 730 million pounds (365,000 tons)

MULLIONS: 730 tons of chrome-nickel steel and aluminum

Caroline Schermerhorn Astor ruled New York's social elite—"The 400," a term invented by her oily cicisbeo, Ward McAllister, who limited upper-crust society to the number of people who could comfortably fit inside Mrs. Astor's ballroom. (The gorgeous ballroom scenes in the Martin Scorsese movie, *The Age of Innocence,* were set in what would have been the old Astor mansion.)

Caroline Schermerhorn's nephew, William Waldorf Astor, erected an elegant hotel, The Waldorf, next door, and when she followed society uptown, her son built the Astoria Hotel on the site of her mansion. The two structures were soon joined (although with connecting halls that could be easily walled off, in case a family feud should erupt), and thus was born the Waldorf-Astoria—the most deluxe hotel in the city from the turn of the century until it was torn down for the Empire State Building in 1929. (The hotel moved to 49th and Park.)

Nineteen twenty-nine was a boom year until the October crash, and America's commercial giants vied with each other to see who could erect the tallest skyscraper. Walter Chrysler had already topped his landmark Art Deco shrine at 77 stories, ending the brief reign of the Bank of Manhattan as the world's tallest building. But John Jacob Raskob, vice president of General Motors and inventor of the installment plan, was not going to take Chrysler's aerial supremacy lying down. He joined with recently defeated Democratic presidential candidate Alfred E. Smith with plans to build a skyscraper to beat them all.

They hired William Lamb of Shreve, Lamb & Harmon to design it, and (on his sixteenth try) he came up with a beautifully pure single tower, with setbacks starting at the fifth floor, perfect Art Deco flavorings, and a crisp, simple dignity.

Two weeks after construction began, the Crash of '29 took the air out of the skyscraper race for a half century, but Raskob was already committed. Work continued at a feverish pace (the *Times* called it a "chase up into the sky"), and the building was completed in an astonishing 19 months.

Opening in the depths of the Depression, the building, as they say, laid an egg. Office space went unrented, so much so that the place was nicknamed the "Empty State Building." The observatories, however, were an immediate hit. The millions of visitors who paid admission to view the world from an impossible height saved the building from bankruptcy.

"They look like ants!" was the cry, about the people below in the street. The height of the 102nd floor observatories put Manhattan into comprehensible, if not sobering, perspective. Actually, from that height, the human form appears to be less than a millimeter long. It's not ants they look like, but lice.

Not everyone came just to gawk: the first suicide off the Empire State came only 18 months after opening day. The cruel-looking fingers of the suicide fence on the observatory terrace, put up in 1947 after a three-week period in which five people tried to jump, testifies to the building's attraction to the self-destructive. In 1979, a woman circumvented the fence, jumped from the 86th floor, and was blown back onto a ledge on the 85th floor. She survived.

But the most amazing catastrophe associated with the building occurred in 1945. On the morning of July 28, visibility was low and the air was foggy, but Lieut. Col. William Smith was scheduled to fly his B-25 bomber from Boston to Newark Airport. Instead, he wound up dodging the plane among the forest of skyscrapers in Midtown. "From where I'm sitting," Smith said, "I can't see the top of the Empire State Building." He barely missed the Salomon Tower before banking away, then climbed abruptly upward. Minutes later, at 9:50 A.M., he crashed his 12-ton bomber into the 79th floor of the Empire State Building. Ground zero was Room 7915, a Catholic war-relief office.

One engine tore straight through the building and out the other side. Another plummeted down an elevator shaft. Burning gasoline poured down the sides of the building to the 75th floor. The three men in the plane and 11 in the building died. But overall the number of fatalities was low because it was Saturday morning and the building was almost empty. One elevator operator survived freefall from the 80th floor; emergency brakes saved her.

The building survived also, enduring through the years as a potent symbol of America's commercial ambition. It had the longest reign of all as the world's tallest building, over 45 years, and its run in the public imagination continues to this day. A trip to its observatory is still an obligatory part of a visit to Manhattan. The World Trade Center is taller, but not by much, and the Empire State Building is much more centrally located. Today, since investor Donald Trump owns a piece of it, tabloids sometimes refer to it as the "Trumpire State Building."

A visit begins at the ticket office in the basement concourse, snakes in a line through a two-phased elevator ride, and finally winds up inside the glass-enclosed 86th floor. There are sidewalk-sized open walkways to the north and south, and more generous terraces on the east and west, with spectacular views all around. The view from the totally enclosed 102nd floor is not sufficiently different to be worth the wait for the elevator, but the curious will always want to take the trip.

One of the most romantic things about the Empire State Building is that it is open until midnight. On a warm spring night, when static electricity gives each kiss a literal spark, and a hand extended beyond the suicide fence might glow with St. Elmo's fire, Manhattan rolls out below like a romantic invitation. There might indeed be places around that are nearer to heaven, but none that are closer to it.

"He adored New York. He romanticized it all out of proportion." —*Woody Allen,* in Manhattan. *A sunset view from the Empire State Building has inspired many a romance. (photo by Katsuyoshi Tanaka)*

M I D T O W N
A N D   T I M E S   S Q U A R E

IF, FOR A LOT OF PEOPLE, MANHATTAN IS NEW YORK CITY, then for an equal majority Midtown is Manhattan. This sacred quadrant, dense with commerce, has attracted the moth-like attentions of countless restaurateurs and other attendants, so bright is the flame of its money. The resulting matrix of watering holes, clubs, galleries, hostelries, boutiques, clothiers, and specialty shops is among the greatest in the world, thus drawing even more wealth to itself and perpetuating its status as a sort of Meta-Manhattan.

Times Square is too integral to the neighborhood (although to call Midtown a neighborhood is a bit like calling New York a town) to be relegated to the status of a support system for Midtown's wealth and prestige, but the "**Crossroads of the World,**" as it styles itself, is still a place to spend money as well as earn it. If you envision Midtown as a giant engine for creating wealth, then Times Square's theater, restaurant, and entertainment district is perfectly poised to siphon off a share.

The two districts create a glorious dipole crackling with excitement and energy. Times Square forms a huge booming canyon of light and neon at the confluence of Seventh Avenue and Broadway, while Midtown represents a picket line of tall buildings stretching almost across the width of Manhattan. The symbiosis does not extend farther west, to **Clinton,** a former slum neighborhood which for much of its life was known as **Hell's Kitchen,** nor quite to **Turtle Bay** and **Sutton Place,** upscale residential areas near the **United Nations,** along the East River.

■ UNITED NATIONS

The ghost of Woodrow Wilson was hovering over San Francisco in May of 1945, when the founding conference of the United Nations was being convened. The U.S. President had labored to bring his League of Nations into being after World War I, only to have it rejected in the isolationist atmosphere of his own country. It took another brutal war and millions more dead before the spirit of cooperation between countries was a sufficiently recognized ideal to spur some sort of action.

What was given form in San Francisco would later land in Manhattan as the United Nations—a wildly optimistic appellation, given the squabbling to which its member nations have frequently descended. Politics was present at the creation of the United Nations, especially in the formation of the veto-empowered Security Council, which included among its permanent seats only the victors of World War II.

Squabbling continues to the present day. Not long ago, when Ed Koch was mayor of New York, he became so enraged at what he felt to be the U.N.'s anti-Israel bias that he threatened to boot it out of the city. He implied that the "swords-into-ploughshares" Biblical motto might in the U.N.'s case be reversed, and its members guilty of beating ploughshares into swords.

When the nascent United Nations began casting about for a suitable site for a headquarters, Nelson Rockefeller, scion of the huge Standard Oil fortune of his grandfather, John D., was still years away from becoming governor of New York State. He was then serving as the point man for Rockefeller Center, the family's sprawling Midtown office project.

Nelson Rockefeller realized he could increase the value of Rockefeller Center and at the same time remove a potential competitor to it in one bold stroke. The last parcel of available Midtown real estate large enough for a U.N. site was called "X City." Encompassing the original Turtle Bay, where a creek the Dutch called Saw Kill debouched into the East River, the area had become a stench-ridden sector of slaughterhouses spread along the East River north of 42nd Street, owned by developer William Zeckendorf.

If Zeckendorf raised office buildings on the site, as he planned, the value of Rockefeller Center would be severely diluted by the competition. But if the U.N. located there, it would have the opposite effect of raising Midtown property values immensely, making Rockefeller Center all the more valuable.

With typical drive, Nelson plunged into the negotiations to lure the U.N. to New York. As the deadline for site selection approached, Nelson was overjoyed when his father, John D., Jr., announced he would donate the entire $8.5 million Zeckendorf demanded for the X City property ("Why, Pa, that's most generous!" Nelson is supposed to have gushed). Thus, because of a depressed Midtown real estate market and the irrepressible energy of Nelson Rockefeller (as well as his Pa's deep pockets), the United Nations is headquartered in New York.

It is a good fit. Manhattan is the one place in the world which best suggests both the possibilities and limitations of cooperation among radically different cultures and people. Geneva, perhaps, might have a more ancient tradition of negotiation and diplomacy, but Manhattan has the bumptious, strident, unnerving challenge of its streets. All the U.N. diplomats need to do for a reality check is step outside their chambers.

Nevertheless, the U.N. still represents an approach to an ideal. It is somehow fitting that an organization which embraces cooperation among all the peoples of humankind be located on an island which is home to so many of them. A visit to the stately precincts of the United Nations is a good place to kick off a tour of the East Side. And while you're removed from the immediate cacophony of Manhattan, you might also want to meditate on the foibles of the human character and the possibilities of peace.

Architecturally speaking, the International-style Secretariat Building plays nicely off the parabolic roofline of the General Assembly, and the whole complex—four buildings in all—renders a distinct and graceful impression. The **U.N. Rose Garden,** behind the General Assembly along the East River, is a glorious, gentle-scented enclave with blooms donated from all over the world. All in all, a stunning setting for a world peace organization.

The visitors' entrance is opposite 46th Street. Almost every nation in the world has donated art for the building, and there are various exhibits inside the lobby—a

The Rose Garden frames the Secretariat Building at the United Nations.

ELEANOR ROOSEVELT ON THE UNITED NATIONS

*I*know that a great many people in the United States and other nations today wonder what is the use of having a United Nations. "It is just a debating society. It doesn't do anything." Those are criticisms one can hear almost anywhere, though to my mind they are quite unjustified.

I would like to ask everyone who has made or been tempted to make some such criticism of the United Nations to remember just one fact: When the United Nations was set up in the spring of '45 we thought that as soon as the war came to an end we would make the peace. And the organization that was set up was to function in a peaceful world, maintaining the new peace and creating an atmosphere in which lasting peace could grow and develop.

The people who wrote the Charter did not assume that peace was going to drop down on us like a beneficent blanket from heaven and be with us forever. They were quite realistic about it. They knew that, even though we made a peace, we would have to work year in and year out, day in and day out, to keep that peace, and to see that the atmosphere of the world was conducive to its growth. They knew that throughout the world there were tremendous difficulties, that it would take a long while, for instance, to make it possible for the people of our country to understand what was happening to someone in South Africa or in India or in Siam.

Finally, if democracy—and the blessings of it both as a way of government and a way of life—are going to win this contest for the support of the peoples of the world, we must have moral conviction and spiritual leadership. . . . That is the challenge that we face in strengthening and making the United Nations work as a whole. Those are the standards that we set ourselves and, in the interest of the future, those are the standards by which we must live.

—Eleanor Roosevelt,
"What I think of the United Nations,"
United Nations World, 1949

Foucault pendulum, a replica of *Sputnik,* a moon rock, displays on the history of the organization itself—to enjoy while you await one of the hour-long tours of the building, which leave every half hour.

The neighborhoods immediately surrounding the U.N. are of a largely staid and expensive residential atmosphere, with many consulates and international offices sited here, too. To the west of the United Nations, 42nd Street passes under (not through) **Tudor City,** a hideaway of 3,000 apartments built in the 1920s and almost totally self-contained, with stores, parks, and restaurants. Tudor City used to be even more self-sufficient, when its grounds featured a miniature golf course, a blandishment its residents must now seek elsewhere.

Comfortably situated amid all the diplomatic offices near the U.N. is the **Ford Foundation** at 320 East 43rd Street, a good place to visit even if you don't have your hand out for a grant, just to experience the amazing 12-story jungle atrium in one of the finest modern buildings in New York. What Henry Ford would have thought about this elegant but progressive design is not known, but he once voiced his concern that excavation of the Empire State Building might affect the rotation of the Earth, so perhaps it's best he didn't live to see what his money had wrought.

Stop for a moment at Third Avenue and 46th Street to recall an uprising that almost tore apart the city during the Civil War. At this corner was the site of the draft office that was the target of anti-conscription gangs, angered at a draft law that allowed rich citizens to buy their way out of the Union army for $300. The infamous Draft Riot, one of the worst civil disturbances in Manhattan history, started here on July 13, 1863. It eventually swelled to include the whole city, resulting in an estimated 2,000 people dead, many of them black.

Just down the block, at 246 East 46th Street, is another notorious site, this one **Sparks Steak House,** where Mafia boss Paul Castellano and chauffeur Tommy Bilotti were gunned down on December 16, 1985. The triggermen were widely believed to be messengers of John Gotti, impatient to take command of the Gambino crime family. The rub-out increased the eatery's popularity exponentially, prompting many idle restaurateurs to dream of a Mafia hit in their own establishments.

North of the U.N., the area changes into a residential neighborhood called Turtle Bay, named after the long-gone East River marsh that was, indeed, full of turtles—at least until the colonial New Yorkers hunted them out for soup. The district is typified by the quiet gentility of **Turtle Bay Gardens,** on the interior of the block surrounded by 48th and 49th streets, Second to Third avenues. Unfortunately, these are not open to the public, but enjoyed rather by residents whose elegant townhouses border them. (Katharine Hepburn lives on East 49th Street.)

Farther north, between First Avenue and the river, are two neighborhoods that exhibit the same air of exclusivity and privilege as Turtle Bay. These are **Beekman Place**, running north from 49th Street, and **Sutton Place**, north from 53rd Street. Both are residential enclaves within easy walking distance from the United Nations and the towers of Midtown. At 23 Beekman Place is the **Paul Rudolph house**, a showcase residence built by a leading force behind modern architecture.

Sutton Place is an especially fine prospect from which to view the Queensboro Bridge; you've seen the terrace at 57th Street in Woody Allen's *Manhattan.* Sutton Place is better known from another film, *The Dead End Kids,* which commemorated the anomalous historical juxtaposition of slum and townhouse when the neighborhood was in transition.

Near Sutton Place, at 58th Street, is **Riverview Terrace**, a rare private street in Manhattan, with the official residence of the Secretary General of the U.N. at the south end, off **Sutton Terrace Square.**

■ 42ND STREET

From the U.N. area, the logical approach to the more bustling center of town is to work east along that celebrated artery, 42nd Street. The thoroughfare, which marks the southern border of Midtown, strings several architectural and cultural pearls along its length. At Second Avenue is the great Art Deco **News Building** (220 East 42nd Street), worth a step inside for the huge spinning globe, bronze geography inlays on the floor, and various meteorological instruments in the lobby. It all effectively recalls the architectural mood of 1930, when the place was built.

For the most glorious incarnation of the Art Deco style, however, there is nothing in the world like the **Chrysler Building** at 405 Lexington Avenue, built by auto magnate Walter Chrysler so his sons would have something to manage if they stayed on in New York. Designed to be the tallest structure in the world ("Make this building higher than the Eiffel Tower," said Walter to architect William Van Alen), the Chrysler Building's exact height (1,048 feet) was kept a secret during its construction to foil competitors in the skyscraper race. At the last moment, its 27-ton crown was hoisted to the top in one piece, and the Chrysler was finally revealed as (briefly) the tallest building in the world.

Van Alen achieved some sort of aesthetic apogee with the Chrysler's exterior, with its stainless-steel-clad façade and lancet crown. Every decorative touch is meant to signify "automobile," from gargoyles resembling 1929 radiator caps to abstract roadster graphics. In 1981, Alen's original lighting plans were rediscovered and implemented, resulting in a nightly Art Deco splash of fluorescence.

The Chrysler Building is best viewed from a distance, from down Lexington Avenue, say, or even from Hollywood: *Ghostbusters, Bonfire of the Vanities,* and the horror flick *Q!* have all featured generous angles of the building. Best is the view you'll get from the observatories at the Empire State Building. The interior, of African marble and chrome steel, is striking, as are the elevators; the mural on the lobby ceiling celebrates transportation and industry.

Just down the block from the Chrysler Building, at 42nd Street and Park Avenue, is one of the architectural, cultural, and transportation anchors of Midtown and of Manhattan itself, **Grand Central Terminal.** It's a building that manages the unlikely feat of combining Beaux Arts fantasy with pure functionalism—after all, it is a working train station. More than that, it reminds present-day Manhattan of a more gracious past. Compare it with the "modern" monstrosity of Penn Station, and you'll know why New Yorkers cherish Grand Central.

The station's exterior is studded with sculpture, including one of railroad magnate Commodore Cornelius Vanderbilt, original developer of the site. The massive clock and statue grouping on the colonnaded south side, by Jules-Alexis Coutans, is visible all the way down Park Avenue.

Note that the east side of Grand Central, the one facing the Grand Hyatt Hotel, is less embellished by architectural ornament. When the building was erected this side fronted slums, the denizens of which were not thought capable of appreciating beauty.

The interior bears out the promise of Grand Central's marvelous façades. A soaring vault decorated with constellations (painted by Paul Hellau and Charles Basing, complete with over 2,500 trompe l'oeil "stars") watches over the scurryings of a half million commuters daily. A recent cleaning project by the Metropolitan Transportation Authority, holder of the Grand Central lease, scrubbed away 50 years of soot and grime to reveal a brilliant cerulean "sky."

The station is built over a complex of railway and subway tunnels, and is itself several stories deep. On lower levels, acoustics along the Guastavino-tiled vaults are such that a whisper spoken into one of the corners will magically be heard across the hallway.

The Chrysler Building catches rays of a setting sun.

For all the glory of the 75-foot arched windows and the grand staircases (patterned after those at the Paris opera), Grand Central is a building that *works*, and works hard. Subways, commuter trains, and serious Midtown foot traffic converge here, with 32 miles of track in total. Fluid pedestrian movement is maintained by ramps and segregated levels. The much-needed renovation promises to brush away some of the seediness and restore past glory, but just as it is, Grand Central is a railroad terminal against which all others may be measured.

"Grand Central Station! Crossroads of a million private lives!" —opening words of the 1937 NBC radio drama, "Grand Central Station."

For a time, in the late 1960s, it looked as if Grand Central would go the way of Pennsylvania Station, demolished in the name of progress. When the terminal's owners, Penn Central railroad, wanted to raze it and build an office tower there, the landmark preservation battle was fought (by Jacqueline Kennedy Onassis, among others) all the way to the Supreme Court. The case resulted in an important six-to-three precedent-setting decision endorsing the concept of landmark preservation.

Located directly to the north of Grand Central (at 200 Park Avenue), and receiving the traffic off its Park Avenue roadway, is the **MetLife Building,** known to stubborn New Yorkers by its former appellation of the Pan Am Building. Controversial from the first, for usurping the "air rights" of Grand Central, the Pan Am monolith went on to greater notoriety when a helicopter fell off its helipad (since closed) onto unsuspecting pedestrians below.

The golden-topped **Helmsley Building** at 230 Park Avenue also stands athwart Park Avenue, but is much more popular. It was built at the same time as Grand Central by the same architects, and only in modern times was absorbed into the hotel and real estate empire of Harry Helmsley. Helmsley, of course, is the husband of Leona, the self-proclaimed "Queen of New York," who went to jail for tax evasion. "Only little people pay taxes," she is said to have proclaimed, until the legal system whittled her down to size.

The United Nations, the Chrysler Building, and Grand Central stand side by side in a neighborhood of superlatives, but if you made us choose the most beautiful, it would be the **New York Public Library** at Fifth Avenue and 42nd Street. The site was formerly the Croton Reservoir, an artificial lake with an Egyptian-style parapet 50 feet high and 25 feet thick, around which it was once fashionable to stroll. Improved water delivery systems eventually made the reservoir obsolete, and one of the grandest libraries in the world was built on the site, financed by the largesse of John Jacob Astor and filled with the book collections of Sam Tilden and James Lenox.

As with Grand Central, the library's architectural style is French Beaux Arts, but its decorative flourishes are less mitigated by the utilitarian pursuits of the building. The result, completed in 1911 and recently refurbished, is a lyrical white marble temple dedicated to reason, education, and beauty. Outside, the lions of Patience and Fortitude (so named by Mayor Fiorello La Guardia) stand guard.

The ornate façade is set off by two flagpoles, their bases riotously embellished in painted bronze. A pair of fountains, labeled Truth and Beauty ("all ye need to know in life," according to Keats), flank the grand entrance steps, which are peopled in warm weather by a carnival gallery of lounging, lunch-eating, gawking New Yorkers. Food kiosks supply sandwiches and beverages.

Inside, the gilded opulence of the library's Astor Lobby immediately straightens the spine of everyone who enters. Directly ahead is Gottesman Exhibition Hall—venture in, look up, and admire the superb ceiling. Down the south hall on the first floor is the DeWitt Wallace Periodical Room (11,000 periodicals in 22 languages from 124 countries), named after the founder of the *Reader's Digest* and graced with great Richard Haas murals celebrating the New York publishing world. A codicil to DeWitt Wallace's will directed that the room be air-conditioned (the only public space in the library that is) in tribute to the long hours he and his wife spent sweating in this room in the muggy New York summers, preparing the first issues of the world's most popular magazine.

This central research library of the New York Public Library system (82 branches, seven million users annually) does not lend out books; rather, users are permitted to order and peruse them in two grand reading rooms on the third floor. The coffered, 50-foot ceilings of these linked rooms feature superb decorative murals crowded with clouds, flying fish, angels, and satyrs. They are the perfect diversion while you're waiting for your books to arrive from the 92 miles of computerized stacks, with over three million books tucked out of sight below nearby Bryant Park.

Bryant Park itself, immediately behind the library to the west, is a great recent success story of New York renewal. Named for poet William Cullen Bryant, it was once a potter's field (some of the bodies moved from Washington Square wound up here), then the grounds of the Crystal Palace Exhibition Hall, which burned down in a spectacular conflagration in 1858. More recently, it was a seedy drug bazaar, but in 1989 it was closed and underwent a total makeover.

The result is one of the friendliest public spaces in Manhattan, patrolled and kept clean, with lively events such as outdoor movies (projected against a giant screen at night) in the summertime. From inside Bryant Park one may meditate on the mysteries of architectural style, since to the south rises the great Gothic pile of the **American Radiator Building** at 40 West 40th Street, and just to the north the sleek vertical curve of the **W.R. Grace Building.**

North of Bryant Park is the "Club Row" of 44th Street: such toney enclaves as the **Yale Club** (50 Vanderbilt Avenue, at West 44th Street), the **Harvard Club** (27 West 44th), and the **New York Yacht Club** (37 West 44th). Tucked away on the same street (at number 20) is the small gem of the **General Society Library of Mechanics and Tradesmen,** a private book collection open for a nominal fee, and one of the great little-known retreats of Midtown. A few blocks north, on 47th Street between Fifth and Sixth avenues, is the **Diamond District,** mostly wholesale, some retail, run by a hermetic group of dealers tantamount to a medieval guild.

■ ROCKEFELLER CENTER

Covering a vast, 22-acre chunk of the most expensive real estate this side of Tokyo (and currently owned by Japanese real estate interests) is Rockefeller Center, bounded by 47th and 52nd streets, and Fifth and Sixth avenues. Probably the grandest Oedipal monument Manhattan has to offer, it was conceived and built by John D. Rockefeller, Jr., a man who constantly labored in the shadow of his father, the Standard Oil tycoon. Rockefeller Center was going to be Junior's self-validation, the family monument that would prove his worth.

It almost ended in a disaster. In 1928, Junior paid $3.3 million for a 24-year lease on a parcel of Midtown that in the nineteenth century was the site of the Elgin Botanic Gardens, and later passed into the hands of Columbia University.

Junior planned a development that would be anchored by the Metropolitan Opera, which was casting about for a new home.

Then the Great Depression hit. The front page of the *New York Times* on October 29, 1929, said it all in two headlines: "Stock Prices Slump $14,000,000,000" and a smaller one below, "Architects Picked to Plan Rockefeller Center." John D.'s timing could not have been worse. The Met bowed out, and the Rockefellers were left holding the bag—a very expensive bag at that. Only John D.'s doggedness, the immense wealth of the Rockefeller family, and the sheer momentum of the building project saved Rockefeller Center from bankruptcy. It didn't turn a profit until well after World War II.

Few can deny the staggering scale of the plan. There were 14 original buildings, including such New York landmarks as the world's largest indoor movie theater, **Radio City Music Hall,** and the **G.E. Building** (formerly the RCA Building). Another five huge office towers were added along Sixth Avenue in a second round of construction beginning in 1957, with Marilyn Monroe throwing the switch to dynamite the hole for the new **Time-Life Building.**

In 1989, a division of Mitsubishi, a Japanese mega-corporation, paid $846 million for a 51 percent controlling interest in the company that owns Rockefeller Center. At the time, the transaction was bemoaned as evidence of the parceling out of the American Dream, what with Honda outselling Ford, Columbia and Universal movie studios coming under Japanese ownership, and the Rising Sun seeming to blot out the sky. Those fears have calmed somewhat, especially since, according to most analysts, Mitsubishi overpaid for Rockefeller Center.

John D. Rockefeller. (Library of Congress)

> *"The view of Rockefeller Center from Fifth Avenue is the most beautiful I have ever seen ever seen ever seen [sic]".* —*Gertrude Stein*

That remains to be seen. Today, Rockefeller Center remains a phenomenon, a thriving "city-within-a-city," with 15 million square feet of rentable space, 240,000 total daily population, 388 elevators, and 97,500 locks to keep it all safe and secure. Some elements of the original design are ingenious, such as the rooftop greens, the underground truck delivery bays, and the vast subterranean promenade connecting the buildings, lined with shops and restaurants.

Clever also is the long sloping design of the **Channel Gardens,** between the **British Empire Building** and **La Maison Française** (the "Channel" between the British and the French), which uses gravity to propel passersby on Fifth Avenue into Rockefeller Center proper. There they'll see the famous Christmas tree and skating rink in winter, the annual flower show in spring, or the open-air restaurants in warm weather.

That sunken skating rink is a quintessential Manhattan scene, especially when the huge Rockefeller Center tree is erected over it during the holidays. There always seem to be more than a few smooth professionals among the wobbly-ankled amateurs, and their circuit of the small rink, breath pluming in the cold air, can be mesmerizing. At least it seems to be so to the gallery of onlookers, who line around the promenade above, sometimes two or three deep during the crowded shopping days around Christmas.

The National Broadcasting Company became one of the first tenants of Rockefeller Center, back when radio was king. Entrances to the NBC Studios are mid-block in the G.E. Building, with tours available. Across the street is NBC's "window on the world," huge picture windows fronting on the set of the "Today Show," "Now," and other programs. Electronic kiosks solicit "people-in-the-street" interviews and passersby can ogle the newscasters inside. Across Sixth Avenue from Radio City Music Hall is **Television City,** a theme restaurant packed with memorabilia.

Be sure to note the Jose Maria Sert murals (*American Progress* on the west wall, and *Time* on the ceiling) in the G.E. Building lobby. Sert had the unenviable job of painting over Diego Rivera's controversial 1933 mural, which was originally commissioned for the space. Rivera, a Communist and iconoclast, began an epic panorama featuring a heroic proletariat triumphing over the very kind of capitalists that built Rockefeller Center. Nelson Rockefeller pulled the plug when the Mexican muralist included a glowing portrait of Lenin. To Rockefeller's credit, he tried to have the Rivera mural moved to the Museum of Modern Art, but that proved physically impossible.

All things considered, and even granting its status as "the heart of Midtown," Rockefeller Center is a little too cold, a little too clean, to invite an enthusiastic embrace. Appreciation, yes, admiration, maybe—but there are limits to the emotions it sparks in the hearts of New Yorkers. Maybe that's because Rockefeller Center has never strayed far from its corporate genesis; it is, after all, a collection of office buildings, no matter how much art or how many amenities it scatters around for the hoi polloi.

The best way to investigate the nooks and crannies of Rockefeller Center is with a self-guided tour, which includes a stop in the development's very own museum, in the basement concourse. Tour map brochures are available in the lobby of the G.E. Building.

■ MIDTOWN

Built on a grand scale—it's the largest Catholic church in the United States—is Rockefeller Center's neighbor across Fifth Avenue, **St. Patrick's Cathedral** (Fifth Avenue, 50th to 51st streets). Begun in 1858 and completed in 1879, St. Patrick's is the spiritual center of New York's vast Catholic population. The interior is even more impressive than the Gothic Revival exterior, especially the Lady Chapel, behind the altar. James Renwick, the primary architect, also designed the Smithsonian Institution in Washington, D.C.

On Madison Avenue, directly across from St. Patrick's rectory, are the wonderful **Villard Houses** (451 and 455 Madison). Now partly incorporated into the New York Palace Hotel, these are the surviving pair of five nineteenth-century brownstones built to resemble an Italian Renaissance palazzo. Inside the north wing at 457 Madison is the **Urban Center**, an active research and preservation group which occasionally mounts exhibits.

A wonderful place to catch up on all those segments of "The Honeymooners" you missed—as well as anything else in a huge collection of news reports, scripts, and radio programs—is the **Museum of Television and Radio** at 25 West 52nd Street. This marvelously modern shrine to television (and, to a lesser degree, radio) hosts lectures and exhibits, but its great appeal are the screening facilities. After a session chuckling at Lucy or witnessing Walter Cronkite get misty-eyed reporting John F. Kennedy's assassination, you can revive your spirits next door at the famed **21 Club** on West 52nd Street.

As long as you accept "Modern" as applying to a defined period—1850 to 1950, say—the **Museum of Modern Art**, at 11 West 53rd Street, is the standard against which all other collections must be measured. MOMA, as it is known in shorthand, seems more than willing to rest on its considerable laurels, leaving the thrashing and brawlings of the contemporary art scene to other museums.

MOMA was founded in 1929 (by John D. Rockefeller, Jr.'s wife Abby Aldrich Rockefeller, among others) in the wake of the stock market crash. It was the first of its kind; contemporary art at that time was consigned exclusively to private galleries. The museum was greatly enlarged during the mid-1980s, its endowment strengthened by the addition of a residential tower next door. The renovated restaurant features excellent food, and the room overlooks the great MOMA sculpture garden.

MOMA is justly celebrated for its bedrock collection of Impressionist, Cubist, and Modern masters, with Van Gogh particularly well represented, and some epochal works of Picasso on permanent display. Picasso's *Guernica* (1937), a great anti-war statement and long a MOMA stalwart, was returned to Spain upon the restoration of democracy in that country, as per the artist's wishes.

Dance *by Henri Matisse is one of the Museum of Modern Art's masterpieces.*

St. Patrick's Cathedral from Fifth Avenue.

However much the rich collection of paintings shine, MOMA's primary contribution to the art world is enlarging its scope, canonizing works from disparate fields of design, film, and architecture. Its film program, based in its basement theaters, features some of the most interesting and vibrant cinema in town. The fourth-floor design collection (to which you are welcomed by a full-size Bell helicopter, hanging above the stairwell), redefines the concept of what art is.

Across the street from MOMA on West 53rd Street is the **American Craft Museum,** featuring ceramics, work in metal and wood, and other media ghettoized under the rubric of "crafts," as opposed to "art." In fact, the whole neighborhood around MOMA has become something of an artistic free-fire zone, with sidewalk artists proliferating on Fifth Avenue and 53rd Street.

In the blocks along Fifth and Park avenues north from MOMA are some of the most notable skyscrapers of Midtown, and many have additional treasures hidden inside them. The **Seagram Building** at 375 Park Avenue is home to power-dining central—The Four Seasons restaurant (see "Restaurants" in "PRACTICAL INFORMATION"). Together with the nearby **Lever House** at 390 Park Avenue, the Seagram is considered the apogee of the post-war International style of "glass-box" architecture.

The **"Lipstick Building"** of Philip Johnson, at 855 Third Avenue, is an odd, oval edifice that was recently voted the most unpopular skyscraper in Manhattan. Nearby, dwarfed by its towering neighbors, is a sole two-story, nineteenth-century holdout, the small, distinctive saloon, P. J. Clarke's at 915 Third Avenue. Universally known as P. J.'s, it is recognizable from Ray Milland's degenerate pub crawl in *The Lost Weekend.*

A distinctive roofline is that of the **Citicorp Center** at 153 East 53rd Street. Its beveled roof was originally meant to be a solar collector, but the real innovation here is the airy, open base of the building, where a church and shopping bazaar are located. Also famous for its profile is **Sony Plaza** (550 Madison), with its "Chippendale" top; in the spacious galleria here is Sony Wonder, an interactive electronic exhibit.

On the Fifth Avenue side of the Sony Plaza block (you can gain entrance through the lobby of what used to be, before hard times forced its sale, the IBM Building, at 590 Madison Avenue) is that great temple of high-end consumerism, **Trump Tower** (725 Fifth Avenue). "The Donald," as Trump is known to gossip columnists and his ex-wife, made this glitzy tower of shops, boutiques, and condos his headquarters. For an easy antidote to the glut of modernism, try the ornate

Crown Building at 730 Fifth Avenue, brilliantly lit at night. Built in 1921, it was the original home (on the 12th floor) of the Museum of Modern Art.

The restored statue of the Civil War's General Sherman in front of the **Plaza Hotel** (Fifth Avenue and 59th Street) often invokes gasps of astonishment, but the gaudy gold-leafing is exactly how the equestrian statue was originally designed. *Pomona,* the mythological lady in the middle of **Pulitzer Fountain,** is only a bit more sedate. The model for the sculpture was the legendary "Suzi," a mainstay of the New York Art Students League, and here immortalized for as long as bronze shall last.

The area around the fountain, more formally called Grand Army Plaza but known to New Yorkers simply by the name of the hotel which fronts it, is one of the few European-style plazas in the city. It is one of the only places in the city to get an ammonia-scented whiff of what New York used to smell like, the product of carriage horses which wait for passengers here. Watch out—some of these beasts are surly, and will bite.

The Plaza Hotel itself has attained a kind of *grande dame* status, indicated by the fact that it is the only Manhattan hostelry to warrant designation as a national historic landmark. Coolness and gentility have held sway here for so long that they have survived repeated assault—from Eloise, the eponymous heroine of the children's book, who is depicted pouring water down the mail chutes; from the Beatles, whose stay here during their original visit to the States sparked a near riot; and from Donald Trump, who bought the Plaza in 1988 and not only failed to transform it into Atlantic City North, as some doomsayers predicted, but with his then-wife Ivana's help actually managed to restore its fading grandeur.

The Plaza displays a convincing civility that is often lacking elsewhere. There is something soothingly classic about taking tea—replete with finger sandwiches—in the graceful central lobby, Palm Court, or consuming beef Wellington in the plush Edwardian Room. There is also no New York experience quite the equal of a martini in the Oak Room bar during the winter holidays, looking out at Central Park as it darkens with the blue light of evening.

Fifty-seventh Street, the main crosstown artery which marks the upper limit of Midtown, is known internationally for its art galleries. This is also the street of **Carnegie Hall** at 156 West 57th Street, with its rather perfunctory Renaissance Revival exterior. But it's been a venue for superb music ever since it was built in 1891, with Tchaikovsky conducting the debut concert.

Incredibly, the hall never managed to turn a profit, and at one time, in the early '60s, it was slated for the wrecking ball. A group of artists, Isaac Stern chief among them, stepped in to save it. A renovation in the late '80s cleared away some of the hall's shabbiness, but some say it destroyed the main auditorium's fabled "warm" acoustics, too.

Carnegie was always known as a classical hall, with Gustav Mahler, Arturo Toscanini, and Leonard Bernstein all conducting there. The New York Philharmonic was in residence until it moved to Lincoln Center in the early 1960s—part of the reason Carnegie fell on hard times during this period. The classical "barrier" was broken by W. C. Handy in 1928, and Benny Goodman a decade later. Today Carnegie hosts a wide variety of acts, but it is still a prime classical venue, especially for visiting orchestras.

Also on 57th Street, just east from Carnegie, two piano stores sit a block apart: **Chickering Hall** at 29 West 57th Street and **Steinway Hall** at 109 West 57th. From the former, Alexander Graham Bell made the first long-distance telephone call; the latter is still a great place to hear a recital on a freshly minted concert grand.

Around the corner, at 58th Street and Seventh Avenue, is the confectionary façade of **Alwyn Court,** its every facet encrusted with terra-cotta ornamentation in

The Manhattan bicycle messenger is a special breed of road warrior.

BICYCLE MESSENGER

I'd picked up a choice run early at the Bank of New York at 48 Wall Street and was booking up to Midtown on the first leg of a round trip, jamming from coffee, 23 minutes gone, but feeling good. No reason I couldn't finish this off fast; no reason at all that it couldn't be a $150 day.

I needed to ratchet up to a harder pace, so I cut across to my favorite route uptown. Lafayette traffic thickens some as you move up it. At first, frustrated drivers who peel off Canal come hurtling up the block, changing lanes, and stomping on the gas like they're chasing a hockey puck—making it a pretty wild ride to Houston.

But above Houston, good, persistent creases form and Lafayette draws riders from all over SoHo, and now I see that there are six on the block with me—slashing uptown between the cars like barracuda sliding through a school of tuna. This is perfect riding through here, and a fast bike can fly all the way to Astor Place and onto Fourth without a single kink. My lungs swell and collapse in relentless steady rhythm played against the breathy swish of my wheels. A magnet draws me up Park Avenue South. My empty head roars with the air in my nostrils and reverberates with the brute desires of the city.

By the time I snap left onto 41st my eyes have become slits, and my veins stand high, barely restrained by skin streaked with grime. Should a jaywalker cross my path now I won't brake. I'll hit him, and flatten him, and I'll leave him there.

The cross-town streets are dangerous. On the avenues, the city shows you what it wants you to see, but on the cross-towns, the city does whatever it wants or needs. Whenever I turn onto one, I feel certain that just ahead something is about to happen. Still, I won't let up on the pace I have made. I'm standing into my pedals, when a white slab of steel suddenly fills my entire field of vision. No way I can stop at this speed. I give a long, involuntary blast on my whistle as the handle bars and my head pass beneath a truck door. The thin sheet metal takes an inch-long, crescent-shaped bite out of the skin on my back. I spit out the whistle to scream at the driver. I could stop and crack this guy in the teeth, but it almost doesn't matter. The danger, the pain in my back, they're small parts of riding in this city. And with 11 minutes left, I'm going to finish this run and catch another.

—Wayne Tucker, New York bicycle messenger, 1989

the style known as François I. The salamander above the corner entryway (and elsewhere on the façade) is a heraldic reference to the French king. In the court-yard of the building, there is a mural by Richard Haas, who did some of the deco-rative work in the New York Public Library.

Near the Alwyn is the **Ed Sullivan Theater** (1697 Broadway), given a $14 mil-lion facelift in 1992 by CBS as a present to its new tenant, David Letterman. Letterman has turned the immediate neighborhood into a sort of talk-show theme park, with regular visits to area stores and events which close down nearby cross streets. Competition for tickets is fierce, and each day the chosen few assemble under the Sullivan's grand marquee to wait for showtime.

The area immediately to the north of Times Square is Hotel-Land (see "Accom-modations"), but there are a few sites of casual interest, such as the **Hearst Build-ing** at 959 Eighth Avenue. The oddly truncated feel to this elaborately orna-mented six-story building can be explained by the fact that it was meant to be the base for a skyscraper, whose builders halted construction when the stock market crashed in 1929.

Another product of the Depression, this one gloriously realized, is the **Thomas Hart Benton mural,** *America Today,* inside the north lobby hallway of the **Equitable Center** at 787 Seventh Avenue. Moved from the New School for Social Research, where it was installed in 1930, this epic painting perfectly embodies the political and artistic flavor of the Depression years. Compared to it, Roy Lichtenstein's giant *Mural with Blue Brushstroke,* also in the Equitable lobby, is mere decoration.

■ TIMES SQUARE AND BROADWAY THEATERS

Originally, the quarter where Broadway slashes across 42nd Street and Seventh Avenue was a dusty district called the Long Acre (after a London neighborhood), with a concentration of carriage houses and riding stables. This evolved into Long-acre Square, changed to its present name in 1904, when the *New York Times* occu-pied its headquarters at **One Times Square.** At midnight on December 31, 1904, the paper threw a fireworks celebration welcoming itself to the area, and the tradi-tion of Times Square New Year's revelry has continued ever since.

One Times Square is still there, although after the newspaper moved around the corner to West 43rd the new owners stripped the ornamentation off the build-ing and sheathed it in a blandly modernistic marble skin. What hasn't changed is

Midnight on New Year's Eve at Times Square. Some would rather watch it on TV than participate. (photo by Katsuyoshi Tanaka)

The Astor Theatre advertises The Great Ziegfeld *during Broadway's heyday in the 1920s. (Library of Congress)*

the "Motogram," the electronic headline sign that wraps the building. At night, looking north from One Times Square, you'll see one of the great spectacles that Manhattan has to offer, a glorious blaze of exuberant, electronic vulgarity, a glitter gulch to rival Las Vegas, the incandescent equivalent of a carnival barker.

Even though advertising styles have changed—the old Camel sign, with its trademark smoke rings, is long gone—the city has attempted to codify the look of Times Square, requiring that all new buildings in the area devote a certain percentage of their façades to illuminated signage. In the late 1980s, a city-backed real estate redevelopment threatened to transform the area from an electric circus into a flavorless corporate no-man's-land, but that was derailed by recession. For now, Times Square remains what it is, a little sleazy, a little wild, but enormously energetic.

It is, of course, primarily a theater district. Since the nineteenth century, Manhattan has been the country's premier showcase for drama, comedy, musicals, and, yes, Shakespearean tragedy. Broadway may now be synonymous with the theater world, but throughout history, several different neighborhoods have played host to the city's major theaters.

In the days when the main stages were to be found in the Bowery, New Yorkers took theater seriously enough to make Shakespearean tragedy come to life. The infamous **Astor Place Theatre Riot** of 1849 is usually presented as a street battle between partisans of the American-born Ned Forrest and English import W. Charles Macready, both cast as Macbeth in competing productions. There were also rumors of insults and an undercurrent of English-Irish enmity to the affair, which didn't end until 22 people were dead and the Seventh Regiment Militia had been called out.

These weren't the last murders associated with theater in New York, but most of the time the slaughter has been figurative rather than literal. A moveable feast, the theater district has migrated north over the years, from lower Broadway and the Bowery to 23rd Street and finally to Times Square. In the '30s and '40s, so-called legitimate theater suffered the indignity of being pushed off Broadway itself by big movie palaces, and relegated to the side streets of Times Square.

There it remains today, a little bruised and battered, chronically wounded in a way to deserve its nickname "the fabulous invalid," but a survivor nonetheless. It might not be as vibrant as it was in the glory days of the Bowery, when people

Ethel Merman in Gershwin's Girl Crazy. *(New York Public Library for the Performing Arts)*

killed over casting, or even during the golden age of the '20s, when Eugene O'Neill cut a swath through American drama for others like Tennessee Williams, Arthur Miller, and Edward Albee to follow.

With a few notable exceptions, Broadway today generally means re-warmed musicals from London, revivals, or middle-of-the-road drama. Whatever the fare, Broadway means billions for New York City—$2.3 billion every year, as a matter of fact. That's how much Broadway theater contributes to Manhattan's economy, luring in 1.7 million tourists and 782,000 people from the suburbs. Those theater-goers spend $35 million a year on cabs alone.

Broadway theater refers not to geography but to a specific level of theatrical contract: union labor, guild-sanctioned agreements, and usually, to attract the audiences to pay for all this, major talent. Thus "Broadway" rarely happens on the street itself. It is usually in Times Square, but might stray as far as Lincoln Center.

Off-Broadway, on the other hand, refers to smaller productions, usually performed at venues scattered all over town (the theaters must, however, be of at least 100-seat capacity). Off-Off-Broadway, so-called "Little Theater," is often experimental or exploratory in nature, and performed in everything from theaters to abandoned movie houses to storefronts to art galleries.

One of the most delightful ways to cut your entertainment expenses and get a dose of Manhattan street life at the same time is through the line at the TKTS booth in **Father Duffy Square** on West 47th Street between Broadway and Seventh Avenue. Father Francis P. Duffy (the "Fighting Priest") served as chaplain of the Fighting 69th and as pastor of nearby Holy Cross Church. Duffy Square features statues both of Duffy and of Broadway great George M. Cohan.

Both statues are somewhat obscured by TKTS (pronounced "tickets"). The distinctive red-and-white canvas booth sells half-priced tickets to selected shows on a first-come, first-served basis on the day of the performance, beginning at 10 A.M. for matinees and 3 P.M. for evenings. Check at the booth to see what shows will be available, then take your place in line.

Spend an hour in the TKTS line on a pleasant afternoon and a phantasmagoria of Manhattan street life will pass in parade. Sometimes it's better theater than what you'll see on stage. There is also a TKTS outlet in the World Trade Center that oftentimes has no line at all, but it misses the electricity of Times Square.

While you're on line at TKTS, you can look up at the façade of the old **I. Miller Building,** on the northeast corner of 46th Street and Seventh Avenue, to see some of the grand dames of Broadway: statues of stage actress Ethel Barrymore, musical star Marilyn Miller, movie icon Mary Pickford, and opera singer Rosa Ponselle are all there, although years of neglect have rendered them almost anonymous. I. Miller, by the way, was a world-famous shoe store, where the stars shopped for footwear.

Meanwhile, a few Broadway theaters are struggling out of decrepitude into the first stages of refurbishment. It will be interesting to contrast the public and private styles of theater renovation—the **New Amsterdam** is slated to be redone by the Disney Company, while the **New Victory** is being remodeled under the auspices of the Times Square Redevelopment Plan.

The two theaters have entrances across the street from each other on a notorious stretch of West 42nd Street which bears the nickname of **"the Deuce."** Through years of redevelopment efforts, the area has stubbornly resisted change. The long-darkened legit theaters, the adult shops, and the bargain movie palaces provided a churning backdrop for a street crowd of random hustlers, shills, and corner preachers. Even though it is the best-patrolled street in New York, the Deuce still manages to exude a faint air of menace.

On the set of the Off-Broadway production of Tony-n-Tina's Wedding.

At the west end of this stretch of 42nd, across from **Show World** at 42nd and Eighth (a kind of supermarket of sex), stand the **Port Authority Bus Terminal** and the old **McGraw-Hill Building.** The former is a large-scale commuter terminal periodically infested with hustlers and scoundrels who prey on the unsuspecting, while the latter is one of the more distinctive architectural gems in Manhattan, not quite Art Deco, not quite full-blown Modern.

■ CLINTON

West of Port Authority, stretching north to 59th Street, is the area that used to boast the flavorful moniker of **Hell's Kitchen.** Hell's Kitchen is an old formulation, known in London in the seventeenth century, but there are some reports that there was a restaurant in the neighborhood, run by a couple named Heil, called Heil's Kitchen—giving the "nabe" its deliberately mispronounced appellation.

Since the 1970s, landlords and most residents have opted for the blander name of Clinton, after a park located on West End Avenue, between 52nd and 54th streets. The park, in turn, was named after Mayor DeWitt Clinton, nephew of Gov. George Clinton. A patrician of one of New York's most prominent families, DeWitt Clinton checked the early rise of the Tammany Society, serving as state legislator and U.S. senator as well as mayor.

Long a district of freight yards, docks, and light industry, Hell's Kitchen had a woesome reputation in the nineteenth century as one of the slumpits of the city. This is the neighborhood of *West Side Story,* and gang activity has often been associated with this hard-fought turf, most recently in the form of the contract killers named the Westies.

The docks remain, and some still play host to trans-Atlantic liners and cruise ships at the NYC Passenger Ship Terminal (Piers 88 and 89, West 49th Street). One permanent guest, berthed at the western end of 46th Street, is the USS *Intrepid,* a decommissioned U.S. Navy aircraft carrier turned into the **Intrepid Sea-Air-Space Museum.** The 900-foot World War II veteran flattop is joined by the *Growler,* a nuclear missile submarine, and the Vietnam-era destroyer, the *Edson,* all open to the public.

On board the *Intrepid* are over 40 aircraft, including a Stealth bomber, as well as space capsules, rockets, and missiles. Recent acquisitions include an Iraqi tank captured in the Gulf War, and a Russian guided missile corvette. Unheralded added attractions are the great views of the harbor from the *Intrepid*'s football-field-sized deck.

San Juan Hill, a rise in Ninth Avenue at 57th Street, was an African-American neighborhood in the early twentieth century. It was supposedly named for a black regiment in the Spanish-American War, but was also the site of vicious street battles, as marauders from the Irish neighborhoods to the south came north to fight. Today, Clinton plays host to a couple of entertainment-related landmarks: the **Film Center Building** at 630 Ninth Avenue, with a great Art Deco lobby; and Lee Strasberg's **Actor's Studio** at 432 West 44th Street, thespian training grounds for stars like Marlon Brando, Dustin Hoffman, and Al Pacino.

REAL ESTATE MAKEOVERS

If you can't sell it, repackage it and hawk it under a different name. That's long been one of the sales strategies of real estate developers. Manhattan has been graced with many of these attempts to gild the lily, some of them ignored by natives—unless pronounced with a sneer.

ORIGINALLY CALLED	NOW CALLED
Loisada	East Village
Lower West Side	TriBeCa
Welfare Island	Roosevelt Island
Hell's Kitchen	Clinton
Lower Fifth Avenue	SoFi
Sixth Avenue	Avenue of the Americas
Avenue A	York Avenue
10th Avenue	Amsterdam Avenue
11th Avenue	West End Avenue

CENTRAL PARK

CENTRAL PARK IS THE WEARY CITY-DWELLER'S SALVATION. It represents a combination escape hatch and exercise yard, an urbanized Eden where everyone's offered a bite of the apple. There are countless reasons to cherish it, not the least of which is that here American landscape architecture and park design were first raised to an art. Imagine how impossibly clogged Manhattan would be without it.

The park was born of the efforts of a pair of obscure geniuses (later catapulted into fame by their work on it), their few stubborn supporters, and a financial panic which pricked the business community into an admission that a public works project was perhaps in order.

Beginning in the 1840s, the poet and newspaper editor William Cullen Bryant campaigned hard for the creation of a great park in what was then the hinterlands beyond the northern edge of the city. He was joined by Washington Irving and other notables, and by mid-century, popular support had rallied behind the idea to the degree that both mayoral candidates in the 1850 elections felt obliged to come out in favor of the park proposal.

The 840-acre site was acquired in 1855 by the city for the then-astronomical sum of $5 million. The next step was a topographical survey. This was not an enviable job, given the presence within the park's boundaries of a good population of squatters, who made their living in such obscure nineteenth-century pursuits as the boiling of bones. They rightly recognized surveyor Egbert L. Viele as a harbinger of eviction, and gave him the bum's rush the first time he ventured into what was then a squatters' no-man's-land.

Yet the survey got done. A journalist named Frederick Law Olmsted, backed by Bryant and Irving, got the rather existential position of superintendent for a park that did not yet exist. His friend Calvert Vaux, an English-born architect, convinced Olmsted that together they should enter the design competition for the park.

Since Olmsted was busy during the day supervising the clearing of the ground, the two had many of their design conferences in the park at night as they trod the territory by moonlight. Olmsted and Vaux called their entry the "Greensward Plan," and it won the $2,000 first prize. With a few notable departures and augmentations, it has been the blueprint of Central Park ever since.

(previous pages) Central Park was developed over a period of 16 years, its 840 acres designed by Frederick Law Olmsted and Calvert Vaux.

Development moved at a snail's pace until the Panic of 1857, which put such a great number of people out of work that the monied classes of the city felt they were faced with a choice of public insurrection or a public jobs program. So the monumental task of making the Greensward Plan a reality began in earnest: five million cubic yards of dirt were moved, part of it through the ministration of ten tons of gunpowder charges; five million trees and shrubs were planted; outcroppings of the famous Manhattan schist were dug up and left artfully exposed. Olmsted faced constant sniping on his bureaucratic flank: he and Vaux submitted their resignations several times during the course of the project.

When the job was completed in 1873, the result was a masterful combination of shaped nature and exuberant wildness. Olmsted's announced goal was to make a place where city dwellers could go to forget all about the city, and to that end he planted the edges and ridges of the site with trees. In the intervening years, of course, the city grew taller than those screens to loom over the park like a far-off barricade.

Also in the intervening years, modifications of the Greensward Plan have detracted from the original purity of its purpose. The automobile has made the most difference, of course, while the rise of team sports has transformed what Olmsted meant as meditative wolds into amateur playing fields. Furthermore, Olmsted detested as "sepulchral" all monuments and statues—suggesting that they be best left to the cemeteries—but currently more than a hundred can be found within the park.

Early days in Central Park. (Library of Congress)

CENTRAL PARK (NORTH)

0   400   800
feet

Blockhouse #1 Site, 2
Cascade, 6
Central Park Police
    Precinct, 12
Charles H. Dana
    Discovery Ctr., 1
Conservatory Garden, 5
Harlem Meer, 3
Lasker Rink/Pool, 4
The Loch, 7
North Meadow
    Security, 8
The Reservoir, 10
South Gate House, 11
Tennis Courts, 9

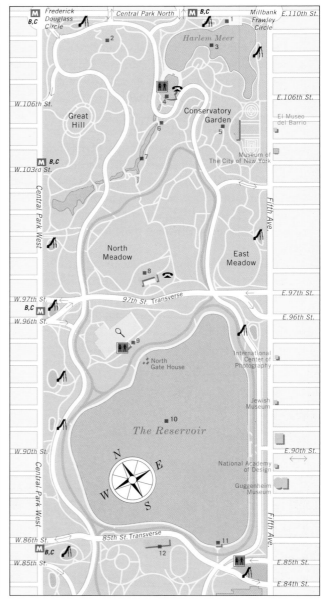

Playground
Public Telephone
Restrooms
Tennis Courts
Bridle Path

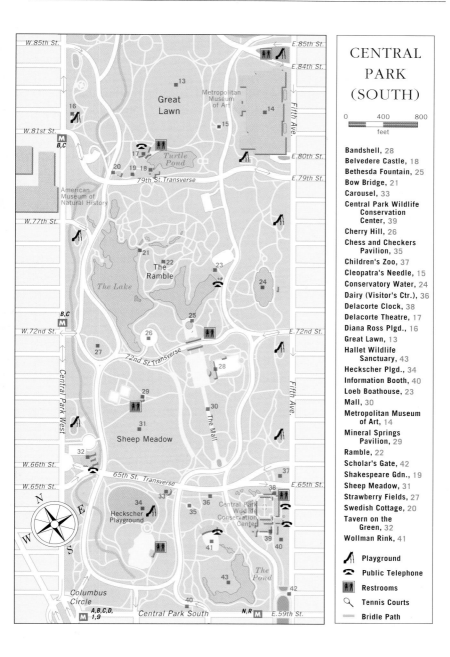

CENTRAL PARK (SOUTH)

0   400   800
feet

Bandshell, 28
Belvedere Castle, 18
Bethesda Fountain, 25
Bow Bridge, 21
Carousel, 33
Central Park Wildlife Conservation Center, 39
Cherry Hill, 26
Chess and Checkers Pavilion, 35
Children's Zoo, 37
Cleopatra's Needle, 15
Conservatory Water, 24
Dairy (Visitor's Ctr.), 36
Delacorte Clock, 38
Delacorte Theatre, 17
Diana Ross Plgd., 16
Great Lawn, 13
Hallet Wildlife Sanctuary, 43
Heckscher Plgd., 34
Information Booth, 40
Loeb Boathouse, 23
Mall, 30
Metropolitan Museum of Art, 14
Mineral Springs Pavilion, 29
Ramble, 22
Scholar's Gate, 42
Shakespeare Gdn., 19
Sheep Meadow, 31
Strawberry Fields, 27
Swedish Cottage, 20
Tavern on the Green, 32
Wollman Rink, 41

Playground
Public Telephone
Restrooms
Tennis Courts
Bridle Path

He viewed all buildings within the park as "deductions" from valuable open space, objecting even to the imposition of the Metropolitan Museum of Art (which to date has eaten up 14 acres of precious parkland).

Robert Moses, the arch-builder who served as parks commissioner under Mayor Fiorello La Guardia, left his inimitable stamp on Central Park, systematically squaring off the intentionally rough edges of the Olmsted plan. One measure which Moses took, however, was undoubtedly long overdue: elimination of a flock of mutant sheep that roamed a meadow in the southern quadrant of the park. Genetically degraded by years of inbreeding, the animals had ceased to be picturesque, bordering instead on the surreal quality of a carnival freakshow.

In the '70s, budget difficulties in New York City contributed to general civic neglect of the park. That decline was effectively halted by the efforts of the Central Park Conservancy, a private organization formed in 1980 which now effectively donates half of the budget for the park's upkeep and refurbishment. Particularly welcome is the attention being paid to the uptown part of the space, north of the Reservoir, originally designated as the "wild" sector in the Greensward Plan. The Conservancy and the Parks Department today are slowly trimming the shabby trails and overgrown brush into usable (but still relatively untamed) parkland.

Some 15 million people use Central Park each year; on an average spring weekend day, 250,000 children and adults flood into these precincts from all over Manhattan, New York, and the world. The park's reputation for danger is seriously overblown, and an awareness of one's surroundings, and common sense about when to visit the park (generally, dawn to dusk), should suffice to protect the wary.

Olmsted and Vaux wanted the southeast quadrant of the park, near the residential precincts of Fifth Avenue, to have the largest number of activities for children. Even though they never designated any part of the park as playgrounds per se, today there are many state-of-the-art facilities all over the park. Concentrated in this quadrant are a vast number of opportunities for the proverbial children of all ages.

Here is also the most popular entry point to Central Park: through the Scholar's Gate (all 22 pedestrian entries to the park are occupationally named, e.g. Mariner's Gate, Hunter's Gate, Miner's Gate) at 59th Street and Fifth Avenue, right behind the equestrian statue of Gen. William Tecumseh Sherman, recently refinished in blindingly bright gold-leaf.

It is a paradox that one of the wildest nooks of the park, a small sanctuary alive with birds, abuts one of the busiest corners of the city, that of the Plaza. Veering left, or west, at Scholar's Gate you will come up against the preserved enclave of **the Pond** and **Hallet Wildlife Sanctuary**; turning north, you will head along the East Drive toward **the zoo**.

Although it's technically named the **Central Park Wildlife Conservation Center**, that epithet will draw a blank stare from most New Yorkers. Ask for "the Central Park Zoo" and you might get directions to the zoo at East 64th Street. **The Children's Zoo,** just north, is currently undergoing renovation, but the Central Park Zoo is itself perfectly proportioned for youngsters to enjoy.

In 1988, a thorough refurbishing transformed the place into a more open, interactive experience. The large central sea lion pool (feeding time, usually at 11:30 A.M. and 2 P.M., is thrilling to watch) is surrounded by three fan-shaped environments: the tropics, the temperate zone, and the polar ice cap. This last, with a trio of polar bears and a flock of penguins, is an enthralling spectacle.

To the east of the zoo, fronting Fifth Avenue, is **the Arsenal,** the only building in the park which predates its founding. It now serves as the headquarters of the Parks and Recreation Department, with a small museum containing the original copy of the Greensward Plan. Don't leave the area without waiting for the quarter hour and the activation of **Delacorte Clock,** above the walkway between the Arsenal and the zoo. The clock—decorated with a fanciful bronze mechanical menagerie of animals, including a dancing bear, kangaroo, and rhino, all tootling on musical instruments—was presented to the city by philanthropist George T. Delacorte.

Delacorte also contributed funds for the establishment of a free theater in the park, and he figures in one of the more bitterly ironic episodes in Central Park lore: at 10 A.M. one winter morning in 1985, the 92-year-old Delacorte and his wife were mugged in a pedestrian tunnel near the clock. The incident reportedly did nothing to dim Delacorte's enthusiasm for the park or his daily walks in it, which he continued until his death six years later.

West of the zoo is **the Dairy,** which used to serve glasses of fresh milk as treats for city children (the cows were kept right there). That building today houses the park information center, but today's Dairy retains something of a kiddie slant, offering a few hands-on games for children inside. You can also get free playing pieces for the nearby **Chess and Checkers Pavilion,** a gazebo-like affair with game tables indoors and out.

ALONE IN CENTRAL PARK

*I*n Central Park the snow had not yet melted on his favorite hill. This hill was in the center of the park, after he had left the circle of the reservoir, where he always found, outside the high wall of crossed wire, ladies, white, in fur coats, walking their great dogs, or old, white gentlemen with canes. At a point that he knew by instinct and by the shape of the buildings surrounding the park, he struck out on a steep path overgrown with trees, and climbed a short distance until he reached the clearing that led to the hill. Before him, then, the slope stretched upward, and above it the brilliant sky, and beyond it, cloudy, and far away, he saw the skyline of New York. . . . there arose in him an exultation and a sense of power, and he ran up the hill like an engine, or a madman, willing to throw himself headlong into the city that glowed before him . . . .

And still, on the summit of that hill he paused. He remembered the people he had seen in that city, whose eyes held no love for him. And he thought of their feet so swift and brutal, and the dark gray clothes they wore, and how when they passed they did not see him, or, if they saw him, they smirked. . . . Then he remembered his father and his mother, and all the arms stretched out to hold him back, to save him from this city where, they said, his soul would find perdition.

—James Baldwin, *Go Tell It on the Mountain,* 1952

(photo by Katsuyoshi Tanaka)

Taking up the pasture where the cows from the Dairy used to graze is **Wollman Rink,** its construction completed with much fanfare (as something like a cross between a public service and a publicity stunt) by developer Donald Trump when the city proved unable to do so. Past Playmates Arch (every structure in the park has a name, although not many New Yorkers may know what it is) turns the great **Central Park Carousel,** beautifully preserved even if sponsors are currently being sought to help spruce it up. The 1870 original was powered by real horses trudging in a circle in a basement pit.

Southwest of the carousel is **Umpire Rock,** so called because it overlooks the baseball diamonds. The ball fields were not in the original Olmsted design, but are nevertheless ragingly popular with cut-throat Midtown publishing, advertising, media, and theater softball leagues. By the rock, **Heckscher Playground,** a great children's area, allows youngsters to scamper over a 400-million-year-old outcropping of Manhattan schist.

North of this is the **Sheep Meadow,** where the ghosts of cacogenic sheep have long since vanished, leaving a vast open lawn (no dogs, no bicycles, no radios) for picnics, sunbathing, or just lounging. **Tavern on the Green,** originally the Sheepfold, represented another trespass against the Olmsted Plan when it was erected by Boss Tweed in 1870, but now it is generally accepted as one of Manhattan's glitziest dining palaces (see "Restaurants" in "PRACTICAL INFORMATION").

More integral to the spirit of the park, and a recent addition that has won intant popularity is **Strawberry Fields.** Honoring John Lennon, who was slain near here, and sponsored by his widow, Yoko Ono, this beautifully landscaped spot has botanical contributions from nearly every country in the world. Set into the sidewalk is a large mosaic that reads "Imagine," from one of the singer's most trenchant lyrics.

On the east side of the Sheep Meadow is the **roller-skating concourse,** a riot of skill and exhibitionism that convenes every warm-weather weekend, and quite a few weekdays as well. To the east of this is a more sedate promenade, one included by Olmsted and Vaux in their original plan: **the Mall,** immediately popular when it opened as a place for *tout* Manhattan to see and be seen. The Mall was originally skewed northwest to provide a prospect of **Belvedere Castle,** to the north, past the Romantic opulence of **Bethesda Terrace.**

Together, the Mall, Terrace, and Castle are the most formal elements in the Greensward design. Bethesda Terrace is a natural viewing point for the pleasure rowboats on **the Lake,** and for the artful grace of Calvert Vaux's **Bow Bridge.** The fountain, the oldest working public one in the city, was built in 1863 to commemorate those who died at sea during the Civil War. It features a statue of *The Angel of the Waters,* which rates notable mention in Tony Kushner's epic drama *Angels in America.*

The Lake itself was deliberately designed to appear larger than it is by winding around out of sight sinuously and mysteriously. Exploring it by renting a rowboat at **Loeb Boathouse** is still one of the most romantic things to do in Manhattan.

Conservatory Water is another Central Park landmark that most New Yorkers know under a less formal name, the **Model Boat Pond,** since here a serious guild of craftsmen convene every weekend at the Kerbs Memorial Model Boathouse to float their tiny ships. Also near this shallow oval of water are two popular children's statues: *Alice in Wonderland,* to the north, and *Hans Christian Andersen,* to the west. The latter site hosts a raucously crowded story hour at 11 A.M. every Saturday in warm weather.

On the north side of the Lake is **the Ramble,** a hill of twisted paths and thickets that comprises a well-known birding mecca, especially for the March 10 "return" when certain birds show up in the same spots each year. North of this, across the

Rollerblading in the park (above). Yoko Ono at Strawberry Fields (right).

79th Street Transverse (all Central Park transverses—there are four—are named for their East Side terminuses; the 79th Street Transverse actually exits the park at West 81st Street) is **Belvedere Castle,** headquarters of the Urban Park Rangers Meteorological Station and Learning Center. Vaux designed the castle on a small scale in order to trick perspective, so that it appears farther off than it really is.

Belvedere Castle is a great stage set for nearby **Delacorte Theater,** another gift to the city from George T. Delacorte and venue for a free summer Shakespeare festival put on by the Public Theater. The ragingly popular shows usually feature a "name" star; new ticketing procedures have eliminated the lines that used to snake all the way around the **Great Lawn.**

West of the Delacorte Theater is the **Swedish Cottage,** where marionette shows are the specialty. At 81st Street and Central Park West is the **Diana Ross Playground,** given to the city after a disastrous free concert in 1983. It featured a literal post-concert bash, with roaming gangs of youths mugging and assaulting concertgoers; Ed Koch, the mayor at the time, dodged some missiles sent in his direction. Bad vibes; nice playground.

The aforementioned Great Lawn was once a reservoir; when it was drained in the 1930s, thousands of homeless drifted into the muddy expanse and set up a Hooverville, one of those shantytowns named in mocking tribute to the Republican President. It is now a collection of playing fields, and in summer is the site of free opera and New York Philharmonic concerts.

To the north is **the Reservoir,** once an integral part of the city's water system, but now the center of a debate over what its future may be. Should it be drained? Given over to boating and swimming? Left as it is? In the meantime, its perimeter continues to be Manhattan's most heavily used jogging track, a well-known haunt of Madonna, John F. Kennedy, Jr., Dustin Hoffman (at least in the movie *Marathon Man*), and other stars. To the northwest of the Reservoir are some of the most heavily used tennis courts in the city.

One Central Park jogger almost didn't live to tell the tale. The still-anonymous woman who was a victim of a "wilding" attack in 1989 was surrounded by a gang of youths in the north of the Park. They beat and raped her, leaving her for dead. She survived to testify against them in a tumultuous trial that received nationwide publicity and contributed to the notoriety of Central Park as a dangerous place to stray after dark. Crimes like this are, thankfully, uncommon, and the park is generally safe—just use common city sense.

Because of topography—the Manhattan schist outcroppings are numerous here, and this was the last part of the park purchased and developed by the city—Olmsted and Vaux did indeed intend that the northern third of the park be wilder than the rest of it. Unfortunately, this and the reputation of nearby neighborhoods has contributed to a plague of neglect and underuse that is just now being addressed.

One exception has always been the superb **Conservatory Gardens** on the East Side, entered through Vanderbilt Gate at 105th Street and Fifth Avenue. Robert Moses added this small paradise to the park after a glass-roofed conservatory building was torn down. The resulting formal gardens, with their fountains and pergola, reflect the taste of their progenitor in their elegance and beauty.

Further north in the park, **Lasker Rink** always features a shorter wait than its sister to the south, Wollman Rink. The new **Charles H. Dana Discovery Center,** opened in fall of 1993 on the shore of **Harlem Meer,** is attracting students, birders, and other naturalists to its ecology exhibits. Finally, the Central Park Conservancy is working to restore the Meer and **the Cascade** that leads to the nearby sinuous body of water, **the Loch.** The Meer, at least, is stocked with fish, and fishing poles are available for loan in Dana Discovery Center.

The prime **bird-watching** season for Central Park is springtime, when species from as far north as the Arctic Circle may be seen passing through Central Park and at least 20 other species are nesting there, including cardinals, downy woodpeckers, eastern kingbirds, gray catbirds, and mallard ducks. Central Park's four best birding areas include the promontory of the Pond near the southeast entrance, the Reservoir, the Loch, and the wild-and-woodsy Ramble on the north shore of the lake. Spring migration begins in March and climaxes in mid-May. In February, look for fish crows and iridescent common grackles; in March, American robins and American woodcocks; in April, ruby-crowned kinglets, blue-gray gnatcatchers, yellow-rumped warblers, brown creepers, black-and-white warblers, and hermit thrushes; and in May, orioles, scarlet tanagers, rose-breasted grosbeaks, indigo buntings, and some 25 brightly colored species of warblers. The fall migration is less concentrated and less colorful because the birds aren't in their mating plumage.

Other good birding spots in Manhattan are Riverside Park and the Heather Garden in Fort Tryon Park. To find out what's been seen where, call the Rare Bird Alert at 979-3070.

CHILDREN IN MANHATTAN

One of the truly great things about being brought up in New York City is that it allows you to go through life with an open mind. —Jimmy Breslin

When Maud Alice Zimmerman Reavill came into the world at Manhattan's Mount Sinai hospital on January 26, 1992—Super Bowl Sunday—her parents were counseled by the sober-minded to decamp the city immediately.

"You can't raise a kid in the city today," they all said. "It's too—" dangerous, expensive, dirty, crowded—fill in the blank.

Maud is still here, and thriving. It is perhaps the worst calumny you can throw at a city, that it's a lousy place to raise kids. Lately, leaving Manhattan after the birth of a child is so common that it's almost cliché. You leave for greener pastures, for somewhere you don't have to watch your kid like a hawk, for suburbia. Maybe it's not so much that the city is bad for kids, but that the suburbs are supposed to be better.

The kids themselves love Manhattan. They are tuned to its frantic pace, its energy, its unpredictability. The city has all the social possibilities of the hive. The complicated caves people live in here are great prospects from which to view the world. Recently, when city workers were digging up the avenue outside our apartment, we almost had to set up bleachers in front of Maud's window, so intent were she and her friends to watch the earth-moving equipment in the street below.

The resources of Manhattan, too, make raising a child here sometimes unexpectedly easy. Central Park has become her backyard. When snowstorms socked Manhattan in during the first winter of her life, Maud was happily learning to walk on the carpeted ramps of the Hall of Gems and Minerals in the American Museum of Natural History. Showing at the time was a short film about the properties and mythologies of gold, narrated by the sonorous tones of George Plimpton, with music from the Nutcracker Suite. Maud found it endlessly fascinating, and she must have watched it dozens of times. She loves the Metropolitan Museum of Art, but especially enjoys the Central Park playground just to the south of it, with great brass bear sculptures by Paul Manschip.

At the moment, Maud has a more extensive social life than her parents—a tribute to her loving babysitter, Magalie Gilson, who is tireless in exposing our daughter to new people and experiences. Maud visits friends for playdates all over the area, and goes to museums, performances, and field trips. While walking down the street in our neighborhood, she is often greeted by name by the neighborhood folk she's met on her endless peregrinations. Ali at the corner newsstand boosts her up on his shoulders whenever he greets her.

This is the true benefit that Manhattan can extend to anyone, not just to children

—an amazing cast of fascinating people who represent, more than museums or parks or anything else, the city's real treasure. We both hope that Maud will grow up to be one of them.

Special Places for Children

American Museum of Natural History. Central Park West at 77th Street, 769-5000.

Aunt Len's Doll and Toy Museum. 6 Hamilton Terrace, 926-4172; by appointment.

Children's Museum of Manhattan. 212 West 83rd Street, 721-1223; three floors of marvelous, mostly interactive exhibits, including finger-painting workshops, video production facilities, a rainforest preserve—lots of fun.

Big Apple Circus. Damrosch Park, Lincoln Center, 268-0055; a seasonal one-ring circus that is a perfect fit for kids.

Central Park Wildlife Center. Central Park at East 64th Street, 861-6030; intimate, well-designed animal environments. Big favorite: the polar bears.

F.A.O. Schwartz. 767 Fifth Avenue, 644-9400. Toy kingdom.

Little People's Theater. Courtyard Playhouse, 39 Grove Street, 765-9540.

Marionette Theater. Swedish Cottage, Central Park at West 80th Street, 988-9093; Saturdays, October through May.

Story Hour. Hans Christian Andersen Statue, Central Park at East 74th Street; 11 A.M. on Saturdays, April through September.

The Nutcracker. New York City Ballet, Lincoln Center, 870-5570; in December.

Paper Bag Players. Broadway and 95th Street, 864-5400.

The polar bear habitat at the Central Park Zoo.

E A S T S I D E

FOR A CERTAIN SPECIES OF CLASS-CONSCIOUS NEW YORKERS, there is simply no other place to live. The West Side is too parvenu, too bourgeois; the Village has all those neo-bohemian flavorings which make it unseemly; everyplace else is out of the question.

Which leaves only the elite East Side. Since early in the century it has been *the* place for Manhattanites who feel themselves defined by their addresses. According to the 1990 census, the blocks between 59th and 110th streets, from Fifth Avenue to the river, retain the highest per capita income of any urban quarter in the nation. Not surprisingly, the area is thick with fine restaurants, boasts a world-class shopping strip in the boutiques and stores of Madison Avenue, and attracts other businesses whose purpose is to serve the rich.

The residential palaces of families like the Astors, the Whitneys, and the Vanderbilts once graced this neighborhood, and have since been transformed into a cluster of museums that must rank among the greatest treasure troves in the world. **Museum Mile** runs along Fifth Avenue roughly from East 70th Street to East 104th Street.

A traditional bifurcation of the district is now fading: the **Upper East Side** (north of 86th Street, or variously, north of 96th Street) and the plain old East Side have become more or less interchangeable, the distinction vital only to an earlier generation of Manhattanites.

There are a few salient dates in the development of the neighborhood as Manhattan's Gold Coast:

1896 Caroline Schermerhorn Astor moves to her mansion at Fifth Avenue and 65th Street; after her comes the deluge of society, making Fifth Avenue the fashionable address it remains today.

1901 Steel magnate Andrew Carnegie occupies his mansion at Fifth and 91st, further extending the boundaries of the acceptable, and christening the neighborhood as Carnegie Hill.

1907 New York Central Railroad electrifies the trains that plough down Park Avenue toward Grand Central, with a railroad tunnel subsequently built beneath the street.

These railroad tracks were long a sooty, unsightly boundary that separated the wealthy (west from Park to Fifth Avenue) from the poor (east to Yorkville and the river). When the tracks were buried out of sight, it removed a stigma and transformed Park Avenue itself into one of the most prestigious residential addresses in the city. The riff-raff were subsequently spooked from Yorkville by high rents, and the East Side became solidly middle class.

■ FIFTH AVENUE AND THE GOLD COAST

The old world of privilege and exclusivity survives on the East Side; this is Clubland, though not in the sense that Elvis Costello sings about in his song of the same title. The **Metropolitan Club** (One East 60th Street), the **Harmonie Club** (4 East 60th Street), the **Knickerbocker Club** (2 East 62nd Street), the **Lotos Club** (5 East 66th Street), the **Union Club** (101 East 69th Street), The **Colony**

INNOCENT RICH

*T*he Beaufort house was one that New Yorkers were proud to show to foreigners, especially on the night of the annual ball. The Beauforts had been among the first people in New York to own their own red velvet carpet and have it rolled down the steps by their own footmen, under their own awning, instead of hiring it with the supper and the ball-room chairs . . . .

Newland Archer, as became a young man of his position, strolled in somewhat late. He had left his overcoat with the silk-stockinged footmen (the stockings were one of Beaufort's few fatuities), had dawdled a while in the library hung with Spanish leather and furnished with Buhl and malachite, where a few men were chatting and putting on their dancing-gloves, and had finally joined the line of guests whom Mrs. Beaufort was receiving on the threshold of the crimson drawing-room.

Archer was distinctly nervous. He had not gone back to his club after the Opera (as the young bloods usually did), but, the night being fine, had walked for some distance up Fifth Avenue before turning back in the direction of the Beauforts' house. He was definitely afraid that the Mingotts might be going too far; that, in fact, they might have Granny Mingott's orders to bring the Countess Olenska to the ball.

—Edith Wharton, *The Age of Innocence,* 1920

UPPER EAST SIDE

0   1100   2200

feet

Abigail Adams Smith Museum, 26
Asia Society, 20
Asphalt Green, 13
Carl Schurz Park, 15
Carnegie Hill, 10
China Institute, 24
Church of the Holy Trinity, 12
Cooper-Hewitt Museum, 7
Frick Collection, 21
Gracie Mansion, 14
Guggenheim Museum, 9
Hospital Row, 25
International Center of Photography, 3
Jewish Museum, 6
Madison Ave., 18
Metropolitan Museum of Art, 17
National Academy of Design, 8
92nd St. Y, 11
96th St. Mosque, 1
Queensboro Bridge, 27
7th Regiment Armory, 23
Squadron A Armory, 4
St. Nicholas Russian Orthodox Cathedral, 2
Synod of Bishops of the Russian Orthodox Church Outside of Russia, 5
Temple Emanu-El, 22
Whitney Museum of Art, 19
Yorkville, 16

Club (564 Park Avenue), and the **Cosmopolitan Club** (122 East 66th Street)—these last two primarily for women—are membership-only havens, most located in fine old East Side mansions.

The irony about these clubs, with their air of inaccessibility, is that many were formed by people who were kept out of other clubs: J. P. Morgan, for example, founded the venerable Metropolitan when the Union Club stiffed him. Groucho Marx ("I wouldn't want to belong to any club that would have me as a member") is relevant here.

A stroll up lower Fifth Avenue is instructive, just to see how the other one percent lived—and to some extent still lives today. At 810 Fifth was the penthouse-cum-aerie of Nelson Rockefeller, longtime governor of New York, scion of one of the largest fortunes ever assembled by one family.

As governor, Rockefeller once wanted to clear a whole block of the West Side for a plaza. Aides were mystified about his dogged insistence on the plan (eventually thwarted), but they should have stood in Rocky's apartment: with the block across the park leveled, he would have had a clear view of the Chagall paintings he had donated to the Metropolitan Opera at Lincoln Center.

An aerial view of the Upper East Side looking over towards Queens.
The Guggenheim Museum is visible near the pond to the right.

A couple of blocks north of Rocky's roost at One East 65th Street is **Temple Emanu-El,** built on the site of the Caroline Schermerhorn Astor mansion that started the turn-of-the-century stampede of society folk to the East Side. In general, this whole neighborhood is filled with what was originally residential architecture, with many of the old mansions since converted to consulates, offices, or clubs.

Those afflicted with altitude sickness over this stretch of Fifth Avenue would do well to head further east, to the area around Bloomingdale's and the Roosevelt Island Tram (see "Boroughs and Islands" chapter). For all its upward mobility, the area is referred to as **East of Eden.**

One indication of the relatively rootless nature of the population is the strip of singles bars along First and Second avenues near the Queensboro Bridge. They cater to the upwardly mobile and unattached who, seeking the prestige (and relative cleanliness and safety) of the East Side, flooded into the area during the 1970s and '80s.

The middle-class flavor of Queens wafting across the **Queensboro Bridge** may clear your head, and may even leave you feelin' groovy, à la Paul Simon's "59th Street Bridge Song." While you're flashing back to the title credits of the television show "Taxi," you can admire the 1909 cantilevered span itself (notice the bizarre finials). With the rest of Manhattan, we're still holding our breath for **Bridgemarket,** the long-aborning project to utilize the superb groin-vaulted space underneath the bridge's Manhattan terminus as a place for shops and food outlets.

North of the bridge, totally blocking the space between York Avenue and FDR Drive, is **Hospital Row,** a concentration of research and health-care facilities. The **Sloan-Kettering Cancer Center** at 1275 York Avenue has a worldwide reputation; it was here that the former Shah of Iran came to die, setting the stage for the Iranian hostage crisis.

Rockefeller University was originally endowed by John D. Rockefeller, Sr., as the Institute for Medical Research. It was put on a graduate university footing by his grandson David, and today ranks as one of the most prestigious medical research facilities in the nation. The grounds, which it shares with the **Cornell Medical Center,** are capacious, with splendid gardens. This area was once part of **Jones Wood,** a huge park that extended from the East River to Third Avenue in the mid-1800s and was once a proposed alternative to the plan for Central Park.

Another spoor of the Rockefeller family—the whole area is thick with it—is the **Asia Society** at 725 Park Avenue, a pet project of John D. Rockefeller III, or JDR III, as he liked to be called. (The five sons of John D. Rockefeller, Jr. supposedly once had a conversation whereby they divided the world: Nelson "got" South America, David got Africa, Laurance got Europe, and JDR III got Asia. Winthrop, the black sheep, was given the Army as his purlieu.)

By all accounts, JDR III had a real sympathy for the refined asceticism of Japan and other Eastern cultures, and it resulted in a lifelong fascination with Asian art. Visitors reap the rewards here, with galleries, films, lectures, theater events, and a bookstore and gift shop on the premises. Similarly, **China Institute,** at 125 East 65th Street, runs an extensive program schedule, and was also endowed by a man with a lifelong interest in the Middle Kingdom, *Time* magazine founder Henry Luce.

The **Seventh Regiment Armory** (66th to 67th streets, Park to Lexington avenues) somehow embraces disparate elements of the East Side mystique within its imposing red-brick fortress. It is the site of the toney Winter Antiques Show, and features interior detailing by Louis Comfort Tiffany (he of the lamps); but the Armory is very much an active National Guard training site. Nearby, in Central Park at 67th Street, is the **Seventh Regiment memorial.**

Which East Side block best represents the neigborhood's brownstone residential architecture is a moot point. The stretch of **67th Street off Fifth Avenue** gets votes for its (mostly) Renaissance Revival limestone façades. **Seventieth Street between Park and Lexington Avenue** also has adherents, for its wonderful diversity of architectural styles: English Gothic, Italianate palazzo, neo-Georgian, Modern, and French

Members of the Seventh Regiment. The gentleman seated on the left is Charles W. Clinton, designer of the Armory. (Courtesy of Margaret Clinton Burt)

provincial, as well as assorted others, all within one block! The townhouse at 171 East 71st Street is instantly recognizable as **Holly Golightly's digs** in the movie version of *Breakfast at Tiffany's*.

■ MUSEUM MILE

So many *objets*, so little time. Museum Mile—roughly from the **Frick Collection** at East 70th Street to **El Museo del Barrio** at East 104th Street—is actually somewhat longer than a mile, more like two. The great concentration of superb, world-class art museums along this stretch can turn Fifth Avenue into something of a cultural marathon for tourist and native alike.

The best advice is not to attempt too much. One splendid gallery in the Museum of the City of New York, say, or a temporary exhibit at the International Center of Photography can be worth more, aesthetically speaking, than a jam-packed schedule of if-it's-two-o'clock-that-must-be-a-Cézanne. Check the schedules before you go, not only for special exhibits, but also for hours. Many of the museums are closed to the public for as many as three days a week.

Stop and smell the flowers at Central Park's exquisite Conservatory Garden. Take your time. Don't overload. Wear comfortable shoes.

■ FRICK COLLECTION

Can a bad man make a good art museum? That is evidently the case with the Frick Collection (One East 70th Street, 288-0700). Henry Clay Frick was one of the most obdurate of the late-nineteenth-century capitalists. As Andrew Carnegie's hatchet man at U.S. Steel, he was a rapacious predator who exploited workers mercilessly, scoured the ranks of his employees for any sign of unionism, and regularly broke strikes with smug relish. But there was no justice, and Frick survived numerous assassination attempts.

So you may want to pause in front of the portal of the Frick Collection, housed in what was Henry Clay's Fifth Avenue mansion, and give a moment's meditation on his indifference to misery. Then put it out of your mind and enjoy one of the most perfect art experiences Manhattan has to offer.

The Frick is not a museum in the sense of most others in the world. It's a private home you've stumbled into (the descendants of Monsieur Frick still sleep over once in a while), a private gallery raised to the Nth power by the magic of money and good taste.

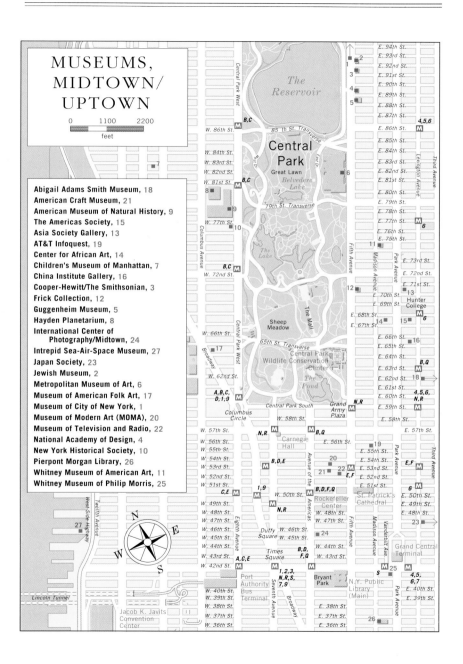

MUSEUMS, MIDTOWN/ UPTOWN

0   1100   2200
feet

Abigail Adams Smith Museum, 18
American Craft Museum, 21
American Museum of Natural History, 9
The Americas Society, 15
Asia Society Gallery, 13
AT&T Infoquest, 19
Center for African Art, 14
Children's Museum of Manhattan, 7
China Institute Gallery, 16
Cooper-Hewitt/The Smithsonian, 3
Frick Collection, 12
Guggenheim Museum, 5
Hayden Planetarium, 8
International Center of
   Photography/Midtown, 24
Intrepid Sea-Air-Space Museum, 27
Japan Society, 23
Jewish Museum, 2
Metropolitan Museum of Art, 6
Museum of American Folk Art, 17
Museum of City of New York, 1
Museum of Modern Art (MOMA), 20
Museum of Television and Radio, 22
National Academy of Design, 4
New York Historical Society, 10
Pierpont Morgan Library, 26
Whitney Museum of American Art, 11
Whitney Museum of Philip Morris, 25

Sit yourself down, says the Frick, make yourself at home, bowl a few frames. It's true: in the basement is **Henry Frick's private bowling alley**—a manual one, no less, meant to be operated by a pin-boy (a non-union pin-boy, no doubt). This is all off limits to the public, of course, but just knowing it's there can lighten one's appreciation of the surroundings.

Some of the furniture is a shade stodgy, and the exhibition seems frozen—never to change or even be rearranged much. But the environment and the art attain a sort of high aesthetic equilibrium that boosts both to a higher plane. The building is spectacular, and it includes a skylit courtyard that has to rank among the city's most perfect trysting spots. One of the best ways to appreciate this romantic atmosphere is with a soundtrack, via the occasional Sunday afternoon chamber orchestra concerts.

The collection concentrates on Old Masters from the fourteenth to nineteenth centuries, with special attention paid to Italian Renaissance greats. Fragonard's *The Progress of Love* is given a whole room of its own, and the series (commissioned by Louis XV's mistress) has the gleaming, confectionary glaze of the French court shining from every canvas. Rembrandt's exquisite *The Polish Rider* is here, too, along with other Flemish masterworks from Van Dyck, Holbein, and Vermeer.

■ WHITNEY MUSEUM OF AMERICAN ART

The Whitney (945 Madison Avenue, at 75th Street, 570-3676) strives to be brash and iconoclastic, fresh and irreverent. If it only occasionally pulls it off, the museum at least manages to stir the froth of modern American art into something resembling life.

The beetling, forbidding façade of the museum belies its egalitarian ideal, and suggests a futuristic castle (complete with moat) rather than a warm and an inviting art space. Based on the collection of Gertrude Vanderbilt Whitney, the museum owns and periodically trundles out samples from a 10,000-piece storehouse of Modern American sculpture, painting, and photography. At times, the museum manages to mount a definitive look at a contemporary artist.

In its struggles to remain current, the Whitney can sometimes stray into the unlikely, but the spectacle of a major arts institution embarrassing itself is not entirely unappealing. The Whitney Biennial, mounted in the spring of odd-numbered years, is intended by the museum to be a plenary look at what's happening on the art scene at that particular time. Picking it apart and taking potshots at the Biennial is a major cottage industry among art critics, but that doesn't make the lines to enter the show any shorter.

The Whitney has the most aggressive outreach program of any museum in town, with satellite galleries in the Philip Morris Building (120 Park Avenue South at 42nd Street, 878-2550), as well as in Stamford, Connecticut.

■ M E T R O P O L I T A N   M U S E U M   O F   A R T

The dilemma here is a glorious one: too much choice. With over three million objects in the Metropolitan Museum of Art (Fifth Avenue at 82nd Street, 535-7710), how can one avoid being buried under the avalanche of culture?

Give yourself time, plan to go when you won't be battling crowds, and allow yourself the luxury of chance meetings with an Etruscan antiquity, a Flemish masterwork, a delicate Chinese vase. Serendipity is an essential part of the Met experience, and to let yourself wander among these treasure trove halls is one of life's greatest pleasures. Is it the world's best art museum? The point is moot. It is without question the premier museum experience in a great museum city, so let's let it go at that.

Begin with the setting, on a healthy tract of precious Central Park land. Frederick Olmsted said later he regretted giving the park over to the Metropolitan's use, but despite the explosive growth of the building over the years, it's been a happy marriage of art and open space. Calvert Vaux's 1880 Beaux Arts building is most impressive when entered from the front steps. Look above the entrance to see the great stone blocks, originally meant to be statues, left uncarved due to vagaries of time and economics. The Met's other entrances are open intermittently, and may reduce the wait in line: through the street-level doors on the left and right of the main entrance, or via the sculpture garden on the west side of the building.

The Great Hall is spectacular, and you get a sense of the type of benefactors the Met has when you realize there's a million-dollar endowment just to keep this superb room in fresh flowers. The list of givers is a veritable roll call of heavyweights: Rockefeller, Morgan, Mellon, and most recently, Walter Annenberg, the *TV Guide* and *Racing Form* mogul. ("Strength goes to strength," explained the never overly modest Annenberg, explaining why he gave his vast collection of Impressionist paintings and other priceless art to the Met.)

Lately, with gifts like Annenberg's and that of *Reader's Digest* founder Lila Acheson Wallace, the Met has been increasing its twentieth-century holdings. It already has the world's greatest collection of medieval antiquities, many housed far uptown in the gorgeous Cloisters, donated to the museum by financier J. P. Morgan. Also impressive is the Egyptian collection, crowned by the Temple of Dendur, an entire 15 B.C. building saved from the rising waters of the Aswan Dam and housed in its own massive wing.

For many people, the only thing to do is to head straight up the main stairway and enter the European painting galleries. The Dutch masters are very well represented here, with Vermeer, Hals, and Rembrandt leading the way for lesser lights to follow. Gallery after gallery, the Met's unequaled collection unfolds like a rose: English painting by Gainsborough and Thomas Lawrence, Italian Renaissance masterworks by Raphael and Botticelli, priceless Spanish canvasses by El Greco and Velázquez. But you're not done yet, for the petals part to reveal an astounding array of Impressionist paintings by Manet, Monet, Cèzanne, Renoir, and Gauguin that can take your breath away.

Strength goes to strength. That's the whole story of the Met collection. Just when you think you've plumbed its depths, you round a corner and are greeted with one more priceless treasure. The nineteenth-century American paintings on

Scenes from inside the Metropolitan Museum of Art. (above and right)

exhibit give a precise measure of the glories and limits of American art during that period. The medieval collection, built upon Morgan's original gift, is so extensive that portions can be housed both here and at the Cloisters with no discernible diminishment to either display.

The Asian art in the museum is arranged around a recreation of a Chinese scholar's courtyard, and indicates the sensitive approach to exhibition that is in evidence throughout. The Michael C. Rockefeller Wing (named for the son of Nelson Rockefeller who disappeared on an art-gathering trip to New Guinea in 1961, to be eaten, some say, by either sharks or cannibals) is a whole museum's worth of art from traditional cultures, displayed in coolly correct new surroundings.

The Met collection sprawls, and there are those who complain that it is not organized in a totally sequential manner—the Lehman Pavilion, for example, has European paintings that might belong to the Great Hall galleries. But one can only answer that sequential organization is impossible in such a large collection.

Repeated application is the only way to enjoy the Met's hidden treasures, its countless nooks and crannies off the beaten path. The building is so huge that it has forgotten corners—like the pistol range in the basement, usually off limits to the public. The period rooms in the American wing, perhaps not the crowd's favorite, can nonetheless transport a visitor as sure as any time machine. The sculpture garden, full of Rodin bronzes, is a gentle place to linger—entering the museum this way is a very different experience from entering through the front door.

The best thing about the Met is that it allows you to develop your own tastes, no matter how idiosyncratic. At the top of the main stairway to the left is a vitrine of Chinese porcelain. Many people pass by it on their way to the twentieth-century wing, say, or the current special exhibition. But we've formed an attachment to this glass case of small, perfect pottery, to the degree that no visit to the Met is complete without it. One expert called it "a sorbet for the eyes, something to clean the palate between courses." Another description is closer to how these vases hit us: "This is the kind of sculpture they have in heaven . . . " The Met is filled with such transcendent objects.

The Met is also open on Friday and Saturday evenings, usually less crowded than the daytime hours. A string quartet plays on the balcony, potential lovers eye each other, and the galleries seem hushed and empty. Another little-known alternative is the weekend brunch in the members dining room, normally closed to the public. The museum's restaurant, arranged around a sunken fountain, is at times hectic, but nevertheless represents a place to recharge one's batteries.

■ GUGGENHEIM MUSEUM

Officially called the Solomon R. Guggenheim Museum (1071 Fifth Avenue, 423-3500), this modern-art mecca is at least as famous for its building as for its collection. Frank Lloyd Wright, who professed to hate cities, got a chance to alter the look of one with his monumental swirl of alabaster concrete. It bulges atop its one-story plinth like a beehive on a gravestone. The Guggenheim represents something of a road not taken for Wright, who perhaps could have rivaled Le Corbusier in forging the modern cityscape. Two later additions did nothing to detract from the drama of Wright's original design.

Inside, the main gallery follows Wright's ramp-like spiral around the outside of the five-floor atrium. Guggenheim was one of the most voracious collectors of the 1920s and '30s, and the permanent exhibit is full of masterpieces by Chagall, Léger, and Kandinsky. For a long time space considerations kept many of Guggenheim's treasures locked away (Wright being a better conceptual architect than a practical one), but a recent addition doubled available gallery space, and some real treasures came out of hiding. Look for the early Picassos in particular.

■ CARNEGIE HILL MUSEUMS

The rise of land from 86th to 96th streets, from Fifth to Lexington avenues, was named Carnegie Hill after Andrew Carnegie's residence, now the **Cooper-Hewitt Museum.** Runners in the New York City Marathon have another name for Carnegie Hill. Because it is near the end of the course, and they arrive exhausted, the runners call this gentle rise "the Wall."

The Cooper-Hewitt (2 East 91st Street, 860-6868), an affiliate of the Smithsonian Institution, is primarily a design museum, with special emphasis on textiles. It suffers from comparison with the Frick, at the other end of Museum Mile, as another exhibit space situated in a millionaire's mansion. The Carnegie Mansion seems thick and turgid next to the spare elegance of the Frick. Curators at the Cooper-Hewitt put on rotating exhibits that make the more everyday design arts accessible to the lay person, who may find astonishing Chinese silks, plush velvets over 1,700 years old, architectural drawings, and decorative metalwork.

Samuel Morse might seem an odd person to found the **National Academy of Design** (1083 Fifth Avenue, 369-4880), but the inventor of the telegraph was also a painter, and in 1825, he realized his life's dream to build a school for artists, run by artists themselves. The original building was at 23rd Street and Park Avenue, and survives in another incarnation as the façade of Our Lady of Lourdes Church

MARK TWAIN WRITES CARNEGIE

Dear Sir and Friend:

You seem to be prosperous these days. Could you lend an admirer a dollar and a half to buy a hymn-book with? God will bless you if you do; I feel it, I know it. So will I. If there should be other applications this one not to count.

Yours
Mark

P.S. Don't send the hymn-book, send the money. I want to make the selection myself.
M.

—Mark Twain, circa 1903, as reprinted in Andrew Carnegie's autobiography, 1920

in Hamilton Heights. The academy features occasional exhibitions, and supports a **School of Fine Arts,** around the corner on 89th Street.

The recently refurbished **Jewish Museum** (1109 Fifth Avenue at 92nd Street, 423-3200) has both historical and contemporary exhibits, plus Cafe Weissman, one of the best museum restaurants in town. The **International Center of Photography** (1130 Fifth Avenue at 94th Street, 860-1777) is the most prestigious venue for photography in the city, perhaps the world. ICP maintains a constantly changing schedule of exhibitions, and there is another branch in Midtown, at 1133 Sixth Avenue at 43rd Street.

Two museums act as the northern end point for Museum Mile. The first is the **Museum of the City of New York** (1220 Fifth Avenue, at 103rd Street, 534-1672), which represents a charming tour of the past as shown through etchings, paintings and other artworks. The charred remnant of Adrian Block's *Tyger,* the first ship to circumnavigate Manhattan, is on display here, brought from where it was discovered during the excavations for the World Trade Center. John D. Rockefeller's bedchamber is available for inspection, too, removed from his townhouse and meticulously reconstructed here.

Also marking the upper reach of Museum Mile is **El Museo del Barrio** (1230 Fifth Avenue, at 104th Street, 831-7272), well situated at the portal of Spanish Harlem. Recently remodeled, the museum marks the contributions of Puerto

Rican and other Hispanic artists, and displays cultural and historical artifacts from New York's huge and varied Latino population.

■ UPPER EAST SIDE

The massive red-brick castle on Madison Avenue at East 94th Street is actually a trick of architecture. What you're seeing is, indeed, the old **Squadron A Armory,** but it's only the shell of the turreted, crenellated, machicolated fortress. On the eastern side, a more modern building takes over: Intermediary School 29, a.k.a. **Hunter High School.** Nearby, at 1180 Park Avenue, is another massive architectural fantasy, the **Synod of Russian Orthodox Bishops,** originally a private residence, incredibly enough.

One of the wellsprings of the neighborhood—culturally, socially, and physically —is the **92nd Street Y** at 1395 Lexington Avenue. As famous for its lectures and classical concerts as it is for its aerobics and gyms, this Y is a branch of the Young

This Gifford Beal painting, Mall in Central Park, 1913, *is part of the collection at the National Academy of Design.*

Men's and Women's Hebrew Association. A short distance away at 1711 Third Avenue is the **96th Street Mosque,** completed in 1991 to address the somewhat embarrassing lack of a world-class Islamic house of worship in Manhattan.

■ YORKVILLE

Yorkville, stretching north from Midtown along York Avenue, was originally a nineteenth-century German-American community discrete from the rest of New York, centered at 86th Street and Third Avenue. In those days York Avenue was called Avenue A, receiving its present-day name not from the city's moniker, but from World War I hero Alvin C. York. Why did a Germanic neighborhood rename its main drag after a one-man army known for having wiped out 35 German machine-gun nests in one day? To defuse anti-German feeling perhaps?

There are but faint reminders of Yorkville's immigrant past today, but check out **Schaller & Weber** at 1654 Second Avenue, an amazing sausage cornucopia, which typifies the neighborhood's Germanic flavor. Also recalling a bygone era are the charming Queen Anne row houses in a cul de sac off East 86th Street known as **Henderson Place.**

Across East End Avenue from Henderson Place is **Carl Schurz Park,** a great riverfront esplanade named for a German immigrant who was a prominent newspaper editor in the nineteenth century. Note the sheet-metal cut-outs that line the southern part of the esplanade (running from 81st to 84th streets, and officially called **Jack Finley Walk,** after yet another newspaper editor, this one from the *New York Times*). The best thing about the park is the view of Hell Gate, the roiling part of the East River where Long Island Sound and the Harlem River meet in a riot of crosscurrents. Across the river is the Roosevelt Island Lighthouse; north are Randall's and Ward's islands (see "Boroughs and Islands" chapter) and the Triborough Bridge.

The northern boundary of Carl Schurz Park abuts the grounds of **Gracie Mansion** at East 88th Street and East End Avenue, the official residence of the mayor since the days of Fiorello La Guardia. The homey, rather homely farmhouse contains elements of the original, an out-of-the-way summer cottage built by Archibald Gracie in 1799. Now considerably expanded and refurbished—with the help of Gracie Mansion Conservancy, which runs a delightful tour of the place—the residence remains unprepossessing, a house rather than a mansion. Yet the sight of a wood-frame house with its new yard, so rare in Manhattan, is altogether enchanting.

Nowhere but in New York would an old asphalt plant be recycled into a deluxe public gymnasium and community center, but that's exactly what happened with **Asphalt Green** at 655 East 90th Street. The distinctive parabolic roofline of the old plant is visible from nearby FDR Drive, and next door, a huge new natatorium has given all the Olympic hopefuls in the neighborhood a new lease on life.

As you pass the unassuming row house at 179 East 93rd Street, you might want to bow your head—or more appropriately, raise it and emit a horse-laugh—in acknowledgment of the **boyhood home of the Marx Brothers.** Chico, Harpo, Groucho and even the hapless Zeppo were raised here, making their first splash on the Times Square vaudeville stage before conquering Hollywood.

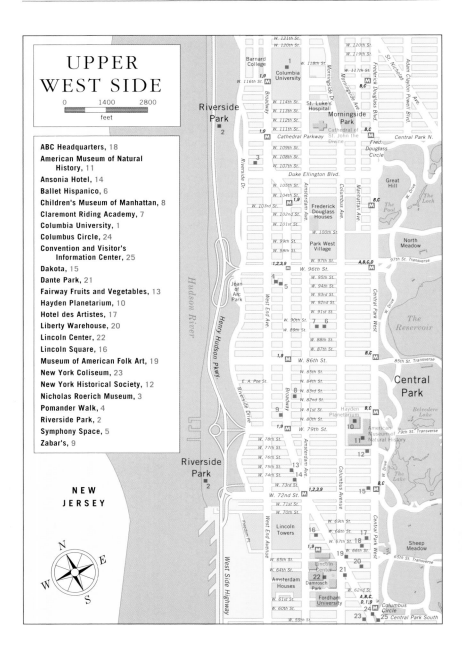

UPPER
WEST SIDE

0   1400   2800
feet

ABC Headquarters, 18

American Museum of Natural
   History, 11

Ansonia Hotel, 14

Ballet Hispanico, 6

Children's Museum of Manhattan, 8

Claremont Riding Academy, 7

Columbia University, 1

Columbus Circle, 24

Convention and Visitor's
   Information Center, 25

Dakota, 15

Dante Park, 21

Fairway Fruits and Vegetables, 13

Hayden Planetarium, 10

Hotel des Artistes, 17

Liberty Warehouse, 20

Lincoln Center, 22

Lincoln Square, 16

Museum of American Folk Art, 19

New York Coliseum, 23

New York Historical Society, 12

Nicholas Roerich Museum, 3

Pomander Walk, 4

Riverside Park, 2

Symphony Space, 5

Zabar's, 9

W E S T S I D E

FOR A LONG TIME THE WEST SIDE was the East Side's poor relation—less prestigious, later to develop, lacking the elite cachet of the neighborhood across the park. Today it presents itself as a viable, less stuffy alternative, a family haven, filled with cultural opportunities and egalitarian pleasures.

The district which would come to be known as the West Side began its urban life as part of the **Thousand Acre Tract,** granted to rich landowners by the first English governor of New York. An old Indian trail bisected the area, and several hamlets and villages grew up along it, among them **Bloomingdale,** an Anglicization of the Dutch town of Bloemendael. Through the eighteenth and much of the nineteenth centuries, the area was sleepy, peaceful, inhabited by poor farmers, and overrun by goats.

The coming of mass transit—the Ninth Avenue Elevated in 1879, and the IRT in 1904—precipitated a mad rush of development. An indication of how much of an outpost the area remained is the **Dakota** apartment building, completed in 1881 and so called because it was "far enough from the center of town to be in Dakota." Broadway was still Bloomingdale Road then (and afterwards, briefly, "the Boulevard"), before it was widened and linked to the downtown thoroughfare.

The Dakota apartment building rises alone on the West Side overlooking skaters in Central Park, ca. 1890. (New-York Historical Society)

Development continued in fits and starts throughout the early twentieth century. The lag behind the East Side might have actually benefited the neighborhood, since by the time it was built up the urban lifestyle had undergone a key shift. Before the mid-nineteenth century it was not considered proper for more than one family to share a roof—that was for the lower classes who lived in the tenements. But relentless population pressure forced a change and gave birth to the apartment house. To entice the burgeoning middle class into them, developers provided incredible luxuries, such as marble lobbies, richly ornamented exteriors, and modern amenities.

Thus the West Side was built up not by millionaire's mansions, as were Fifth Avenue and Carnegie Hill, but by classic apartment houses. The Dakota, the Ansonia, the Belnord, the Kenilworth—along Central Park West and Broadway these magnificent structures survive, testimony to a new order of urban existence. The area west of Broadway, however, was left to degenerate into a slum.

Lincoln Center, one of the largest—and most high-handed—urban renewal projects of twentieth-century Manhattan, cleared a vast swath of those slums, dropping an enormous cultural complex down in their place. John D. Rockefeller III followed in his father's Rockefeller Center footsteps here, with New York's own master builder Robert Moses, as his *éminence grise*. The West Side, long a neighborhood of artists, became a neighborhood of the arts as well.

The West Side is bounded by 59th Street to the south and 110th Street (Cathedral Parkway) to the north, braced by Central Park on the east and Riverside Park along the Hudson. The **Upper West Side**, sometimes extended all the way to West 120th Street to include Morningside Heights and Columbia University (see the chapter "HARLEMS AND UPPER MANHATTAN"), has much more currency as a name than its twin across town. It begins, variously, at 86th or 96th Street, and includes Manhattan Valley, a localized neighborhood built up with housing projects.

■ COLUMBUS CIRCLE

Casting a towering shadow over the southwest corner of Central Park is the **Paramount Communications Building**, formerly Gulf & Western Plaza and notorious for its shoddy workmanship—the whole thing is tilting, and pieces keep falling off. Donald Trump is redeveloping the building (with architect Philip

Squatters' houses perched along what is now "Millionaire's Row" and Central Park West above 59th Street in 1859. (New-York Historical Society)

Johnson's help) into some of the priciest residential condos in the world. One bonus for people living there will be watching pedestrians attempt to negotiate the confusing traffic tangle of Columbus Circle.

On street level, Columbus Circle represents the intersection of Broadway, Eighth Avenue, Central Park West, and Central Park South. To get across it safely represents a crash course in urban survival skills. It used to be called Grand Circle, but in its center is the reason for its renaming: the **monument to Christopher Columbus.** A majestic obelisk visible all the way down Eighth Avenue, the 80-foot tall, 700-ton statue-topped monument was erected in 1892 with donations from New York's Italian-American community, to commemorate the 400th anniversary of the explorer's voyage.

The distinctive building on the south side of Columbus Circle was originally meant to be A&P heir Huntington Hartford's Gallery of Modern Art, but he was bought out by Gulf & Western, who donated it to the city. It is now the **Convention and Visitors Bureau** (2 Columbus Circle, 397-8222), a place to surfeit your hunger for brochures, get your traveler's questions answered, pick up free live-audience TV show tickets, and find out about current events. Also on Columbus Circle is the **New York Coliseum,** a former convention space (superseded by the sprawling glass-façaded **Jacob K. Javits Convention Center,** on 11th Avenue at 35th Street) currently locked up in a fight over just who (and what) will get to replace it.

■ LINCOLN CENTER

Just up Broadway from Columbus Circle is the vast cultural enclave of Lincoln Center. Its genesis began when, in 1957, a board member of the Metropolitan Opera suggested to John D. Rockefeller III that there was an interesting conflation afoot in the cultural and real estate worlds of Manhattan. The New York Philharmonic was getting the boot from Carnegie Hall, and the Metropolitan Opera was looking to move from its longtime home on 39th Street. Meanwhile, Robert Moses was razing a 12-block expanse of tenements on the West Side that might provide the perfect site for both cultural institutions.

JDR III donated almost $45 million of Rockefeller family money ($10 million from himself) and, with Robert Moses acting as midwife, ushered Lincoln Center through the birthing process. The project grew until it included not only the Philharmonic and the Met but a grab-bag of cultural institutions including the Juilliard School of Music, the New York City Opera, the New York City Ballet, and the Film Society of Lincoln Center. This last is housed in a new project completed in 1992, Lincoln Center North, which includes a massive high-rise condominium building and a new home for the Library and the Museum of the Performing Arts.

But it was Moses's original slum-clearance project that created the most controversy. When 18 square blocks were razed, more than 800 businesses were displaced and 7,000 families lost their homes. The eerie sense of a neighborhood sucked dry of life is captured in the film version of *West Side Story* (1961), which was shot on the deserted area streets before Moses brought in the bulldozers. Whatever its origins, the development of Lincoln Center shifted the whole social equation of New York City and provided a transforming boost to the West Side.

It's there, it's used, but is it loved? The angular, travertine chilliness of Lincoln Center's buildings—some of them built in a style so austere it is called Brutalist —has always tempered the feelings that New Yorkers hold for the massive cultural Acropolis. The complex of theaters, auditoriums, libraries, and cultural facilities represents convenience above all, the consumer equivalent of one-stop shopping for the arts.

"Well, there's always an excitement in the air—whether it comes from the slight chance of being mugged or the slight chance of seeing Pavarotti at Lincoln Center." —Bernadette Peters

Lincoln Center's most prestigious tenant is the Metropolitan Opera, which moved into its impressive new quarters in 1966. The Met (it shares the appellation with the art museum across town, so context must determine which you are talking about) has prospered well in Lincoln Center, raising itself to rank among the most well-respected opera houses in the world.

Also performing here is the New York City Ballet, whose seasons run from November through February and April through June. Under the leadership of George Balanchine, NYCB became internationally known for the precision and depth of its corps de ballet.

The Met faces Columbus Avenue, presenting its 10-story fenestrated façade to the plaza, fountain, and passersby. In the morning, its windows are shaded to protect the priceless artwork within: huge, vibrant Chagall murals which, at night, transform the building into an inviting oasis of color. Inside, all is elegance and high culture, the royal red carpet set off by modern starburst chandeliers. The four-tiered theater is plush but not elaborately ornamented—an opera house brought successfully into the twentieth century. When the auditorium's chandeliers ascend to the ceiling like angels, clearing the sight lines and at the same time dimming the interior, it is difficult not to feel a corresponding rise in expectation.

With its enormous stage and even bigger budget, the Met mounts productions that tend to be grand and diva-studded. There's also New York City Opera, kitty-corner in the **New York State Theater:** it runs a different spring season from the Met's and is more likely to show lighter fare—a musical, say, or an operetta. The ticket prices here are half of what they are in the big house across the way. When the opera ends in April, the **American Ballet Theater** takes the stage until June. Known for its renditions of story ballets and star dancers, ABT spends much of the year touring with a wide-ranging repertoire.

Avery Fisher Hall, opposite the New York State Theater, is the home of the New York Philharmonic as well as such crowd pleasers as the Mostly Mozart Festival and the Serious Fun avante-garde performance festival. **Alice Tully Hall** is a smaller, more intimate hall for recitals and chamber music. For a long time it was also the home of the Film Society of Lincoln Center, but that has now moved to new digs in the Lincoln Center North development, the Walter Reade Theater.

Also part of the Lincoln Center complex are the Juilliard School and the New York Public Library's Performing Arts branch. Two theaters, the **Vivian Beaumont,** a 1,100-seat Broadway venue, and the 290-seat **Mitzi Newhouse,** are nestled

A performance of Mama I Want to Sing *at the Heckscher Theater.*

behind a reflecting pool that features a Henry Moore sculpture. The Beaumont has had a problem-plagued history since it opened in 1962. It has recently settled into a series of extremely successful productions under creative director Gregory Mosher.

The Newhouse is the Beaumont's smaller, somewhat more adventuresome sidekick, mounting such productions as *Waiting for Godot* played as it was written, as comedy, with Robin Williams and Steve Martin, and sending such stellar new plays as Wendy Wasserstein's *The Sisters Rosensweig* to Broadway.

Lincoln Square, the confluence of Broadway and Columbus Avenue from which Lincoln Center takes its name, has of late been the focus of some intense high-rise development. Located here at 2 Lincoln Square (at 66th Street) is the gallery and gift shop of the **Museum of American Folk Art** which displays quilts, furniture, and so-called primitive art, its homey contents sometimes a welcome counterpoint to the hustle-bustle of the urban square outside.

There is nothing on the whole island quite like the monster development Donald Trump has planned for the old Penn Railyards, which stretch from 59th all the way to 72nd Street along the Hudson and are the last major vacant land parcel in Manhattan below the Harlems. In 1985, the builder announced he would erect something he called Television City, a sprawling communications, commercial, and residential complex that would have included the world's tallest building. Community (and financial) pressure has since toned Trump's grandiosity down, but his **Riverside South** project still entails building a 57-acre mini-city.

Across the double avenue from Lincoln Center, past the sculpture of Dante holding his *Commedia* in Dante Park (63rd Street and Broadway), is the block that was slated for the Lincoln Plaza project, the abandoned 1970s plan that would have totally razed the space. The **Westside** YMCA at 5 West 63rd Street was the only tenant of the block that refused to budge, thus scuttling the whole project. A block north at 43 West 64th Street is **Liberty Warehouse,** topped with a scale model of the Statue of Liberty (one of Bartholdi's originals) complete with an interior stairway. Contributing to the neighborhood's cultural pretension, if not its culture, are the ABC and WABC headquarters at 30 West 67th Street (at Columbus), and 56 West 66th Street, which sometimes offer free tickets to tapings.

A little more stately, and right down the street, at One West 67th Street, is the **Hotel des Artistes,** proof that the area's artistic bent predates Lincoln Center. Built in 1918 with double-height ceilings to accommodate painters' studios, and not a hotel at all but an apartment building, it has played host to such celebrity tenants as Norman Rockwell, Noel Coward, and Isadora Duncan. One resident, the pin-up illustrator Howard Chandler Christy, painted the extravagant murals in the building's famed restaurant, Café des Artistes (see "Restaurants" in "PRACTICAL INFORMATION"). The whole street is sometimes known as "Studio Row," for the half-dozen buildings on the block that were designed as artists' studios.

■ CENTRAL PARK WEST

At 72nd and Central Park West is probably the most famous apartment house in the world, the **Dakota** at One West 72nd Street. It's gained notoriety not only as the centerpiece of such diverse films as *Rosemary's Baby, House of Strangers,* and the cult novel *Time After Time,* but also because it was here in 1980 that John Lennon was shot to death in the 72nd Street driveway. Other residents over the years have included Judy Garland, Boris Karloff, Leonard Bernstein, and Lauren Bacall, who still calls it home.

The Dakota was built by Singer Sewing Machine heir Edward S. Clark, who had the sense of humor to turn a barb about the far-flung location of the place into its actual name. A recent buff-job has refocused attention on the building's marvelous architectural details, some with a Wild West theme (in jocular reference to its name), and some baroquely neoclassical, like the Zeus sculptures on the balustrade.

A walk along this section of Central Park West (OR CPW, as it's known in Manhattan shorthand) north from the Dakota is worth it for a look at some classic apartment buildings, all built in the early years of the twentieth century, including the **Langham** (135 CPW) and the **Kenilworth** (151 CPW).

Most impressive for its bulk, but also for the trend it set on Central Park West for twin-towered silhouettes, is the **San Remo** (145-146 CPW). Once in the news because its co-op board turned down an application from Madonna (fearing she would bring in too many screaming fans), the San Remo is East Coast home to such Hollywood celebs as Steve Martin, Dustin Hoffman, and married couple Demi Moore and Bruce Willis.

Farther north at 170 CPW is the **New-York Historical Society,** a superb but threatened repository for early documents relating to the history of the city and state of "New-York," as the name used to be hyphenated. Some of the treasures here include the original watercolors of naturalist John James Audubon.

Recently, the resources of the society have become strained and its future has become uncertain: exhibitions have been curtailed, and although the library remains open to the public, services are limited. The arrival of a new director and a new infusion of funds from the state, however, may help to put the New-York Historical Society back on firm footing.

■ AMERICAN MUSEUM OF
NATURAL HISTORY

Across 77th Street from the historical society is the sprawling **American Museum of Natural History** (CPW at 77th Street), a great hulking Barosaurus of a place, which ate four square city blocks and now stands grandly looking around for more. As the repository for an astounding 35 million objects of potential interest to the anthropologist, archaeologist, naturalist, or to anyone who is the least bit curious about the world, this museum needs more space.

Not as sexy as its sister museum, the Met, across the park (the two were originally designed as a matched set), the Museum of Natural History nevertheless exhibits a kind of anachronistic, daffy charm, especially in rooms featuring dioramas of animals stuffed 60 years ago. But while gallery after gallery seems devoted to

The ever-popular dinosaur exhibit at the American Museum of Natural History.

*Manhattan still offers a traditional alternative to the taxicab or subway.
(photo by Katsuyoshi Tanaka)*

well, dead things, many others sparkle with liveliness—if not *life*. In the Hall of
Minerals, priceless gems (including the glowing Star of India sapphire) and glittering geodes fill the glass cases.

We like the 77th Street entrance, not only because that whole side of the museum
is an impressive red-brick Romanesque delight, but because the lines here are usually
shorter. The main entrance, on Central Park West, is watched over by an equestrian
statue of Teddy Roosevelt, spiritual founder of the museum. Be sure to check out
the other statues on the pediment, too, ranked above the entrance like sentries.

A group of three dinosaur skeletons in the main entrance hall welcomes visitors
and immediately demonstrates the staggering size of these beasts. A *tableau vivant*
features a gape-jawed Tyrannosaurus rex about to devour a baby Barosaurus, and a
mother Barosaurus rearing up on her hind legs to defend her offspring.

Little matter that some paleontologists debate whether the huge, hulking Barosaurus could, in fact, rear up at all—the arrangement is a spectacular opening to
the treasures of the museum (the 77th Street entrance has an impressive Chumash
warrior canoe).

Directly to the north of the Barosaurus is a small cul-de-sac which is among the least visited rooms in the museum, but demonstrates its cracked charm quite well. The room features a collection of rather frowzy seabirds, mostly gathered during a nineteenth-century expedition to the South Seas. Here they are, held out of time, decaying slowly over the years, a frozen tribute to a bygone age of muscular, can-do naturalism—before species started to vanish left and right.

After the dinosaurs, the most popular exhibits are the dioramas, such as the African mammals room, straight ahead past the Barosaurus from the main entrance. The fourth floor, devoted to fossils and dinosaurs, is reopening in stages (helped along by a donation from Stephen Spielberg's profits from *Jurassic Park*) after being closed for renovations. Given the evidence of the Hall of Mammals, the refurbished exhibits promise to be more impressive than ever. The current revamping includes the opening up of windows in the galleries, providing more natural light (and lovely views of Central Park) to wanderers here.

One great attraction of this museum, as with the Met, is exploring its out-of-the-way spaces. Strolling through the Hall of the Pacific Peoples on a gloomy winter day, one feels oneself transported, not necessarily to the South Seas, but to some twilight zone out of time—or at least out of Manhattan.

An adjunct to the American Museum of Natural History is **Hayden Planetarium**, which offers varied programs ranging from straight astronomy to heavy-metal-rock-and-laser extravaganzas. The Museum also houses the **NatureMax Theater**, with an 80-foot-tall screen, and a constantly changing series of film attractions.

■ NORTH ON BROADWAY

Broadway, too, has its share of classic constructions from the golden age of the apartment building, and none finer than the **Ansonia.** Rising like an astonishing vision at 2109 Broadway, its history is as outrageous as its Beaux Arts ornamentation. Builder William Earle Dodge Stokes, heir to a mining fortune, was an iron-willed eccentric who demanded that the place be built not only fire-resistant but fireproof—and the Ansonia has never had to carry fire insurance.

Along with the seals who cavorted in a pool in the lobby, Stokes kept a whole menagerie on the Ansonia's roof, at least until the health department made him quit: 500 chickens (he sold half-price eggs to his tenants), a tame bear, and a flock of hybrid geese which used to fly over and terrorize Central Park, biting passersby.

The three-foot-thick walls of the Ansonia, part of the fireproofing scheme, soon attracted musicians because the rooms were virtually impervious to sound. Arturo Toscanini, Igor Stravinsky, and Lily Pons all stayed there, but not, as is widely reported, Enrico Caruso. Impresarios Florenz Ziegfeld and Sol Hurok were longtime tenants.

The basement swimming pool, the wonder of Manhattan when the Ansonia opened, was in recent times turned into a gay bathhouse, the Continental Baths, where Bette Midler got her start as a cabaret singer to the betoweled clientele. Later the pool became Plato's Retreat, the renowned heterosexual swinger club. The Ansonia is the star of the movies *Three Days of the Condor* and *Single White Female,* but its interior has not kept up with its lavish exterior, and renovations over the years have dulled it down considerably.

The stretch of Broadway north of the Ansonia, like its parallel stretch of Columbus Avenue one block over, is redolent with West Side flavor and features many shops that are neighborhood favorites. **Fairway** at 2127 Broadway is worth a step inside just to see how crazy (and exhilarating) the simple act of produce shopping can get in Manhattan. Some swear by **H&H Bagels** at 2239 Broadway to the degree the shop gets FedEx orders from all over the world. **Zabar's** (2245 Broadway) is an internationally known emporium for cookware (second floor) and, more to the point, smoked fish and other comestibles (ground floor). It has been reported that Zabar's—pronounced "zay-bars"—sells an average of 1,000 pounds of smoked salmon a week.

■ UPPER WEST SIDE

Riverside Park, which undulates along the Hudson on the western flank of the West Side, runs all the way from 72nd to 159th Street, over three miles. Designed by the same team responsible for Central Park, architect Calvert Vaux and landscape designer Frederick Law Olmsted, this park's wide promenades are punctuated by monuments and memorials, including one of the only New York City statues erected to honor a twentieth-century woman, Eleanor Roosevelt, at 72nd Street.

The **Soldiers and Sailors Monument,** at 89th Street, with its huge Corinthian columns, massive dome, and stern eagles, features an empty niche that was once filled by a life-size bronze sculpture of George Washington, since removed to the safety of City Hall. To the immediate south of the monument, at 83rd Street, is **"Mount Tom,"** named by Edgar Allan Poe after his landlord's son, and a place where the author of "The Raven" used to go to contemplate the Hudson.

Something of a historical throwback is **Claremont Riding Academy and Stables** at 175 West 89th Street, the only source of horses for the bridle paths of Central Park. Near the park, at 94th and Broadway, is one of those charming hideaway mews that are sprinkled all over Manhattan. This one, **Pomander Walk,** is modeled after a stage set of the ragingly popular play of the same name, which opened on Broadway in 1911. **Symphony Space** at 2537 Broadway was the brainchild of Oscar-winning director Allen Miller and Isiah Sheffer, who took a run-down movie theater and made of it a landmark concert and lecture hall that has helped to foster the cultural revival of the whole neighborhood. The place is famous for hosting day-long classical concerts (usually concentrating on a single composer), short-story fests, and the annual dramatic reading of James Joyce's *Ulysses.*

In general, the Upper West Side, north of 86th Street, is more ethnically diverse, less homogenized than its sister precinct to the south. The neighborhood still struggles to balance the social needs of its citizenry with the quality-of-life issues that make some blocks resemble open-air mental clinics. But there are some startling finds here, also, such as the huge, open-air **statue of Buddha,** the largest in Manhattan, that greets passers-by at the Buddhist Church at Riverside Drive and 106th Street.

Zabar's purportedly sells 1,000 pounds of smoked salmon each week (above). A patron from the Claremont Riding Stables pauses in the glow of a spring afternoon (right).

The housing projects of Manhattan Valley, as the area around 100th Street and CPW is known, symbolize an old-style government approach to the area's social diversity. Somewhat more human-scale is the huge government project that designated the West Side Urban Renewal Area: it resulted in the renovation of side-street brownstones, landmark status for Claremont Stables, and a new home for **Ballet Hispanico,** in two renovated carriage houses at 167 West 89th Street.

NEWS ITEM—NEW YORK CITY JULY 13, 1917:

"Machine Gun Can be Mounted on Ordinary Auto for Defense Purposes"

If you own an automobile, you have a likely defense weapon in your possession. The photo shows Mr. and Mrs. H. M. Busch in their automobile showing how a machine gun can be mounted on the car to be used for defense purposes. It is proposed as a Home Defense Measure to station machine guns at points throughout the cities and suburban sections, so that in case of necessity, the people with automobiles can rush to these points, get the guns, mount them on their machines, and be ready for action. Every automobile that will not be used for other military purposes can be converted into a fighting machine.

■ CULTURAL TIMELINE ■

1732 First city theater opens. Sign posted prohibits spitting.

1842 Charles Dickens visits New York City, and finds the slums as bad as London's.

1849 British actor Charles Macready begins a riot by stating that Americans are vulgar. A mob storms the Astor Place Opera House during Macready's performance of Macbeth and 22 people die.

1880 Metropolitan Museum of Art opens.

1883 Opening of the Metropolitan Opera. Total wealth of audience is estimated at $500 million; the Vanderbilts alone occupy five boxes.

1891 Carnegie Hall opens with a performance by Pyotr Ilich Tchaikovsky.

1895 Olympia Theater is the first to open in the Broadway area.

1907 First *Ziegfeld Follies*.

1910 Arturo Toscanini becomes conductor of the Metropolitan Opera.

1913 Armory Show. An international Modern art exhibit (displaying works by Picasso, Duchamp, Matisse) held at the 69th Regiment Armory on Lexington signifies the emergence of American Modern art.

Thomas Edison demonstrates the first talking motion picture (a scene from Shakespeare's *Julius Caesar)* in a New York theater.

A group of New York painters (George Bellows, Edward Hopper, John Sloan, among others) form the Ashcan School, so named for the artists' unidealized depictions of city life.

New York World prints first crossword puzzle.

1916 Marcel Duchamp and several painters from the Ashcan School climb to the top of Washington Square's Memorial Arch and declare Greenwich Village the New Bohemia. The mayor sends in the militia.

1919 F. Scott Fitzgerald moves to New York City, begins work in advertising and writes a laundry detergent slogan, "We keep you clean in Muscatine."

1925 Harold Ross founds *New Yorker* magazine and starts the famous "Round Table" tradition at the Algonquin Hotel.

1927 Martha Graham performs "Revolt," a dance about social protest.

Mae West fined $500 for her performance in the racy Broadway show, *Sex.*

continues

1929	Museum of Modern Art founded by a trio of patrons including Abby Aldrich Rockefeller, wife of John D. Rockefeller, Jr.
1930	Establishment of the Guggenheim Museum.
1931	Ira Gershwin wins a Pulitzer prize for his song, "Of Thee I Sing."
1932	Radio City Music Hall opens with celebrities including Charlie Chaplin, Clark Gable, and Amelia Earhart in attendance.
1934	Apollo Theatre headlines Duke Ellington, Billie Holiday, and Bessie Smith. Amateur nights introduce Sarah Vaughan and James Brown.
1939	Picasso takes his painting *Guernica* out of Spain, in political protest against Franco, and donates it to the Museum of Modern Art. The painting remains in New York for 40 years and then returns to the Prado.
1942	Painter John Graham arranges a show where the works of Jackson Pollock, Lee Krasner, and Willem de Kooning hang beside paintings by Matisse, Braque, Picasso, and Modigliani. New York celebrated as the new art capital.
	Anaïs Nin rents a loft at 144 MacDougal Street, purchases a used printing press and prints three of her books.
	Frank Sinatra makes his solo debut in New York City.
1943	*Oklahoma* premieres, the first Broadway musical hit by Richard Rodgers and Oscar Hammerstein. Future collaborations include: *Sound of Music, South Pacific, Carousel,* and *The King and I.*
1945	Tennessee Williams's *The Glass Menagerie* opens.
1958	Leonard Bernstein joins the New York Philharmonic.
1964	Beatles play at Shea Stadium during first American concert tour.
1967	Hippie musical *Hair* opens Off-Broadway.
1971	Whitney Museum hosts pop artist Andy Warhol's retrospective show.
1974	Mikhail Baryshnikov debuts with the American Ballet Theater.
1978	Isaac Bashevis Singer receives the Nobel Prize for Literature.
1992	*Angels in America* premieres—an epic treatment of the era of AIDS.
1993	David Letterman moves his late night-talk show from the NBC studio in Rockefeller Center to CBS's Ed Sullivan Theater on Broadway.

*The Solomon R. Guggenheim Museum was designed by architect
Frank Lloyd Wright in the 1940s and '50s.*

HARLEMS AND
UPPER MANHATTAN

THERE ARE WHOLE BLOCKS, WHOLE NEIGHBORHOODS of Harlem that rank among the most beautiful in Manhattan, and would grace any district of the city. These areas are buried beneath Harlem's virulent reputation as Manhattan's crime-ridden ghetto, and that is a real shame.

Yet there is a burning curiosity about Harlem on the part of tourists and residents alike, a sense of longing on the part of those looking across the absurd fence of race and suspicion. Busloads of tour groups visit Harlem every day. If this largely untapped desire to know more were fulfilled, Harlem would be the popular tourist mecca it deserves to be.

More than a third of the length, if not the area, of Manhattan lies to the north of Cathedral Parkway, or 110th Street. Here topography has defeated the best efforts to subdue it, and the island retains many of the dips and hills that were leveled out during the development of its lower two-thirds. Harlem is an area of ridges and valleys, of heights and flatlands. The far upper reaches of the island finally vanquish the grid plan altogether, with the streets surrendering to the contours of the land.

Dutch settlers claimed Harlem Valley in 1636 as a tobacco plantation on the site of an abandoned Indian village. Peter Stuyvesant, the governor general of the colony, stepped in when area farmers each lobbied to name the place after their own home towns in Holland. None of them came from the Dutch city of Haarlem, though, so Stuyvesant named the area Nieuw Haarlem to avoid a squabble.

In the 1840s, after rail service connected it to downtown, Harlem became New York's first suburban community. Rich downtowners fled the heat of the city to gain the river-cooled breezes on the ridges of the heights along the Hudson. These would soon be known as Morningside, Hamilton, and Washington heights, each a distinctive neighborhood with superb river views.

The IRT subway extension in 1904 prompted another wave of real estate speculation, but this time the developers overbuilt. As their new apartment houses stood empty, their only option was to rent to Manhattan's burgeoning African-American population—at three times the normal rent. Thus the black capital of America was born out of a rent-gouging landlord's cold heart. A suitable enough genesis, some say, given the real estate speculation that has been rife in the area ever afterwards.

Harlem bloomed with the black renaissance in the wake of World War I, and received a tremendous influx of southern rural blacks migrating north after World War II. What they found were economic apartheid and a Jim Crowism venomous enough for the newcomers to label their new home sardonically "Up South"— same bigotry, different latitude. Despite adversity, Harlem as a center of black life prospered, eventually consuming precincts to the east, Italian Harlem and Spanish Harlem.

Today, the area is roughly divided between East and West Harlem by the commuter rail tracks of Park Avenue, with 125th Street (Martin Luther King, Jr. Boulevard) running the breadth of island as a main economic thoroughfare. East Harlem is a little more Hispanic, its black districts a little more poverty-stricken than those in West Harlem, which has more middle-class neighborhoods and a greater preponderance of historical sites.

A lot has been made of "Harlem light," a quality of airiness and openness that is unmatched anywhere else on Manhattan. This has much to do with the wide boulevards and the relative lack of high-rise buildings, but the exposed topography contributes also. As is happening elsewhere in New York, a battle continues in Harlem over the future look of the neighborhood, with groups in favor of more landmarking and low-rise zoning facing off the real estate interests that have been the bane of Harlem's existence for almost a century.

On the western edge of the district, rising above the Hudson, are Morningside Heights, home of Columbia University, and Hamilton Heights, home of City College of New York. Together they comprise Harlem Heights, while farther north the same ridgeline is called Washington Heights. At the island's northern tip is Inwood, more topographically varied than the rest of the island. With rude outcroppings of Inwood marble and Fordham gneiss, this neighborhood is probably the only place in Manhattan where a visitor can hope to experience the land the way the Algonquians saw it.

■ MORNINGSIDE HEIGHTS

Constructed in fits and starts since 1892 and still unfinished, the **Cathedral Church of St. John the Divine** at Amsterdam Avenue and West 112th rides the crest of Morningside Heights like a celestial spaceship. When and if it is ever completed, this Episcopalian edifice will be the largest cathedral in the world (it'll still be smaller than St. Peter's in Rome, but that is technically not a cathedral). While

Near the northern tip of Manhattan rests the Cloisters, a "mock" monastery assembled from various medieval sites in Italy.

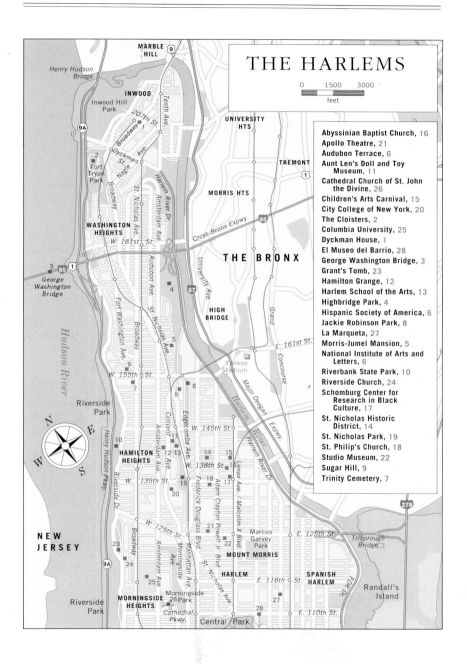

THE HARLEMS

0   1500   3000
feet

Abyssinian Baptist Church, 16
Apollo Theatre, 21
Audubon Terrace, 6
Aunt Len's Doll and Toy Museum, 11
Cathedral Church of St. John the Divine, 26
Children's Arts Carnival, 15
City College of New York, 20
The Cloisters, 2
Columbia University, 25
Dyckman House, 1
El Museo del Barrio, 28
George Washington Bridge, 3
Grant's Tomb, 23
Hamilton Grange, 12
Harlem School of the Arts, 13
Highbridge Park, 4
Hispanic Society of America, 6
Jackie Robinson Park, 8
La Marqueta, 27
Morris-Jumel Mansion, 5
National Institute of Arts and Letters, 6
Riverbank State Park, 10
Riverside Church, 24
Schomburg Center for Research in Black Culture, 17
St. Nicholas Historic District, 14
St. Nicholas Park, 19
St. Philip's Church, 18
Studio Museum, 22
Sugar Hill, 9
Trinity Cemetery, 7

work halted during the Depression and World War II, it has lately recommenced in earnest. A master English stonemason, James Bainbridge, is training a corps of neighborhood youths in the fine art of gargoyle production.

They follow a French Gothic master design modified from the original by Ralph Adams Cram in 1911. The architect was true to his name, and crammed an enormous amount of ornament and elaboration upon this massive building. The towers are getting the most attention now, but inside the Gustavino vaulting (the same used in Grand Central Station), the massive wooden Altar of Peace and the varied chapels off the apse show that Cram got plenty of help from other visionaries. For an idea as to how the whole will look, check out the model in the cathedral's gift shop.

The fact that their house of worship is a work in progress has not halted the St. John's congregation from pursuing a vigorous course of social and ecumenical activism. This includes a wide menu of events, concerts, theater, and lectures at the cathedral, among them an annual Blessing of the Animals, whereby the whole neighborhood turns out with their pets. Classical and jazz concerts within the soaring space of the cathedral's interior are also widely popular.

If the cathedral is the gateway to Morningside Heights, **Columbia University** is its main tenant. The campus officially stretches from 114th to 120th streets between Amsterdam and West End avenues, but Columbia's influence swells into the whole area, filling the streets with students, acting as the neighborhood's largest landlord. Any college built upon the site of an insane asylum (as Columbia was, relocating from downtown to the grounds of the Bloomingdale Asylum for the Insane) might be expected to carry on a tradition of lunacy—and fans of the nation's losing-est college football team might attest to participating in some of that.

While its sister institution, Barnard College, remains one of a handful of women-only schools, Columbia College, its undergraduate counterpart, only recently converted from single-sex to coed. The whole university lends an Ivy League cachet to the more fundamental education that comes with living in Manhattan. The center conduit of the campus is **College Walk,** a pedestrian extension of 116th Street. Low Memorial Library—not a library at all, now, but the main administration building—sits across a college green from Butler Library. The whole campus is honeycombed with underground steam and electrical tunnels. These came of use to students protesting the war in Vietnam, when they took over the campus in 1968—they circumvented police barricades by using the tunnels to get from building to building.

Cross to the west side of Broadway to enter the Barnard College campus; the main gate is at 117th Street. The northwest corner of Barnard abuts two magnificent specimens of theological architecture, the **Union Theological Seminary** (north of Barnard on Broadway) and **Riverside Church** (at West 120th Street, between Broadway and Riverside Drive). Riverside Church, with its mighty carillon belltower, also has an observation deck for excellent views of Harlem, Lower Manhattan, the Palisades, the Hudson River, and the George Washington Bridge. The Seminary has a similar little-known attraction, an interior courtyard that seems a million miles away from the city outside.

In Riverside Park, directly below Riverside Church, is the subject of New York's most famous trivia question: Who is buried in Grant's Tomb? The monument itself, under the care of the United States Park Service, has seen better days, and is the target of a recent beautification effort. Inside are the matching black tombs of Ulysses S. Grant and his wife, Julia—hence the trick answer to the quiz. The mosaic-covered benches of the plaza were made by local youngsters.

A traditional but illegal method of keeping cool during the summer. (Library of Congress)

Brave amateurs at the Apollo Theatre.

■ MANHATTANVILLE AND WEST HARLEM

Through a gap in Morningside Heights ran an old road that led to the docks for the New Jersey ferry, and along this road grew up a village called Manhattanville. The gap represents a geologic fault line—not, thankfully, an active one. Today that road has become the western dogleg of Martin Luther King, Jr. Boulevard—also known as 125th Street and the heart of commercial Harlem. Manhattanville has survived as a neighborhood but not as an identity separate from Harlem itself.

The time to visit **125th Street** is during the day on weekends, when progress down the street takes on the flavor of a walk through a bazaar, so thick are the vendors. Apart from the name, the present-day incarnation of the **Cotton Club** (666 West 125th Street) has not much in common with the classic Jazz Age nightclub—that was located on Lenox Avenue. **Theresa Towers** (2090 Seventh Avenue at 125th Street) is now just an office building, but has a storied past as Hotel Theresa, where Fidel Castro stayed during his visit to the United Nations in 1960, in a snub to the "capitalist" hotels of Midtown.

The **Apollo Theatre** at 253 West 125th Street still hosts a raucous amateur night every Wednesday, and is still one of the cultural landmarks of West Harlem.

When Elvis Presley first came to New York, the Apollo was the one place he wanted to see; likewise the Beatles. It opened in 1914 as a whites-only opera house, showcasing talent like Bessie Smith, Billie Holiday, Fats Waller, Duke Ellington, and Louis Armstrong. New owners took over in 1935 and opened the audience to blacks and subsequent generations witnessed people like James Brown, B. B. King, Diana Ross, Michael Jackson, and George Clinton.

Like most of New York City, the Apollo hit hard times in the 1970s, closing briefly before being saved by Harlem mover and shaker Percy Sutton. He renovated the decayed structure into a 2,000-seat, double-balconied theater. In the lobby, there is a hall of fame and a small museum. Backstage is the preserved trunk of the famous "tree of hope," touched for luck by performers in the 1920s (when it stood in front of another club), and now used for the same purpose by the Apollo's rap, comedy, soul, jazz, and rock acts. Most likely in need of a good-luck charm are the brave souls who venture out on amateur night: audience derision can be scathing.

Other cultural meccas in the neighborhood are the **Studio Museum in Harlem** at 144 West 125th Street, the **National Black Theater** at 2033 Fifth Avenue, and the **Schomburg Center** at 103 West 135th Street. The first is a prestigious venue for shows of African and African-American art, while the National Black Theater is a longstanding venue for great, music-infused theater, including its recurring gospel show, *Legends.*

Dancing at the Savoy in the 1930s.

The Schomburg Center library, meanwhile, is the repository of the research collection of Arthur Schomburg, who had the foresight and tenacity to collect documents pertaining to African-American history when it was being largely ignored by white academia. Here is where Alex Haley researched much of his book, *Roots,* and where today a thriving research library and cultural center (including the Langston Hughes Auditorium, named for the famed Harlem poet) is located. Schomburg's original collection of 10,000 books, manuscripts, and artifacts has grown to more than five million items, including runaway slave notices, the first black newspaper (*Freedom's Journal*), the holograph of Richard Wright's *Native Son,* and many of Duke Ellington's original scores.

Around the corner, at 187 135th Street, is **where James Weldon Johnson lived** when he wrote "Lift Up Every Voice and Sing," now known as the black national anthem. Adam Clayton Powell, Jr. Boulevard, originally Seventh Avenue and renamed for the crusading U.S. congressman, embraces a historic stretch of former speakeasies and nightclubs that was known as "Harlem's Beale Street" or "Jungle Alley" during the height of the Jazz Age. **Small's Paradise** (2294 Adam Clayton Powell, Jr. Boulevard), a famous Prohibition "speak," or speakeasy, is boarded up, but **Well's Jazz and Supper Club** (2247 Adam Clayton Powell, Jr. Boulevard) remains open and active.

In front of what used to be Connie's (originally at 2221 Adam Clayton Powell, Jr. Boulevard), between 131st and 132nd streets, was **the site of the Tree of Hope,** a sort of good luck charm that was traditionally touched by the jazz club performers before they went onstage. Nearby, at 134th Street and Adam Clayton Powell, Jr. Boulevard, is **St. Philip's Church,** one of the reasons Harlem is what it is today. St. Philip's was formerly located in the Tenderloin, on the site of what was to become Penn Station. When the congregation was bought out for the construction of the station, they moved their church up here, and with their buy-out money bought a large stretch of 135th Street. This housing formed the core of an African-American neighborhood out of which came the famed Harlem Renaissance of the 1920s.

Representing 106 buildings encompassing two streets, the **St. Nicholas Historic District** (138th and 139th streets, Adam Clayton Powell, Jr. to Frederick Douglass boulevards) is better known by the rather patronizing nickname of **Strivers' Row** —but that's not what the residents ever called it. Once more, here is a product of real estate speculation, but this one somehow worked. The townhouses were

THE WEARY BLUES

Droning a drowsy syncopated tune,
Rocking back and forth to a mellow croon,
 I heard a Negro play.
Down on Lenox Avenue the other night
By the pale dull pallor of an old gas light
 He did a lazy sway. . . .
 He did a lazy sway. . . .
To the tune o' those Weary Blues.
With his ebony hands on each ivory key
He made that poor piano moan with melody.
 Oh Blues!
Swaying to and fro on his rickety stool
He played that sad raggy tune like a musical fool.
 Sweet Blues!
Coming from a black man's soul.
 Oh Blues!
In a deep song voice with a melancholy tone
I heard that Negro sing, that old piano moan—
 "Ain't got nobody in all this world,
 Ain't got nobody but ma self.
 I's gwine to quit ma frownin'
 And put ma troubles on the shelf."
Thump, thump, thump, went his foot on the floor.
He played a few chords then he sang some more—
 "I got the Weary Blues
 And I can't be satisfied.
 Got the Weary Blues
 And can't be satisfied—
 I ain't happy no mo'
 And I wish that I had died."
And far into the night he crooned that tune.
The stars went out and so did the moon.
The singer stopped playing and went to bed
While the Weary Blues echoed through his head.
He slept like a rock or a man that's dead.

     —Langston Hughes, *The Weary Blues,* 1923

designed by three separate architects, including ones on the north side of 139th Street by Stanford White. Note the sign on "Gate No. 6" on 138th Street: "Walk your horses."

These blocks have something that most of the rest of Manhattan lacks, something that is taken for granted in many urban areas: alleyways. (Alleys allow deliveries and garbage disposal through back doors, thereby decreasing traffic jams and litter exponentially.) The St. Nicholas District has been enthusiastically adopted by a whole new generation of urban professionals, ranging from surgeons to rap stars (and, rumor has it, Bob Dylan). The lovely, townhouse-lined streets are some of the prettiest and most serene on the island.

Just east of the St. Nicholas District is the **Abyssinian Baptist Church** at 132 West 138th Street, long a religious and political locus of Harlem life, and the pulpit of such high-profile reverends as Adam Clayton Powell, Jr., his father before him, and the present-day activist reverend, Calvin Butts. The baptismal font here features a Coptic Cross brought from Ethiopia by none other than the Lion of Judah, Haile Selassie himself. The choir here is justly famous for its superb renderings of gospel hymns.

Growing out of a church into a blockbuster cultural and educational force, the **Harlem School of the Arts** at 645 St. Nicholas Avenue encompasses the old St. James Presbyterian Church but has sprawled to encompass much of the block. The school's Suzuki classes are famed for teaching grade-schoolers the violin and other classical instruments.

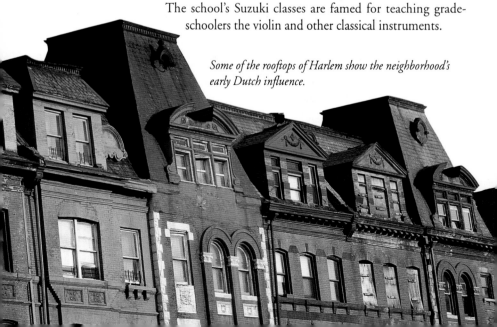

Some of the rooftops of Harlem show the neighborhood's early Dutch influence.

A series of parks stud the escarpment between the valley of Harlem and the heights to the west. North to south, the first three are **Morningside Park,** below Columbia University, **St. Nicholas Park,** below City College, and **Jackie Robinson Park** (also known as Colonial Park) below Sugar Hill. All are thin, rocky strips of greenery on steep gradients, and serve more to punctuate the neighborhoods than provide meaningful open space.

Alexander Hamilton's country home was in what is now a Harlem neighborhood. (Library of Congress)

■ HAMILTON HEIGHTS

Dominating the ridgeline of Hamilton Heights is **City College,** a branch of the City University of New York. The Gothic eruptions of such City College buildings as Shepard Hall and North Academic Center are visible from all over Harlem Valley. The darker stones are Manhattan schist excavated during the building of the IRT subway line, while the lighter limestone was quarried by the inmates of Sing-Sing penitentiary.

Hamilton Grange, Alexander Hamilton's country home above St. Nicholas Park at 287 Convent Avenue (to the north of City College), is now crammed onto the grounds of St. Luke's Episcopal Church. The church fathers bought the house, originally located 100 yards to the north, and moved it here for use as a rectory, lopping off the porches and reorienting it, front to back, in the process.

The Grange was Hamilton's home during the last years of his life, before he was killed in a duel with arch-rival (in love as well as in government) Aaron Burr. There is a proposal afoot to move the place to St. Nicholas Park; as it is now, under the custodial care of the National Park Service, the house is much diminished inside and out.

On Hamilton Terrace are **Aunt Len's Doll and Toy Museum** (6 Hamilton Terrace), a personal collection open to the public by appointment, and the **Children's Arts Carnival** (62 Hamilton Terrace), where a large percentage of the youth of Harlem gets its first exposure to arts and crafts. Like Hamilton Terrace, Convent Avenue, a block west, is known for its terrific concentration of row houses. With subtle variations in style and coloration, the residential architecture on the blocks of Convent Avenue between 140th and 144th streets is some of the finest in Manhattan.

Also superb are the sunny precincts of **Sugar Hill,** on the Hamilton Heights ridgeline north of 145th Street. Centered along Edgecombe Avenue, this was the most prestigious address in the Harlem of the 1920s. Cab Calloway, Duke Ellington, Thurgood Marshall, W. E. B. Dubois, and Langston Hughes all lived here. They once overlooked the **Polo Grounds** on 155th Street along the Harlem River, the old home of the New York Giants, and now the site of a public housing project.

Along the Hudson River in West Harlem is perhaps the strangest hybrid public structure ever erected. Only in Manhattan would a state park be located on top of a sewage treatment plant, but that's exactly the odd conflation that occurred at **Riverbank State Park,** from 137th to 145th streets along the Hudson River. Underneath the ballparks, swimming pool, and playgrounds of this concrete riverside platform is the **North River Water Pollution Control Plant.** The park was meant to appease community activists who protested the siting of the waste plant in the neighborhood, but the plant continued to emit foul odors, and the city had to outlay vast amounts of money to render the park usable.

Trinity Cemetery (West 153rd to 155th streets, Riverside Drive West to Amsterdam Avenue) is the permanent home to some of the most prominent families of nineteenth-century society: Astors, Schermerhorns, and Bleeckers; here is where the celebrated "400" came to rest. It is sited on the former farm of the great naturalist and ornithologist John James Audubon, who is buried here also. The grave that draws the most visitors (at least at Christmastime) is that of Clement Clarke Moore, who, as the author of "A Visit from St. Nicholas" (a.k.a. "Twas the Night Before Christmas"), receives visits from carolers every year.

Directly north of the graveyard at 155th Street and Broadway is **Audubon Terrace,** a collection of classical buildings that once housed museums and the **National Institute of Arts and Letters.** The institutions that remain here today are even more lonely than before, since the Museum of the American Indian decamped for Washington's Smithsonian Institution and the U.S. Customs House downtown. Still open to visitors, though, is the **Hispanic Society of America.**

The area surrounding the exquisite **Morris-Jumel Mansion** (1785 Jumel Terrace, at 161th Street and Edgecombe Avenue) is filled with townhouses, private residences, and row houses which, because they weren't destroyed by development fever, perhaps retain the most nineteenth-century feel of any Manhattan neighborhood. The streets of Jumel Terrace, Sylvan Terrace, and West 160th Street are worth a stroll just to soak in the atmosphere of a bygone era: check out the wooden houses at 20 Sylvan Terrace.

Chief among the area's pleasures is the Morris-Jumel mansion itself, a Federal-style home with stunning views, a widow's walk, and an overall feeling of gentility and calm. It was built as a summer home for the Roger Morris family, but was taken over by George Washington during his doomed defense of Manhattan during the fall of 1776.

Later the mansion was the home of Stephen Jumel, a wine merchant, and his celebrated beauty of a wife, Elizabeth Bowen (she reportedly faked a deathbed scene to get him to propose). When Jumel died in a street accident, he left Bowen in possession not only of the mansion, but of a sizable fortune besides. She went on to marry and immediately divorce Aaron Burr, her longtime beau and the rival who killed Alexander Hamilton in a duel.

This far north, Manhattan is barely 2,000 yards wide, and from the Jumel Mansion you can easily sight the **Highbridge Tower** along the Harlem River at West 174th Street. This was once part of the city's water supply system, and now marks the end of **Highbridge Park,** along the Harlem River.

■ EAST HARLEM

"El Barrio"—the neighborhood. East Harlem has always had a large Hispanic population, especially Puerto Ricans who were part of the Latino influx into the city after World War II. El Barrio largely displaced Italian Harlem, and blended into black Harlem to the north and west.

El Museo del Barrio at 1230 Fifth Avenue is the traditional anchor for the neighborhood, a cultural center as much as a museum. The district that stretches north from this is one of the most troubled in Manhattan, with few historical landmarks to underpin and emphasize its continuity. It is a relatively flat area of housing projects, with plans to exploit the **Harlem River waterfront** delayed in eternal planning stages. A literal bright spot here is the **footbridge to Ward's Island** at 103rd Street which gets periodic coats of Day-Glo paint.

Graffiti with a message fronts a Harlem street.

Saturday afternoon in Harlem.

The real flavor of El Barrio is present in **La Marqueta,** the open-air Spanish marketplace between 111th and 116th streets, beneath the elevated tracks of Park Avenue. Stalls selling mangoes, plantains, and other tropical fruits, ready-made *empanadas* and *pastellis,* colorful clothing, and handicrafts, are jam-packed together in an "everyday's-a-holiday" atmosphere. Founded by Mayor Fiorello La Guardia in 1936, La Marqueta was recently slated for a total overhaul.

Just south of 125th Street, athwart Fifth Avenue, is **Marcus Garvey Memorial Park.** Marcus Garvey, the black nationalist of the early twentieth century who founded a popular "back to Africa" movement, was long associated with Harlem: he had his offices here, and his followers conducted many parades and rallies in the area. Built around **Mount Morris,** which the Dutch called Snake Hill, the park named after him anchors a neighborhood of gracious townhouses and churches. On top of Mount Morris is the **city's only remaining fire tower,** an elegant cast-iron concoction with a spiral staircase and bell, visible from all over the surrounding area.

■ INWOOD AND UPPER MANHATTAN

Glance at a map of Manhattan and you'll see the city's vaunted grid system of streets stutter and stop at 179th Street, just north of the approach to the George Washington Bridge. That's because the hills of this part of Manhattan were simply too much for a linear pattern to handle. Broadway, a rogue thoroughfare in itself, suddenly makes a startling turn east. The northern tip of the island, a favorite haunt of the Algonquians, has been given over to wild parkland, as if the urban impulse had exhausted itself through too much exertion farther south.

The major boundary line for this neighborhood is the slash of the Cross-Bronx Expressway (here briefly and optimistically called the Trans-Manhattan Expressway), a habitually clotted artery that leads to the **George Washington Bridge.** The soaring suspension bridge rivals the Brooklyn Bridge as architecturally the finest link to Manhattan, and echoes the distant parabolas of the Verrazano-Narrows Bridge to the south. In this neighborhood, though, the bridge stands alone and steals the show, a marvel of engineering and design.

Completed in 1931, the bridge had a lower level (which New Yorkers snidely dubbed "Martha Washington") added in 1962. A prime New York experience, and one not for the faint of heart, is to step across the pedestrian walkway, facing into the swirling winds of the harbor. Beneath the bridge, invisible to those who are rushing across it, is the Jeffries Hook Lighthouse, famous from the children's book, *The Little Red Lighthouse and the Great Gray Bridge,* by Hildegarde Hoyt Swift and Lynd Ward.

Fort Tryon Park, at 192nd Street from Broadway to Riverside Drive (the entrance is on Fort Washington Street), graces the ridge of **Washington Heights.** Here General Washington made his last stand against the Hessian troops who were dogging his footsteps north as he tried to move his army from New York in the fall of 1776. In a lost platoon action of that battle, a Revolutionary heroine was born, when Margaret Corbin took over her fallen husband's gun mount and fought for a full day.

The park is a gift to the public from the ubiquitous Mr. Rockefeller (John D., Sr. this time), in exchange for which the city did him a favor: it eliminated traffic thoroughfares through the campus of his Institute for Medical Research (later Rockefeller University). Beautiful flower gardens are what Fort Tryon is known for, that and for being the site of yet another Rockefeller bequest, the Cloisters.

■ THE CLOISTERS

What a few dollars will buy you: the Cloisters, at West 190th Street at Fort Washington Avenue, represents various architectural elements purchased by Rockefeller, hauled over from France and Spain, and reconstructed on the northern tip of Manhattan. J. P. Morgan's medieval art collection, made up of pieces so rare as to be of incalculable value, was donated to the Metropolitan Museum of Art in 1917, and is mostly housed here.

The one-two punch of Rockefeller and Morgan produced a serene refuge unlike any other museum in Manhattan. Even the grounds, with their meticulous plantings of herbs and flowers, give out a sense of order and anachronism. Rockefeller owned the land across the river, too, so there are no messy developments to mar the spectacular views of the Hudson.

Inside, the low-ceilinged galleries follow one another in chronological order. The Unicorn Tapestries are brilliantly alive and justly celebrated, but the spectral sepulcher of Ermengol VII is impressive in a darker way. The Treasury has one of the greatest illuminated *Book of Hours* this side of Dublin's *Book of Kells,* and is filled with other oddities that demonstrate the strange medieval turn of mind— like a single rosary bead upon which the whole scene of the Passion is carved.

Near the Cloisters is one of the few surviving symbols of Dutch Manhattan: the **Dyckman House** at 4881 Broadway. The last eighteenth-century Dutch farmhouse on the island, it was rebuilt by William Dyckman in 1783 after the British burned the original during the Revolutionary War. A real plus is the interior, filled with the Dyckman family furniture and other period pieces—check out the floor, made from varying widths of chestnut planks.

Baker Field, home of Columbia University's hapless football team, is snuggled in a bend of Spuyten Duyvil Creek on the northern tip of the island. The rechanneled creek is home also to the university's crew, which sometimes encounters random floating objects (tires, discarded sofas, drowned raccoons) during its training runs. Next to the playing field, rising on an escarpment that used to be favored turf for Algonquian Indians, is **Inwood Hill Park.** Wild, inaccessible, penetrated only occasionally by such urban emissaries as addicts and the homeless, here is a small, mostly ignored enclave of nature, a sylvan coda to the strenuous allegro of Manhattan proper.

STRANGE CASE OF MARBLE HILL

When is Manhattan not Manhattan? When it's in the Bronx.

That's the bizarre predicament of Marble Hill, which used to be a proud part of the borough of Manhattan. In 1895, however, the Army Corps of Engineers rechanneled the meandering Spuyten Duyvil Creek, lopping off Marble Hill from the rest of the island, joining it to the Bronx with landfill from the excavation for Grand Central Station. Politically, Marble Hill is still considered part of Manhattan. Residents still vote in Manhattan elections, and are considered residents of that borough. Geographically, it is part of the South Bronx, an island betrayed by its stream.

(following pages) A magnificent view over Central Park on a clear day.

BOROUGHS AND ISLANDS

WE'VE GOTTEN OFF ON A WRONG FOOT right from the start. The folks who live in the Bronx, Queens, Brooklyn, and Staten Island might take umbrage at the term "the boroughs." After all, they point out, Manhattan is itself a borough.

In the constantly shifting allegiances of New York City, Manhattan is a source of both resentment and pride to those who live in the "outer boroughs" (again, a Manhattan-centric phrase). They wince under the sneer that they're only "BTs": bridge and tunnel people. But the fact remains that when a Queens resident (or one from the Bronx, Brooklyn, or Staten Island) travels to Manhattan, he or she will say, "I'm going into the City."

Absence of first-hand knowledge on the part of many visitors means that the other boroughs are known primarily by reputation, which is a shame, since the boroughs are characterized by such variety that it is difficult for any one rubric to describe them. The boroughs are simply governmental jurisdictions—each borough is the equivalent of a county or parish. But political boundaries have hardened into stereotypes.

The Bronx, for example, is widely known for the urban wasteland of its southern tier—the rubble-strewn lots of such movies as *Fort Apache, the Bronx*. Yet the borough also has some of the most countrified neighborhoods in the city, suburban oases where raccoons are not unknown. **Queens**, also, is stereotyped as a vast middle-class sprawl, "a little bit of Akron picked up and dumped in the middle of New York City," as Jimmy Breslin says. But it also has vibrant, ethnically mixed neighborhoods, like Astoria and Flushing.

Brooklyn is perhaps the most famous of the boroughs—or more accurately, the most famous borough from which to come. The "City of Churches" has played mother to a host of errant children, among them Woody Allen, Mel Brooks, and Beverly Sills. Finally, **Staten Island** (or Richmond, as she is classically known), is the wallflower of the boroughs—but paradoxically, the first one to talk about leaving home. Home to Mafia dons, New York's largest garbage dump (the Fresh Kills landfill, soon to be the highest promontory on the Atlantic coastline), Staten Island can also be a region of calm amid the amphetamine hustle of New York City.

The pronounced focus of this book on Manhattan is not meant to indicate any lack of marvelous attractions in her sister boroughs. We'll plead space limitations, and point out that the sites of interest in the outer boroughs are spread out across the city's low-density sprawl. Here's a baker's dozen of the best of them, listed alphabetically by boroughs.

■ BEST OF THE BOROUGHS

Bronx Zoo, a.k.a. International Wildlife Conservation Park. Fordham Road and Bronx River Parkway, Bronx; (718) 367-1010. One of the best zoos on the East Coast, with an increasing trend toward *in situ* animal displays. There's a monorail ride through an "Asian" forest, and a great children's petting zoo.

New York Botanical Garden. Southern Boulevard and 200th Street, Bronx; (718) 817-8705. A lovely haven on the northern edge of the Bronx, with many special shows and exhibits throughout the year.

Brooklyn Botanic Garden. 1000 Washington Avenue, Brooklyn; (718) 622-4433. Near Prospect Park, the Brooklyn Library, the Brooklyn Museum, etc. A walled enclave in the middle of Brooklyn.

Brooklyn Museum. 200 Eastern Parkway, near Washington Avenue, Brooklyn; (718) 638-5000. Worth the journey for the collection of Egyptian art alone, but its iconoclastic contemporary exhibitions are noteworthy, too.

Luna Park was part of Coney Island's amusement arcades at the turn of the century. (Library of Congress)

Coney Island. Take D train (subway) to Brooklyn from Manhattan. Though a faded landmark today, some of the old rides are still here, and there's always the beach. During the summer check out Sideshows by the Seashore, at the Boardwalk at West 12th Street; (718) 372-5159. A wonderful on-going performance piece masquerading as a carnival freakshow.

New York Aquarium. Surf Avenue at West 8th Street, Coney Island; (718) 265-3400. Not just a collection of fish tanks, but a spirited and energetic introduction to the wide world of sea life. Its population of 20,000 aquatic creatures is headed up by performing dolphins, seals, and beluga whales.

Prospect Park. Take 2 or 3 subway to Grand Army Plaza, Brooklyn. Over 500 acres, and another masterpiece from Olmsted and Vaux, the team that designed Central Park. This one is wilder, more forested, with a great, children-oriented zoo.

Richmondtown Restoration. 441 Clarke Avenue, at Arthur Kill Road, Staten Island; (718) 351-1611. A concentration of restored historical buildings dating from colonial or Revolutionary War times, with some activities—blacksmithing, milling, etc.—being recreated by workers in period dress.

Tibetan Museum. 338 Lighthouse Avenue, Staten Island; (718) 987-3478. Officially called the Marchais Center for Tibetan Art, this gallery-sized institution is a real pearl hidden in the residential anonymity of Richmond.

American Museum of the Moving Image. 36-01 35th Avenue, at 36th Street, Astoria, Queens; (718) 784-0077. Television, video, and film—all heralded here in a spot not far from where the first movies were made.

Isamu Noguchi Garden Museum. 32-37 Vernon Boulevard, Long Island City, Queens; (718) 204-7088. In what was once Noguchi's workshop, exhibits of his graceful, elegant sculpture are displayed, both in a loft and in an outdoor garden.

World's Fair site. Union Turnpike at 44th Avenue, Flushing, Queens. The ghost of the 1939 World's Fair still haunts this site, with the Unisphere from the 1964 reprise still standing. Check out the Queen's Museum of Art (718) 592-2405, with its amazing New York Panorama—a small-scale reproduction of the entire city of New York.

Liberty Science Center. Liberty State Park, 251 Phillip Street, Jersey City, New Jersey; (201) 200-1000. Okay, so it's not strictly in a borough of New York—it's just across the river in New Jersey, opposite Ellis Island and the Statue of Liberty. But this opulent museum, with intriguing, superbly designed and constructed exhibits (many of them interactive), is well worth the journey, especially for youngsters.

■ OTHER ISLANDS OF NEW YORK CITY

Test your knowledge of geography: Which of the five boroughs of New York City is not located on an island? Manhattan we know is, and Staten Island gives itself away (the sneaky will call it by its other name, Richmond). Of the other three, only the Bronx is on the mainland—Queens and Brooklyn representing the western extremity of Long Island.

Manhattan is surrounded by islands large and small. **Ellis and Liberty islands** are covered in the "Lower Manhattan" chapter, but the rest are listed here. Some of them figure in the history of the area, and some are just green flecks in the stream, prompting the occasional bemused passerby to wonder, "What's that little island called?"

■ GOVERNOR'S ISLAND

Currently the providence of the U.S. Coast Guard, Governor's Island is a serene little community in the shadows of Wall Street. Kids don't lock their bikes here, and the twice-daily ferry is open only to residents. A Motel 6 located on the island may be Manhattan's best housing deal at $27 per night, but it's only available to those who furnish military ID.

Planes of the 11th Bombardment Wing of the First Air Division fly over Governor's Island during maneuvers in the early 1930s. (Underwood Photo Archives)

It was called Nooten Eylandt (Nut Island) by the Dutch for the trees that grew there, and it was actually where the first colonizers settled—before they moved over to Manhattan. In 1698 it was set aside as a sort of personal bailiwick of New York's governors. Later, it was fortified with Castle Williams during the War of 1812—like its twin, Castle Clinton in Battery Park, it never fired a shot against the British. This fort, nicknamed "the Cheesebox" and clearly visible from Lower Manhattan, was designed by Ben Franklin's nephew, Lt. Col. Jonathan Williams, for whom Williamsburg, Brooklyn, is named.

The only way for civilians to experience the gracious pleasures of Governor's Island—which seems if only by comparison to its behemoth neighbor to be locked in some sort of '50s time warp—is via a semi-annual open house. The island's nineteenth-century buildings—the Admiral's House and Fort Columbus, among others—and its sole eighteenth-century survivor, the Governor's House, are all open for tour. It's a great picnic outing. For dates, call (212) 668-7000.

■ ROOSEVELT ISLAND

It is not recorded what the Algonquians called the pencil of land in the East River, but European settlers named it Blackwell's Island, after a farm family who lived there from 1660 until 1828. Later on, as the city used it as a dumping ground for public works projects, it held a smallpox quarantine station, poorhouses, asylums, hospitals, and jails—thereby earning itself the appelation of Welfare Island.

But that much real estate that close to the East Side was too hard for developers to resist. You can still see the remains of the smallpox hospital at the island's southern tip, Manhattan's only landmarked ruin, and Blackwell's farmhouse has been preserved. The most salient features of Roosevelt Island today are the residential developments erected, beginning in the 1970s, by New York State's Urban Development Corporation.

These came in two successive waves, representing Southtown and Northtown, and are connected by a vehicle-less thoroughfare called—of course—Main Street. In fact, although there is a bridge connecting Roosevelt Island with Queens, cars are relegated to a main garage (called "Motorgate") and banned on island streets. Banned also are garbage trucks, due to Roosevelt's ingenious system of zapping its refuse from each apartment house to a central receiving station via pneumatic tubes.

One of the best things about Roosevelt Island is the ride over, via a Swiss-designed aerial tram which leaves from East 60th and Second Avenue, and is one of Manhattan's cheapest thrills at the price of a subway fare. The promenades which encircle the inhabited part of the island give out some of the best views of the East Side. On the northern tip of the island stands a lighthouse that was, legend has it, the work of an inmate of the insane asylum.

■ MILL ROCK

Due east of 96th Street in the East River, it is less than an acre even at low tide, and identified on maps as a park. A park for whom, or what, is not explained. Seagulls, perhaps?

■ U THANT ISLAND

Opposite the United Nations in the East River, and originally called Belmont Island, it was renamed in 1971 upon the retirement of the Burmese Secretary General of the United Nations, of whom it was said, when he left New York, "U Thant go home again."

■ WARD'S AND RANDALL'S ISLANDS

These were originally two separate islands, but now are joined by landfill. Most New Yorkers consider them simply part of the support structure for the Triborough Bridge, which crosses over Randall's. But Downing Stadium, on Randall's, hosts soccer meets and the annual Festival of San Juan, the patron saint of Puerto Rico. On Ward's Island are the training center for the city's firefighters, the Manhattan Psychiatric Center, and perhaps the saddest structure in all Manhattan, the Children's Treatment Center for retarded, insane, or emotionally disturbed kids.

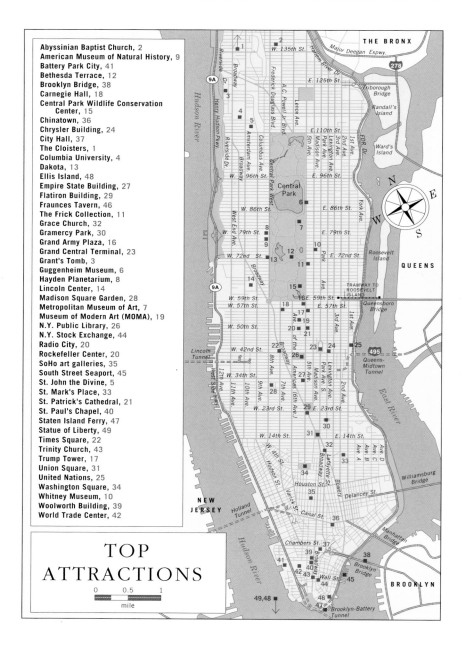

TOP
ATTRACTIONS

0   0.5   1

mile

PRACTICAL INFORMATION

NOTE: Compass American Guides makes every effort to ensure the accuracy of its information; however, as conditions and prices change frequently, we recommend that readers also contact the local visitors bureaus for the most up-to-date information—see "Information Resources."

■ AREA CODES

All phone numbers listed in this book, unless otherwise noted, are in the **212** area code.

■ CLIMATE

Manhattan weather can be a study of extremes, especially in the sopping, muggy heat of August or the fierce blizzards of February. Yet, the city is liveable for long stretches of time. The prime periods in Manhattan are fall and spring. In September, there is a palpable excitement over the dawn of a new "season"—the arts and cultural activity that quicken the pulse of the city. In May, there is the surging sense of having finally shucked off winter, and the street scenes get lively again.

But it is the winter holidays which somehow show off Manhattan at its best. Perhaps it is the interregnum in the blustery city cynicism, or the jangling of all those cash registers. *The Nutcracker,* the tree at Rockefeller Center, the windows at Saks—the holiday traditions never seem to grow tired.

| | AVERAGE MAXIMUM | | AVERAGE MINIMUM | |
	Fahrenheit	Centigrade	Fahrenheit	Centigrade
January	39°	4°	26°	-3°
February	40°	5°	27°	-3°
March	48°	8°	34°	1°
April	61°	16°	44°	6°
May	71°	21°	53°	11°
June	81°	27°	63°	17°
July	85°	29°	68°	19°
August	83°	28°	66°	18°
September	77°	25°	60°	16°
October	67°	19°	51°	10°
November	54°	12°	41°	5°
December	41°	5°	30°	-1°

■ METRIC CONVERSIONS

1 foot = .304 meters (m)
1 mile = 1.6 kilometers (km)
1 acre = .4 hectares (ha)

■ GETTING THERE

■ BY AIR

New York City is currently served by three major airports. **La Guardia,** in northern Queens, is the most intimate and the closest in. It is near to the Triborough Bridge, lending access to all areas of New York City. **John F. Kennedy International Airport,** in southern Queens, handles arrivals from other countries and some domestic flights. **Newark International,** in New Jersey, is the up-and-coming alternative for international and domestic arrivals, although it is farther from Manhattan than either La Guardia or Kennedy.

For information on bus service to and from New York area airports, call Port Authority's Air-Ride line (800) 247-7433.

LA GUARDIA
- Information: (718) 533-3400 ▪ Parking: (718) 533-3850
- Ground transportation: (718) 533-3766 or (718) 533-3765

Bus transportation from La Guardia to Midtown is available from private carriers, and an MTA shuttle-bus connects to subways. A taxi ride from La Guardia to Midtown should cost around $25-$30 depending on traffic. There is also the Delta Water Shuttle, to and from Wall Street's Pier 11, a 25-minute trip timed to coincide with departures of the Delta Air Shuttle. Call (800) 544-3779.

KENNEDY
- Information: (718) 244-4444 ▪ Parking: (718) 656-5699

Bus transportation is available from Kennedy to Midtown, Wall Street, and other locations throughout the boroughs. There is a free shuttle bus operated by the Metropolitan Transit Authority connecting to the subway. A taxi ride from Kennedy to Midtown should cost $35-$40 depending on the traffic.

NEWARK
- Information: (201) 961-6000 ▪ Parking: (201) 961-4751
- NJ Transit Express: (800) 772-2222

Buses are available to Midtown. Taxis are usually non-New York City cabs; it is best to establish price beforehand. A ride to Midtown should cost around $40–$50.

HELICOPTER TRANSPORTATION
There are three commercial heliports in Manhattan:
Wall St. (248-7240), **E. 34th St.** (889-0986), and **W. 30th St.** (563-4442).
New York Helicopter (charter service): (800) 645-3495.

▪ BY BUS
Port Authority Bus Terminal (between Eighth and Ninth Aves., 40th to 42nd Sts., 564-8484) serves 55 million riders a year, mostly commuters who travel on the three dozen bus lines which operate out of it. George Washington Bridge Bus Station (Broadway between 178th and 179th Sts., 568-5323) primarily serves northern New Jersey. Both terminals connect with subway lines.

■ BY TRAIN

Amtrak trains depart from Penn Station to points west, Grand Central to points north; call (800) 872-7245. Amtrak's Metroliner is a shuttle service to Washington, D.C., with reservations required; call (800) 872-7245.

Commuter rail lines service the immediate metropolitan area. They include Metro-North 532-4900, or (800) 638-7646 outside of NYC; the Long Island Railroad (718) 217-5477; and NJ Transit (800) 772-2222 from New Jersey, (201) 762-5100 from outside of New Jersey.

The Port Authority also operates the PATH (Port Authority Trans-Hudson) trains, a commuter subway line that connects New Jersey (Hoboken, Jersey City, and Newark) and Manhattan (stations along Sixth Ave. at 33rd St., 23rd St., 14th St., Ninth St., Christopher St., and another at the World Trade Center).

■ BY CAR

The best advice? Don't bring one. Fleets of taxis wait to take you wherever you want to go; limousines are at your beck and call. Parking in a garage is expensive. Parking on the street is a nightmare and dangerous to the health (if not the continued presence) of your car.

If you must drive, traffic reports are available from WINS (1010 AM) Shadow Traffic Network or Metro Traffic Control. For street parking information, call 566-4121. Driving on Manhattan streets is not for the tame.

■ GETTING AROUND

■ BY SUBWAY

The most extensive underground system in the world (722 miles of active track), the New York subway is the target of much preconception. The simple reality is that the subway is cheap, reliable, and fast. The litany of complaints voiced by New Yorkers about the subway has some substance in fact. It could be cleaner—it's an old system. The trains are too loud, and there are sporadic delays. Safety is a factor and you must take common-sense precautions. Daytime hours are generally safer than after 9 P.M., but a petty-crime "bump" occurs around the hour school lets out (3 P.M.). It's a good idea to avoid flashy jewelry when riding on the subway and avoid the last car, especially late at night.

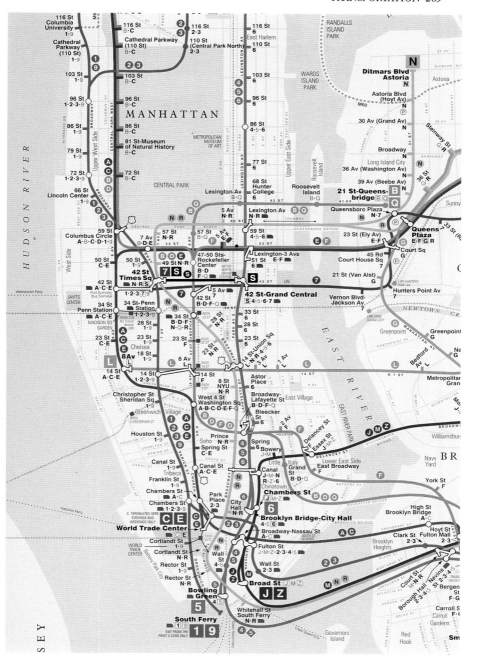

An early New York subway interior.
(Underwood Photo Archives)

All that said, the subway can be a terrific ride. You might want to try to catch the first car in the train, since the view out the front window, as the subway careens through subterranean New York, is one of the best free shows in the city. Subway tokens (currently $1.25) are available at toll booths and selected other locations throughout the city, as are subway maps. For more information, call the Travel Information Center of the New York Transit Authority at 330-1234.

■ BY TAXI

Today's taxi driver is sometimes a newly arrived immigrant, experiencing difficulty with both English and the layout of the city streets. But drivers are just as likely to be consummate professionals who have been driving all their lives.

For safety's sake and in case you leave something behind, it's a good idea to note the medallion number of the taxi you are getting into, prominently displayed on the rooftop light. That light also indicates whether the cab is available (when lit), occupied (light is off), or off-duty (off-duty light is on). There are some areas of Midtown (near Grand Central in particular) where taxis may stop only in specified zones. The current meter "drop," or immediate charge, is $1.50, with charges added every one-tenth mile or every minute while waiting in traffic. There is also a 50-cent nighttime surcharge from 8 P.M. to 6 A.M. The NYC Taxi and Limousine Commission may be reached at 221-8294.

■ BY CAR / LIVERY SERVICE

Although not empowered to pick up street hails, livery cabs often will. Drivers of yellow cabs may not legally refuse to take you anywhere within the boroughs, Westchester and Nassau counties, or to Newark Airport, but in practice it may be difficult to get a yellow cab to take you to an outlying address. Livery cabs ("We're not yellow, we go anywhere") have taken up the slack, servicing many neighborhoods where yellow cabs fear to tread.

■ BY BUS

New York City has an extensive bus service, slower but perceived by many to be safer than the subway—and a great way to view the passing parade. Tokens or exact change required. For information, call (718) 330-1234.

Levels of transit. A sectional diagram of 33rd Street at Sixth Avenue and Broadway. (New York Municipal Archives)

SHOPPING MANIA

Friends send people to me. Really. It's gotten to be quite the running joke among a certain circle of people I know. It usually begins with a hesitant late night phone call. "Laurie? Hey doll! How's New York? Listen, are you in town around the weekend of the 21st? Great! I've got this wonderful friend from Kansas who is *dying* to meet you, and I've told him that you're the *Zagat's* of what to do, where to go, and *where to shop* in New York."

Appealing to my sense of mass consumerism is hitting below the belt, I remind her—even though I'm already beginning to plan the coming weekend in my head, as any good commanding officer preparing for battle would.

That's how it begins. I've learned through the years that I've no control over these visitations, and that most people share my favorite vice: conspicuous consumption.

Where to find everything from the latest couture collections for body and home (**Barney's** uptown at 65th and Madison) to the best plastic dashboard saint that glows in the dark (**Little Rickie's** on First Avenue), loom large in my feeding chain.

One of my oldest friends and shopping enablers refers to it as "a visual thing." I like that. It makes sense—especially as I wander aimlessly down Madison Avenue several hundred dollars later, clutching a microscopic, adorable Barney's bag to my chest, muttering this to myself like some sort of uptown version of a Buddhist chant.

After a shopping blackout such as the aforementioned experience, you may want to wander downtown to a kinder, gentler, *trendier,* neighborhood: SoHo. The mecca of art, fashion, and coffee.

Prince Street is an ideal starting point. It is one of the main drags of the neighborhood: many shops are located there, and it's great for people watching. One of my favorite shops, **APC**, located just off the corner of Prince and Mercer, specializes in Parisian basics: the perfect white cotton T-shirt, unbleached denim jeans, baby sweaters, and oiled leather jackets.

T Salon, a "salon du the" in the new SoHo branch of the Guggenheim, is a refreshing stop for lunch or just a pot of tea. The adjoining boutique stocks all sorts of unique tea accouterments, as well as over 30 different kinds of loose tea, including Mariage à Frères.

continues

"The trouble with New York is it's so convenient to everything I can't afford." —Jack Benny (left) A shop window at Barney's.

Freelance footwear, at 124 Prince between Greene and Wooster, is every foot fetishist's dream—beautifully well-made shoes for women, ranging from classical oxfords to outrageous platforms and pumps.

Replay Country Store at 109 Prince is one-stop shopping Euro-style in a visually captivating setting. The unisex clothing is made in Italy with a nod to 1950s American basics: jeans, jackets, chambray work-shirts, and well-worn motorcycle boots rule.

Stussy, the surfer/skateboard/homeboy shop at 104 Prince (via L.A.) is always hopping. Packed with the phattest trendy gear from team jackets to baseball caps, the price is right. No item escapes the stamp of the Stussy logo . . .

Kelly & Ping, just off Prince on Greene Street, is a must for any adventurous foodie. Upon entering, you'll feel as through you've stepped into a Marquerite Duras novel. Ceiling fans slowly circle, as Asian spices and brightly colored packaging tingle the senses. Simple items, a pot or pan, become beautiful objects—and the open kitchen offers Thai, Vietnamese, and Chinese cuisine.

AD HOC and **Portico,** both on Prince Street, are ultra-luxurious bath stores, stocking everything from Egyptian cotton sheets to handmade English soaps and Italian glassware.

From SoHo, keep wandering south toward **Canal Street,** where Rolexes, Tag Heuer, Cartier, and any number of high-end sport watches of the *faux* variety abound, and may be had for less than 20 dollars. Chanel, Gucci, Hermes, and Louis Vuitton "goods" tumble from every stall—some of which are amusing hybrids of two distinctly different designers' "lines." Take that Vuitton baseball cap, for instance . . .

Shop around from stall to stand before you buy and don't be afraid to bargain. It's expected. Next, wander east up Canal, past the fruit and seafood markets, through the crashing bustle of Chinatown, and remember, "It's a visual thing . . ."

—Laurie Wolfe, art director at *Women's Wear Daily*

■ ACCOMMODATIONS

There is no thrill in the world quite like checking into a solid Manhattan hotel, in a room with a view and with a restaurant that offers room service. Some experiences—like the Plaza, the new Four Seasons, the Algonquin—have strayed beyond simple accommodation into the world of myth. The bars in these places are events in themselves. A martini never tasted so crisp.

Price listings are based on a double room with bath per night, before sales tax. Rates can vary according to season, day of the week, and special promotions, so verify with each hotel.

As for location, the vast majority of New York hotels are concentrated in a single neighborhood, north of Times Square in Midtown. Fine for those who have business in the area, but it leaves a lot of others out in the cold. We've tried to include below alternatives in all neighborhoods of the city.

Prices

$ = under $75 $$ = $75–$150 $$$ = $150–$225
$$$$ = $225–$275 $$$$$ = upwards of $275

The Algonquin. *Midtown* 59 W. 44th St. (bet. 5th and 6th Aves.); 840-6800
Identified with the flapper era's scathing Dorothy Parker and her literary Round Table buddies, the Algonquin consciously seeks to evoke that era while providing up-to-date service and facilities. There is no hotel lobby-bar in the city that is more comfortable for drinking and chatting, with its deep-dish armchairs and silver service-bells. $$$

Banana Bungalow. *Upper West Side* 250 W. 77th St. (at Broadway); 769-2441
New York City does have youth hostels; this one offers rooms that sleep six for a penny-pinching $12 per person per night. $

The Beacon. *Upper West Side* 2130 Broadway (bet. 74th & 75th Sts.); 724-0839
Convenient place to stay if you'd like to just roll out and catch a concert at the next-door theater of the same name. $$

Box Tree Hotel *Midtown* 250 E. 49th St. (bet. Second and Third Aves.); 758-8320
Two brownstones were combined to create a luxurious, 15-room inn (with its own restaurant). Expect marble, crystal, fur—the works. But leave kids under 10 at home. $$$$

Carlton Arms Hotel *Gramercy Park* 160 E. 25th St. (bet. Third and Lexington); 679-0680
It's a poor man's Chelsea Hotel, if you can imagine that. Many of the rooms have been "decorated" by local artists. $

MANHATTAN ACCOMMODATIONS

0   1000   2000

feet

Algonquin, 83
Ameritania, 63
Banana Bungalow, 2
Barbizon, 13
Beacon, 4
Bedford, 94
Beekman Tower, 37
Best Western, 73
Beverly, 39
Box Tree Hotel, 38
Broadway American, 1
Carlton Arms Hotel, 105
Carlyle, 9
Chatwal Inn, 80
Chelsea Hotel, 110
Comfort Inn, 101
Consulate, 69
Days Hotel Midtown, 71
Days Inn, 23
Doral Court, 92
Doral Inn, 42
Doral Park, 95
Doral Tuscany, 93
Dorset, 56
Drake Swissotel, 33
Dumont Plaza, 100
Eastgate Tower, 90
Edison, 76
Elysee, 51
Embassy Suites, 74
Empire, 21
Essex House, 24
Excelsior, 5
Fitzpatrick, 11
Four Seasons Hotel, 32
Gorham, 58
Gramercy Park Hotel, 107
Grand Hyatt , 87
Helmsley Middletowne, 45

Helmsley Windsor, 26
Herald Square Hotel, 104
Holiday Inn Crowne
    Plaza, 70
Hotel Inter-Continental, 47
Hotel Iroquois, 84
Hotel Macklowe, 81
Hotel 17, 106
Hotel Wentworth, 82
Howard Johnson, 64
Kitano, 98
Le Parker Meridien, 59
Lexington, 43
Loews Summit, 40
Lombardy, 34
Lowell, 17
Lyden Gardens, 12
Lynden House, 36
Madison Towers, 97
Mark, 6
Marriott East Side, 41
Mayfair Baglioni, 15
Mayflower, 20
Michelangelo, 68
Milburn, 3
Milford Plaza, 78
Millenium, 109
Morgans, 96
New York Helmsley, 88
New York Hilton and
    Towers, 57
New York Marriott
    Marquis, 79
New York Palace, 49
New York Vista, 111
Novotel, 65
Omni Berkshire Place, 50
Omni Park Central, 62
Paramount, 77

Park Lane, 30
Peninsula, 53
Pierre, 18
Plaza, 31
Plaza Athénée, 16
Plaza Fifty, 35
Ramada, 72
Ramada Hotel
    Pennsylvania, 102
Ramada Renaissance, 75
Regency, 14
Rihga Royal, 61
Ritz-Carlton, 27
Roger Smith, 46
Roosevelt, 86
Royalton, 85
Salisbury, 25
Shelburne Murray Hill, 91
Sheraton City Squire, 66
Sheraton New York Hotel &
    Towers, 67
Sheraton Park Ave., 99
Sherry Netherland, 19
Shoreham, 54
Southgate Tower, 103
St. Moritz, 29
St. Regis-Sheraton, 52
Stanhope, 7
Surrey Hotel, 8
Tudor, 89
United Nations Plaza, 44
Waldorf-Astoria, 48
Warwick Hotel, 55
Washington Sq. Hotel, 108
Wellington, 60
Westbury, 10
Westpark Hotel, 22
Wyndham Hotel, 28

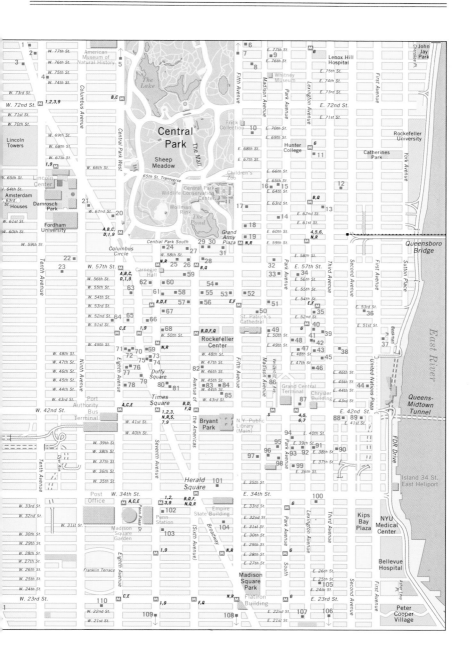

The Carlyle *Upper East Side* 35 E. 76th St. (on Madison); 744-1600
Old-world style and Bobby Short downstairs in the Cafe Carlyle. $$$$$

Chelsea Hotel *Chelsea* 222 W. 23rd St. (bet. Seventh and Eighth Aves.); 243-3700
Probably the only place in the world where Mark Twain and Sid Vicious were
housed under the same roof. $$

Days Hotel Midtown *Midtown* 790 Eighth Ave.; 581-7000
Rooftop swimming pool in the middle of the Theater District. $$$

Four Seasons Hotel *Midtown* 57 E. 57th St. (bet. Park and Madison); 758-5700
Sleek and stylish, this I. M. Pei-designed palace was an instant New York landmark.
The staff, rooms, and restaurants measure up to the grand design, and views aren't
too shabby, either. Brings hotels into the twenty-first century. $$$$$

The Franklin *Upper East Side* 164 E. 87th St.; 369-1000
Charming, yet somehow sinister—à la David Lynch. Beds with gauzy white canopies,
time-trapped elevators, and a young, eccentric staff. $$

Gramercy Park Hotel *Gramercy Park* 2 Lexington Ave. (at 21st St.); 475-4320
Each guest gets something to make him or her the envy of *tout* Manhattan—a key to
private Gramercy Park, one of the town's most coveted oases. $$$$

Hotel Elysée *Midtown* 60 E. 54th St.; 753-1066
Gloriously civilized and stylish. The piano room contains Vladimir Horowitz's old
Steinway, no less. $$

Hotel Inter-Continental *Midtown* 111 E. 48th St. (bet. Lexington and Park); 755-5900
An old-fashioned, bustling place whose lobby sports Tiffany-style glass shades and
throngs of Japanese business travelers. Rooms have been spruced up. $$$$

Hotel 17 *Gramercy Park* 225 E. 17th St.; 475-2845
This former SRO (stands for Single Room Occupancy)—or welfare hotel—has been
renovated. Budget travelers and the "transient chic" (models, musicians) share a
hallway bathroom and phone. $

Hotel Wales *Upper East Side* 1295 Madison Ave. (at 92nd St.); 876-6000
An appealing place to curl up with tea, butter cookies, and a Sherlock Holmes
mystery (just a few of the fetching details at this hotel). $$

The Lowell *Upper East Side* 28 E. 63rd St. (bet. Madison and Park); 838-1400
Intimate, tasteful, comfortable as your home, with cozy fireplaces, plants and
flowers, marble baths—doesn't sound like your home? Go ahead, pretend. $$$$$

The Mark *Upper East Side* 25 E. 77 St.; 744-4300
Suite-hotel convenience combined with understated, effortless luxury. $$$$

Mayfair Baglioni *Upper East Side* 610 Park Ave.; 288-0800
European-style apartment hotel, with a marble-and-mahogany lobby. Everything, from the impeccable staff to the in-house restaurant—Le Cirque, no less—smacks of monied comfort. $$$$$

The Mayflower *Upper West Side* 15 Central Park West (at 61st St.); 265-0060
Pleasant hotel overlooking Central Park. $$$

The Millenium *Lower Manhattan* 55 Church St. (at Fulton St.); 693-2001
Views showcase South Street, Battery Park, the Hudson River, and the Statue of Liberty at the 58-story Millenium. Features a glass-enclosed pool. $$$$

New York Hilton and Towers *Midtown* 1335 Ave. of the Americas (at 53rd St.); 261-5732
This stalwart chain member's great if you don't mind finding yourself confused from time to time whether you might be in Dubuque . . . or Las Vegas . . . or . . . But familiarity is exactly what some travelers value most. (See other hotel chains listed below.) $$$

The Paramount *Midtown* 235 W. 46 St. (bet. Broadway & Eighth Ave.); 764-5500
The ultra-chic Philippe Starck design can't mask the fact that the rooms are painfully small. In Texas, they'd call this kind of place "all hat and no cattle"—but a hip, young crowd likes it anyway. $$$$

Le Parker Meridien *Midtown* 118 W. 56th St. (bet. Sixth & Seventh Aves.); 245-5000
Hard-core jocks will love the rooftop pool, squash and raquetball courts, jogging track, and health club. $$$$

The Peninsula *Midtown* 700 Fifth Ave.; 247-2200
This elegant and gracious hotel offers an excellent health club and spa, as well as a rooftop bar with smashing views of Midtown. $$$$$

The Pierre *Upper East Side* 2 E. 61st St. (at Fifth Ave.); 838-8000
Perfection, at a price. $$$$

The Plaza *Midtown* 768 5th Ave. (at 59th St.); 759-3000
The renovations under the recent regime of Monsieur Trump have buffed up its faded glory. $$$$

The Regency *Upper East Side* 540 Park Ave. (at 61st St.); 759-4100
A business person's hotel, with "power breakfast" in the restaurant de rigeur. Staff might have a problem with "strange" requests—like putting up a crib or bringing an ironing board. $$$$

Roger Smith *Midtown* 501 Lexington Ave. (at 47th St.); 684-7500
A self-styled haven for artists. The owners have installed a lobby gallery of painting and sculpture, and weekend guests get passes to MOMA. $$$

The **Ritz-Carlton** *Midtown* 112 Central Park S. (bet. Fifth and Sixth Aves.);
757-1000
Breathtaking Central Park views and sublimely comfy beds. The Ritz-Carlton
is a favorite among people you wouldn't expect—like Aerosmith. $$$$

Rihga Royal *Midtown* 151 W. 54th St. (bet. Sixth and Seventh Aves.); 307-5000
A Japanese hotel group is responsible for the all-suite accommodations here,
which are lavish in a subdued, simple, almost Zen style—note the single fresh
tulip posed by your bathroom sink. For true luxury, try the 24-hour Suite
Dining at a table in your room set with linen, china, crystal, and silver. $$$$$

The **Royalton** *Midtown* 44 W. 44th St. (bet. Fifth and Sixth Aves.); 869-4400
Another Ian Schrager/Philippe Starck production in which luxe is offset by a
touch of zany. Power lunch in the lobby restaurant attracts an A-list crowd.
$$$$

The **Sherry-Netherland** *Midtown* 781 Fifth Ave.; 355-2800
A Jazz Age baby perfectly preserved for the delectation of the late twentieth-
century hordes. $$$$$

The **St. Regis** *Midtown* 2 E. 55th St.; 753-4500
Built by John Jacob Astor back in 1904, this Beaux Arts beauty doesn't show
her age, especially after a recent $100 million restoration. Make sure to catch
the Maxfield Parrish murals at the King Cole Bar. $$$$$

The **Stanhope** *Upper East Side* 995 Fifth Ave.; 288-5800
Bask (on your room's Louis XVI-style furnishings) in the reflected glory of the
Metropolitan Museum of Art, just across the street. $$$$

Surrey Hotel *Upper East Side* 20 E. 76th St.; 288-3700
Genteel, sophisticated comfort. Known as the place Manhattan's upper-crust
husbands decamp to while waiting for the divorce papers to go through. $$$$

United Nations Plaza *Midtown* One United Nations Plaza; 355-3400
Chrome and marble modernity greet visitors to this skyscraper hotel, which
boasts not only a 27th-floor glass-enclosed swimming pool but a 38th-floor
indoor tennis court—the only hotel tennis court in Manhattan. $$$$

The **Waldorf-Astoria** *Midtown* 301 Park Ave. (bet. 49th and 50th Sts.); 355-3000
Once the largest hotel in the world, and the first to invent room service. Today
you can expect premium lodgings, but it is more staid grandfather than spritely
trend-setter, and there is a slight air of corporate name-tagitis hovering about
the busy public areas. $$$$$

Washington Square Hotel *West Village* 103 Waverly Pl.; 777-9515
Tiny but charming rooms distinguish this prize in the heart of Greenwich Village. Bob Dylan slept here, and Joan Baez sang about it. $$$

The Westbury *Upper East Side* Madison Ave. at 69th St.; 439-4834
Built in the 1920s as a residential hotel by the family of an American polo player, the Westbury exudes elegance and quiet privilege. $$$$$

Wyndham Hotel *Midtown* 42 W. 58th St.; 753-3500
The best-kept secret in town is the owner-occupied, extremely homey Wyndham. Take off your shoes and stay a while. $$

■ ADDITIONAL LISTINGS

The Barbizon
Upper East Side 140 E. 63rd St.; 838-5700 $$$

Doral Tuscany
Murray Hill 120 E. 39th St.; 686-1600 $$$

Essex House
Midtown 160 Central Park South; 247-0300 $$$$

Herald Square Hotel
Chelsea 19 W. 31st St.; 279-4017 $$

Hotel Dorset
Midtown 30 W. 54th St.; 247-7300 $$$$

The Edison
Midtown 228 W. 47th St.; 840-5000 $$

Hotel Macklowe
Midtown 145 W. 44 St.; 768-4400 $$$$

The Michelangelo
Midtown 152 W. 51st St.; 765-1900 $$$$

The Milburn
Upper West Side 242 W. 76th St.; 362-1006 $$

Iroquois
Midtown 49 W. 44th St.; 840-3080 $$

Ramada Renaissance
Midtown 2 Times Square; 765-7676 $$$$

St. Moritz
Midtown 50 Central Park South; 755-5800 $$$$

Warwick Hotel
Midtown 65 W. 54th St.; 247-2700 $$$

Wellington
Midtown Seventh Ave. at 55th St.; 247-3900 $$

■ MORE HOTEL CHAINS

Embassy Suites
  1568 Broadway; 719-1600 $$$
Grand Hyatt
  Park Ave. at Grand Central Terminal; (800) 233-1234
New York Marriott Marquis
  1535 Broadway (at 45th St.); (800) 228-9290
Ramada Hotel
  401 Seventh Ave. (bet. 32nd and 33rd Sts.); (800) 223-8585
Sheraton New York Hotel and Towers
  811 Seventh Ave. (at 53rd St.); (800) 223-6550
Manhattan East
  All-suite hotels, including the Shelburne Murray Hill, Dumont Plaza, Lyden Gardens, Lyden House, Eastgate Tower, and Southgate Tower Suites; (800) 637-8483.

■ RESTAURANTS BY CUISINE

New Yorkers just love food, whether standing up, sitting down, eating in, ordering out, or taking out to eat in the park. You can actually find people eating while they walk, which most of the world finds completely disgusting. People think it's because New Yorkers are in a rush—it's not. New Yorkers just don't want to stop. They don't want to stop eating.
                                                                —Hal Rubenstein

Along with talking and making money, consuming food is part of Manhattan's holy trinity. It was always thus: when you hear stories of Diamond Jim Brady devouring 26 dozen oysters in one sitting (along with various steaks, chops, and fowls), and that his prowess with a knife and fork somehow translated into renown as a gambler, satyr, and bon vivant, you know that the nineteenth century was not for the gustatorily timid.

Like Diamond Jim shoveling it in, New York is a great consumer not only of food but of cuisines. There is no such thing as "New York food" or a "Manhattan" restaurant in the way a place can be a French restaurant. That's because all food —from French cordon bleu to Jamaican jerk chicken—is New York food. New York's trademark eats, the bagel and the knish—which some folks insist you cannot get a good version of west of the Hudson—are products of an immigrant culture. Even something as foreign to New York as California cuisine has found a home here—and not a few artful practitioners.

Manhattan knows all, embraces all. The "foodies" of the island sniff out new trends and are on them like white on rice. Not for nothing was the *Zagat's Guide* born here, a kind of gourmet grapevine in book form, wherein restaurants are voted upon by those who actually patronize them and the consensus tabulated, as if this were a political election or a popularity contest.

In a sense, it is. When Chinese food grabbed the attention of food trendies in the 1970s, the Asian community suddenly found that restaurant jobs were plentiful, and there was a resulting infusion of money into the immigrant community. Even the rats in Chinatown got sleeker. The stomach, as Bertolt Brecht points out, is a political organ.

Mostly, Manhattan avoids the garnish and goes straight for the main course. Street food is a prime anomaly of the island, not found to such a degree elsewhere, not even in the other boroughs. The city's French restaurants have long been justly hailed as among the best in the world, especially for those graced with an expense account. Italian, Chinese, Korean, Thai, soul, Japanese, Jewish, Ukranian, Mexican, Tex-Mex, even such unlikely but delicious New York–bred amalgrams as Cuban-Chinese all crowd the island with heady flavors.

Price listing is meant to be a general guide, not an exact standard, and includes meals for one, without drinks or tip.

Restaurants by Cuisine

Prices

Meal for one, without drinks or tip.

$ = under $10 $$ = $10–$20 $$$ = $20–$35
$$$$ = $35–$50 $$$$$ = upwards of $50

Classic New York

Boathouse Cafe *Upper East Side* E. Park Dr. N. and 72nd St.; 517-3623
Location is all here, and with its recent refurbishment it takes its place as a classic New York eatery. $$$

Café des Artistes *Upper West Side* 1 W. 67th St. (bet. CPW and Columbus Ave.); 877-3500
Romantic, elegant, cozy, with a soupçon of the risqué thanks to the murals on the walls. What Manhattan means, what civilization is. $$$$

Carnegie Deli *Midtown* 854 Seventh Ave. (bet. 54th and 55th Sts.); 757-2245
Is that a Buick built of corned beef or a sandwich? Staggering portions of classic deli fare, gussied up with celebrity names. An eternal survivor in the deli wars. $–$$

Elaine's *Upper East Side* 1703 Second Ave. (bet. 88th and 89th Sts.); 534-8103
It's not eating so much as social preening, with a constant parade of movie and music people checking each other out. A friend of ours dining here once lit Woody Allen's hair on fire—by mistake. $$$

The Four Seasons *Midtown* 99 E. 52nd. St. (bet. Park and Lexington Aves.); 754-9494
Effortless and grand, with enough cool ambition in menu and setting to match the power crowd you'll find here. The beaded window curtains undulate, the ice rattles in your glass, the waiters lay down the perfect seasonal offerings. Manhattan takes on a golden glow. $$$$$ (prix fixe dinner $$$)

Lutèce *Midtown* 249 E. 50th St. (bet. Second and Third Aves.); 752-2225
With 31 years of haute cuisine history in Manhattan, French owner and chef Andre Soltner often makes the rounds of tables, suggesting luxurious dishes like caviar over sour cream and vodka, served in an eggshell. $$$$$

The Russian Tea Room *Midtown* 150 W. 57th St. (bet. Sixth and Seventh Aves.); 265-0947
Excuse me, Dustin, but you have a glob of caviar on your chin . . . Celebrity sighting among the blinis, with the movers and shakers still coming after all these years. Ordinary mortals can enjoy it, too. $$$$

The Ballroom, a lively cabaret, serves savory tapas and other Spanish cuisine at its premises on 28th Street near Eighth Avenue.

The "21" Club *Midtown* 21 W. 52nd St. (bet. Fifth and Sixth Aves.); 582-7200
When the movers and shakers of Midtown put away their childish things, the ceiling of the grill room at 21 is where they wound up. A tradition that revives itself fresh every day, in a classic brownstone that was once a speakeasy. $$$$$

Gourmet

Alison on Dominick Street *TriBeCa* 38 Dominick St.; (bet. Varick and Hudson Sts.); 727-1188
Put your ear to the wall in the basement of this charming, romantic hideaway and you'll hear the distant rumble of Holland Tunnel, next door. But you'll have to tear yourself away from the food first. $$$$

Le Bernadin *Midtown* 155 W. 51st St. (bet. Sixth and Seventh Aves.); 489-1515
To all those who don't believe food preparation is an art, or think gourmandizing is coarse and sinful—come to dinner here, it will make a believer out of you. The freshest of seafood prepared in the most imaginative ways, with brilliant desserts to linger over. $$$$$

Bouley *West Village* 165 Duane St. (bet. Greenwich and Hudson); 608-3852
A lot of people call David Bouley the most imaginative chef working in Manhattan, and with the wait for reservations, who are we to argue? French cuisine modified by American and Californian impulses. Go for lunch, or try the fabulous tasting menu. Either way, you may meet the personable chef himself. $$$$$

Le Cirque *East Side* 58 E. 65th St. (bet. Fifth and Madison Aves.); 794-9292
The name conjures up images of Jackie O dining on trufflles and champagne. But even without the celebrity gloss, this restaurant would shine for dishes ranging from simple Angus steak to the more elaborate sea bass roasted in slivered potatoes. $$$$$

Union Square Cafe *Chelsea* 21 E. 16th St. (bet. Fifth Ave. and Union Sq.); 243-4020
Danny Meyer is a restaurateur who makes people feel at home, and then dazzles them with splendid food, artfully presented. His place is proof that Manhattan esprit didn't perish with the last generation. $$$$

French

Cafe Loup *West Village* 105 W. 13th St. (bet. Sixth and Seventh Aves.); 255-4746
A favorite Village place, moved from its low-slung original venue to this blander spot, but still serving good, moderate meals. $$$

La Luncheonette *Chelsea* 130 Tenth Ave. (at W. 18th St.); 675-0342
Way out west, but worth the trek. Cozy decor sets off fine French provincial fare. $$$

Peacock Alley *Midtown* Waldorf-Astoria Hotel, 301 Park Ave. (bet. 49th and 50th Sts.); 872-4895
Invigorated by a new chef, and serving classic French provincial fare with a contemporary twist, along with the only crème brulée in the city made from duck eggs. Leading the way in the new trend toward quality hotel dining. $$$$

Raoul's *SoHo* 180 Prince St. (bet. Sullivan and Thompson); 966-3518
The kind of place that makes people want to adopt it as their own. Classy, intimate, energetic, with straight-ahead French food that brings you back again and again. $$$$

Views and Ambience

The Rainbow Room *Midtown* 30 Rockefeller Plaza, 65th Floor (bet. 49th and 50th Sts.); 632-5100
Can't decide if you feel like eating or dancing or just swooning at a view? Here's the place for you, newly buffed but with the same old vintage romance. Jacket and tie required. $$$$$

The Terrace *Morningside Heights* 400 W. 119th St. (bet. Amsterdam Ave. and Morningside Dr.); 666-9490
Fabulous views and food in this uptown aerie. Beautifully appointed and well staffed. $$$$$

The Water Club *Murray Hill* 500 E. 30th St. (on East River); 683-3333
A welcome reminder that Manhattan is a river city. A floating restaurant with great views, especially in summer, from the deck. A romantic place to ask someone to marry you. $$$$

Cheap Eats

Real New Yorkers draw their sustenance from these places, and they offer great meals for travelers on a budget.

Brunetta's *East Village* 190 First Ave. (bet. 11th and 12th Sts.); 228-4030
This was long known as the Italian block of this stretch of lower First Avenue, and Brunetta's partakes a little of that social club atmosphere. Cheap, delicious, authentic. $

Cabana Carioca *Midtown* 123 W. 45th St. (bet. Sixth and Seventh Aves.); 581-8088
One of the best moderately priced eateries in Times Square, with its three levels getting progressively cheaper as you ascend. Latin-American fare, with crunchy, garlic-infused suckling pig out of this world. $

Cafe Con Leche *Upper West Side* 424 Amsterdam Ave. (at 81st St.); 595-7000
Upscale version of the Dominican coffeeshop. Oxtail stew heaven. $

Tavern on the Green (top) in Central Park is illuminated at Christmastime. A dining alcove at Sign of the Dove (bottom), one of the city's best restaurants. (top photo by Katsuyoshi Tanaka)

Chez Brigitte *West Village* 77 Greenwich Ave. (at Seventh Ave.); 929-6736
Everyone quotes the sign ("Capacity 250, 11 at a time") but what they come back for is the cheap, authentically French cutlets and stews, served at a cheery counter by Brigitte herself. **$**

Christine's *Gramercy Park* 438 Second Ave. (at 25th St.); 684-1879
East Village 208 First Ave. (bet. 12th and 13th Sts.); 254-2474
Oh, that white borscht soup. And the pierogies with fried onions. And the . . . well, you'll have to see for yourself. Home-style, Ukranian dishes, inexpensive. **$**

Corner Bistro *West Village* 331 W. Fourth St. (at Jane St., near Eighth Ave.); 242-9502
Char-broiled burgers matched in size by succulence. **$**

Papaya King *Upper East Side* 210 E. 59th St. (at Third Ave.); 753-2014
Some New Yorkers say the franks here are "better than filet mignon." Know what? At the price, they're right. Wash one down with an alcohol-free piña colada that will make you want to take off your shoes and hit tar beach. Other outlets of the same chain or competitors (e.g. **Gray's Papaya**, 2090 Broadway, at 72nd St.) all over Manhattan. **$**

Sucelt *West Village* 200 W. 14th St. (at Sixth Ave.); 242-0593
The sugar cane stacked up against the corner of this shoebox-sized counter spot lets you know its *comidas Latinos* are the real thing. Order one of the 10 or more different tamales, a hearty meal of a soup, or the quivering octopus salad, but leave room for the creamy fruit shake called a *batido*. **$**

Two Boots *East Village* 37 Ave. A (bet. Second and Third Sts.); 505-2276
Quirky, yes, with its combo Cajun-Italian cookin' (spicy crawfish-topped pizza?) but a low-key, high-energy ambience that suits its downtown crowd. A New York restaurant that goes out of its way to welcome young kids. **$**

Cafes and Bistros

Café Un Deux Trois *Midtown* 123 W. 44th St. (bet. Sixth and Seventh Aves.); 354-4148
It's hip, crowded, urbane, and has always been that way. A classic serving basic frites-style bistro food to pre- and post-theater crowds. **$$$**

Odeon *TriBeCa* 145 W. Broadway (bet. Worth and Duane Sts.); 233-0507
The "Ur" late-night bistro, famous by Andy Warhol's reign. It still cooks. **$$$$**

Delis

Katz's Deli *Lower East Side* 205 Houston St. (at Ludlow); 254-2246
This place's "Send a salami to your boy in the Army" slogan is a Manhattan classic. All that's no reason to ignore the food, which is bountiful, flavorful, and reasonably priced. **$$**

Ratner's *Lower East Side* 138 Delancey St. (bet. Norfolk and Suffolk Sts.); 677-5588
Okay, so Meg Ryan showed Billy Crystal how women fake orgasms here in *When Harry Met Sally* . . . You can still enjoy Jewish dairy specialties like *matzo brei* and baked egg barley without embarrassment. $$

Second Avenue Deli *East Village* 156 Second Ave. (at 10th St.); 677-0606
This used to be the Yiddish Rialto, and today's *echt* Jewish deli has a sidewalk of fame for the stars of a once-vital, now-vanished theater scene. The pastrami is not too bad, either. $$$

Taverns

Chumley's *West Village* 86 Bedford St.; 675-4449
Wow your friends by slipping into this ex-speakeasy through the unmarked Bedford Street entrance. Blazing fireplaces, decent food, ear-splitting decibel levels, and a collegiate crowd. $$

Lion's Head *West Village* 59 Christopher St. (bet. Sixth and Seventh Aves.); 929-0670
More a fragment of Village Zeitgeist than a restaurant, this tavern is a literary hangout, a neighborhood joint, a classic. $$$

McSorley's Old Alehouse *East Village* 15 E. Seventh St. (bet. Second Ave. and Bowery); 473-9184.
A venerable old-timers saloon, yet a younger set has recently discovered the crusty charm. $$

Old Town Bar *Gramercy Park* 45 E. 18th St. (bet. Broadway and Park Ave. South); 473-8874
Art directors love the retro flavor of this unregenerate tavern, which used to serve neighborhood truckers and close at night and on weekends. Then a younger crowd discovered it, and it's been going strong ever since, dishing up serviceable bar fare. $$

Pete's Tavern *Gramercy Park* 129 E. 18th St. (at Irving Pl.); 473-7676
Take its food and its historical claims ("New York's oldest tavern") with a grain of salt, and go for the scene instead, which can get raucous. $$$

P. J. Clarke's *Midtown* 915 Third Ave. (at 55th St.); 759-1650
The kind of classic, sawdust-strewn pub they used to call a joint, where bankers rub elbows with regular Joes. A great place to grab a late-night, post-movie brew and burger. $$$

Round-the-Clock

Brasserie *Midtown* 100 E. 53rd St. (bet. Park and Lexington Aves.); 751-4840
The city that never sleeps needs a classic bistro open 24 hours, and here it is. $$$

Florent *West Village* 60 Gansevoort St. (bet. Washington and Greenwich Sts.); 989-5779
A lifeline tossed into the black sea of bobbing, late-night club-crawlers, this 24-hour
bistro is lost in the bowels of the meat market. $$$

American

America *Union Square* 9 E. 18th St. (bet. Fifth Ave and Broadway); 505-2110
A vast barn of a place, with a multifarious menu (listing an entrée from every state, as
well as fluffernutters and "Dagwood" sandwiches) and an eclectic crowd. $$$

Amsterdam's *Upper West Side* 428 Amsterdam Ave. (bet. 80th and 81st Sts.); 874-1377
SoHo 454 Broadway (bet. Grand and Howard Sts.); 925-6166
Classic American bistro fare, with delicious variations on rotisserie chicken. The
crowd at both spots gets hip and loud later on, but families come early. $$$

Ben Benson's *Midtown* 123 W. 52nd St. (bet. Sixth and Seventh Aves.); 581-8888
Big-portion aged steaks in soothing, though somewhat bland suroundings. $$$$

Bridge Cafe *Lower Manhattan* 279 Water St. (at Dover St.); 227-3344
A neighborhood place that attracts politicos from nearby City Hall. This was Ed
Koch's favorite watering hole when he was mayor. $$$

Broome Street Bar *SoHo* 363 W. Broadway (at Broome St.); 925-2086
The burger's the thing here, with blue-cheese-stuffed monsters definitely the way
to go. $$

Coffee Shop *Union Square* 29 Union Square West (at 16th St.); 243-7969
The food is flavorful Brazilian fare. But the people are prettier than the plates, so it's
easy to get distracted. $$$

Dock's Oyster Bar *Upper West Side* 2427 Broadway (bet. 89th and 90th Sts.); 724-5588
Midtown 633 Third Ave. (at 40th St.); 986-8080
An unpretentious dining experience for fans of fresh seafood. Be sure to check out
the exotic vodka collection at the bar; you'll want an extra-dry martini to chase those
oysters on the half shell. $$$

Elephant & Castle *West Village* 68 Greenwich Ave. (bet. Seventh Ave. and 11th St.);
243-1400
Burgers and brunch. It's all rather precious, but comfortable, reliable, and, for a MOR
Village crowd, inevitable. $$

Flamingo East *East Village* 219 Second Ave. (bet. 13th and 14th Sts.); 533-2860
Excruciatingly chic see-and-be scene just south of shabby East 14th Street. They
serve food, too. $$$

44 *Midtown* Royalton Hotel, 44 W. 44th St. (bet. Fifth and Sixth Aves.); 944-8844
The decor, like the attitude, is thick enough to be cut with a knife—if you can get one out of your back. Just the way the trendy publishing crowd likes it for lunch. **$$$$**

Frank's Restaurant *West Village* 431 W. 14th St. (bet. Ninth and Tenth Aves.); 243-1349
Want a great steak? Go to the source. Located in the heart of the meat-packing district, and frequented at breakfast by meatpackers, during the day by butchers who know their beef, and at night by lucky insiders clued into this unassuming hideaway. **$$$**

Friend of a Farmer *Gramercy Park* 77 Irving Pl. (bet. 18th and 19th Sts.); 477-2188
You'll wait on line with the other weekend brunchers for the giant, down-home muffins and omelettes served in a skillet. The only trick is squeezing out from behind the tiny tables once you've eaten your fill. Cash only. **$$**

Good Enough to Eat *Upper West Side* 483 Amsterdam Ave. (bet. 83rd and 84th Sts.); 496-0163
Homey country fare, with omelettes a specialty and the tea always served up perfectly. **$$**

Gotham Bar & Grill *East Village* 12 E. 12th St. (bet. Fifth Ave. and University Pl.); 620-4020
A revelation when it first opened, and some say it's stronger than ever with its French-influenced new cuisine in spectacular surroundings. **$$$$**

Jackson Hole *Upper East Side* 232 E. 64th St. (bet. Second and Third Aves.); 371-7187
Upper West Side 517 Columbus Ave. (at 85th St.); 362-5177
Upper East Side 1270 Madison Ave. (at 91st St.); 427-2820
Upper East Side 1611 Second Ave. (bet. 83rd. and 84th Sts.); 737-8788
Murray Hill 521 Third Ave. (at 35th St.); 679-3264
One star in the great burger constellation of Manhattan. Is this the best? It's close enough, dishing up great sizzling cannonballs of beef to its numerous fans at its numerous locations. **$$$**

Jerry's *SoHo* 101 Prince St. (bet. Greene and Mercer Sts.); 966-9464
Is SoHo trendy, or what? The coolly understated surroundings and unpretentious fare may lull you into a false sense of security, but the model types, art world honchos, and young film stars who frequent the place will disabuse you of any notion of egalitarianism. **$$$**

Memphis *Upper West Side* 329 Columbus Ave. (bet. 75th and 76th Sts.); 496-1840
Southern-accented cuisine in chic but comfortable surroundings. On weekend nights, a velvet rope goes up out front and the bar rages. **$$$**

Old Devil Moon *Lower East Side* 511 E. 12th St. (bet. Ave A and Ave B); 475-4357
A funky yet civilized oasis in Alphabet City. $$

Old Homestead *West Side* 56 Ninth Ave. (bet. 14th and 15th Sts.); 242-9040
Guns 'N' Roses favorite New York steakhouse, which tells you absolutely nothing
about the decor (red-velvet-flocked wallpaper and mahogany). For epicurians, they
serve kobe beef, at a C-note a steak, from the steers hand-massaged in Japan. $$$$

The Oyster Bar *Midtown* Grand Central Station, Lower Level (bet. Vanderbilt and
Lexington Aves.); 490-6650
A treasure hidden in plain sight, and superb from its sprawling Californian wine list,
its gut-warming pan roasts (sit at the counter and watch the chef slosh that cream
into your oyster stew), right down to the gruff attitude of the waiters. Perfect, if
pricey. $$$$

Sign of the Dove *East Side* 1110 Third Ave. (65th St.); 861-8080
The dynamic kitchen keeps topping itself, putting out superb French-flavored but
classically American cuisine. $$$$$

Sylvia's Restaurant *Harlem* 328 Lenox Ave. (bet. 126th and 127th Sts.); 996-0660
A New York institution, and one taste of these fall-off-the-bone ribs and you'll see
why. Transcendent soul food at a venue that's been around forever. $$$

Chinese

Little Szechuan *Chinatown* 31 Oliver St. (off Chatham Square); 349-2360
Leave the beaten track to find revelatory squid and shrimp with hot peppers, ginger,
scallions, and garlic. The orange chicken will spike your taste buds. $$

Mandarin Court *Chinatown* 61 Mott St. (bet. Canal and Bayard); 608-3838
The dim-sum palace par excellence, featuring bargain prices on an amazing array of
bite-sized Cantonese delicacies. $$

Ollie's *West Harlem* 2957 Broadway (at 116th St.); 932-3300
Upper West Side 2315 Broadway (at 84th St.); 362-3712
Midtown 190 W. 44th St. (bet. Broadway and Eighth Ave.); 921-5988
Huge bowls of Cantonese meat and noodle soup, customized to your liking, among
other Chinese specialties. $$

Phoenix Garden *Chinatown* #15 in Arcade (bet. Bowery and Elizabeth Sts.); 233-6017
Crowds of devotees return again and again just for the crispy salt-and-pepper shrimp,
but you may find your own addiction. $$

Shun Lee Palace *Midtown* 155 E. 55th St. (bet. Lexington and Third Ave.); 371-8844

Shun Lee West *West Side* 43 W. 65th St. (bet. CPW and Columbus Ave.); 595-8895
Uptown Chinese, so with the proper caveats of paying triple for what you'd get cheap in Chinatown, these sister restaurants serve up delicious food in stylish settings. $$$$

Italian

Baci *Upper West Side* 412 Amsterdam Ave. (bet. 79th and 80th Sts.); 496-1550
Baci is Italian for kiss, and you'll want to kiss the chef who comes up with the pasta dishes at this upscale neighborhood eatery. $$$

Canastel's *Gramercy Park* 229 Park Ave. South (at 19th St.); 677-9622
It won the battle of the trattorias in this burgeoning part of SoFi, partly on the basis of its rollicking after-work bar scene. $$$

Il Cantinori *East Village* 32 E. 10th St. (bet. Broadway and University Pl.); 673-6044
The number of exceptional meals put out by the kitchen of this elegant Northern Italian place approaches an alarming percentage. Their tiramisu inspired writer-director Nora Ephron in the screenplay of *Sleepless in Seattle*. $$$$

Carmine's *Upper West Side* 2450 Broadway (bet. 90th and 91st Sts.); 362-2200
"Family-style," which here doesn't necessarily mean ankle-biters but large servings that everyone shares. You'll leave here stuffed with classic Italian dishes. $$$

Contrapunto *Upper East Side* 200 E. 60th St. (at Third Ave.); 751-8616
A haven for Bloomingdale groupies and the pre-movie crowd, with better-than-average pastas and thin-crust "personal" pizzas. $$$

John's Pizzeria *West Village* 278 Bleecker St. (bet. Sixth and Seventh Aves.); 243-1680
East Side 408 E. 64th St. (bet. First and York Aves.); 935-2895
West Side 43 W. 65th St. (bet. Broadway and CPW); 721-7001
For some people, the Village joint is the only one, but the coal-burning ovens burn bright at all three. Unquestionably the best pizza in New York, a pizza town. They don't sell by the slice, but you couldn't eat just one, anyway. $$$

Le Madri *Chelsea* 168 W. 18th St. (at Seventh Ave.); 727-8022
As elegant a setting as you will find for pasta and pizza prepared the way Mama used to. And a short hop from Barney's. $$$$

Luna's *Little Italy* 112 Mulberry St. (bet. Canal and Hester Sts.); 226-8657
Popular, loud Little Italy standby for a good plate of pasta. Prepare to stand in line. $$$

Il Mulino *West Village* 86 W. Third St. (bet. Thompson and Sullivan Sts.); 673-3783
The decor ain't much, but the huge portions of tasty dishes like osso bucco and chicken with artichokes pack in the crowds. Try not to fill up on the house crostini. $$$

Puglia's *Little Italy* 189 Hester St. (bet. Mulberry and Mott Sts.); 966-6006
Diners share long tables at this 75-year-old Sicilian classic. $$$

Rao's *East Harlem* 455 E. 114th St. (at Pleasant Ave.); 534-9625
It's up in El Barrio, but this tiny remnant of Italian Harlem lures the rich and famous with its classic *paisan* fare. Warning: reserve at least three months in advance. $$$$

Supreme Macaroni Co. *Midtown* 511 Ninth Ave. (bet. 38th and 39th Sts.); 502-4842
A garlic-wafting hideaway that sells groceries up front, and a wide range of pasta dishes in a restaurant in back. $$$

Umberto's Clam House *Little Italy* 129 Mulberry St. (at Hester); 431-7545
Joey Gallo died for your sins. $$$

Il Vagabondo *Upper East Side* 351 E. 62nd St. (bet. First and Second Aves.); 832-9221
It's a little cracked, having a bocci court in a restaurant, but it sure is fun. Get a table in the long, narrow dining room beside the court, and after the regulars leave, toss a few balls yourself. $$$

Japanese

Fujiyama Mama *Upper West Side* 467 Columbus Ave. (bet. 82nd and 83rd Sts.); 769-1144
Wow! Crazy place, crazy crowd—what's this superb sushi doing on my plate? $$$

Honmura An *SoHo* 170 Mercer St. (bet. Prince and W. Houston Sts.); 334-5253
Come to this sleek soba parlor for refined and authentic Japanese noodle soups. $$

Japonica *The Village* 90 University Pl. (bet. 11th and 12th Sts.); 243-7752
New York University students study the technique of the sushi chef at this neighborhood place and pronounce it sublime. $$$

Mexican, Tex-Mex, Southwestern

Arizona 206 and Cafe *Upper East Side* 206 E. 60th St. (bet. Second and Third Aves.); 838-0440
Creative Southwestern fare attracts shoppers and movie-goers in the evening, power-lunch types during the day. $$$

Benny's Burritos *East Village* 93 Ave. A (at Sixth St.); 254-2054
Delicious, Mission-style concoctions of rice, beans, and anything else you want to jam in. The first of a whole wave of down-scale burrito palaces. $$

Blue Moon *Chelsea* 150 Eighth Ave. (bet. 17th and 18th Sts.); 463-0560
Upper East Side 1444 First Ave. (at 75th St.); 288-9811
Successful, reliable, if somewhat routine Mexican menu. $$

Cowgirl Hall of Fame *West Village* 519 Hudson St. (10th St.); 633-1133
Good, down-home food, with trinkets scattered all over the walls. A Tex-Mex fun-house. $$$

Mesa Grill *The Village* 102 Fifth Ave. (at 15th St.); 807-7400
The popular place to go for zesty Southwest fare. $$$

El Teddy's *TriBeCa* 219 W. Broadway (bet. Franklin and White); 941-7070
Exuberant, extravagant, entertaining. What other restaurant keeps a Tarot reader on the premises? The crowd is fast and young, the margaritas cold and furious, the food scrumptious and nouvelle Mexican. $$$

Other Ethnic Fare

Alcala *Upper West Side* 349 Amsterdam Ave. (bet. 76th and 77th Sts.); 769-9600
The best thing about this West Side Castillian mecca is the tapas bar, featuring the traditional style of the flavorful, bite-size appetizer morsels. $$$

Indochine *East Village* 430 Lafayette St. (bet. Fourth St. and Astor Pl.); 505-5111
They wrote it off a few years ago, but this trendy Thai restaurant is back, with celebs, satay, and chic surroundings. $$$

Periyali *Chelsea* 35 W. 20th St. (bet. Fifth and Sixth Aves.); 463-7890
Fans of fresh, robust Greek cuisine swear by this rustic yet elegant place—try the stunning grilled prawns. $$$$

Sugar Reef *East Village* 93 Second Ave. (bet. Fifth and Sixth Sts.); 477-8427
Festive food for parrot-heads and anyone else who might want to venture into a restaurant where an impromptu conga line might erupt at any minute. The food, jerk chicken and the like, is good enough to dance about. $$

Veselka *East Village* 144 Second Ave. (at Ninth St.); 228-9682
Ukranian soul food, fueling successive generations of bohemian-wanna-bes with hearty, cheap fare. $

Vegetarian

Angelica Kitchen *East Village* 300 E. 12th St. (bet. First and Second Aves.); 228-2909
This macro mecca in the East Village serves up great steaming "dragon bowls" of brown rice, beans, seaweed, and soba. $$$

Health Pub *Gramercy Park* 371 Second Ave. (21st St.); 529-9200
Can a gourmand be satisfied with health food? The answer here is an unqualified yes, with the soy burger particularly flavorful. $$

Theme Restaurants

Hard Rock Cafe *Midtown* 221 W. 57th St. (bet. Broadway and Seventh Ave.); 459-9320
If you have adolescent kids, you have no choice but to go. Bring earplugs and you'll enjoy the burgers. $$

Harley-Davidson Cafe *Midtown* 1370 Sixth Ave.; 245-6000
Biker chic goes whole hog. Not quite as much variety as at other theme restaurants, but once you've said "Harley," you've said it all. Food is sturdy bar fare. $$$

Planet Hollywood *Midtown* 140 W. 57th St.; 333-7827
"Hollywood is a town that has to be seen to be disbelieved," said Walter Winchell, and the same goes for this place. The food is a surprise, with great burgers. $$$

■ RESTAURANTS BY NEIGHBORHOOD

Restaurants below are also listed in preceding "Restaurants by Cuisine" with more complete descriptions.

Lower Manhattan

Bridge Cafe. *American* 279 Water St. (at Dover St.); 227-3344. $$$

Lower East Side

Katz's Deli. *Deli* 205 Houston St. (at Ludlow); 254-2246. $$
Little Szechuan. *Chinese* 31 Oliver St. (off Chatham Square, Chinatown); 349-2360. $$
Luna's. *Italian* 112 Mulberry St. (bet. Canal and Hester Sts., Little Italy); 226-8657. $$$
Mandarin Court. *Chinese* 61 Mott St. (bet. Canal and Bayard, Chinatown); 608-3838 $$
Old Devil Moon. *American* 511 E. 12th St. (bet. Ave A and Ave. B); 475-4357 $$
Phoenix Garden. *Chinese* #15 in Arcade (bet. Bowery and Elizabeth Sts., Chinatown); 233-6017. $$
Puglia's. *Italian* 189 Hester St. (bet. Mulberry and Mott Sts., Little Italy); 966-6006. $$$
Ratner's. *Deli* 138 Delancey St. (bet. Norfolk and Suffolk Sts.); 677-5588. $$
Umberto's Clam House. *Italian* 129 Mulberry St. (at Hester, Little Italy); 431-7545. $$$

TriBeCa and SoHo

Alison on Dominick Street. *Gourmet* 38 Dominick St. (bet. Varick and Hudson Sts.); 727-1188. $$$$
Amsterdam's. *American* 454 Broadway (bet. Grand and Howard Sts.); 925-6166. $$$
Broome Street Bar. *American* 4363 W. Broadway (at Broome St.); 925-2086. $$

Honmura An. *Japanese* 170 Mercer St. (bet. Prince and W. Houston Sts.); 334-5253 **$$**
Jerry's. *American* 101 Prince St. (bet. Greene and Mercer Sts.); 966-9464. **$$$**
Odeon. *Cafes and Bistros* 145 W. Broadway (bet. Worth and Duane Sts.); 233-0507. **$$$$**
Raoul's. *French* 180 Prince St. (bet. Sullivan and Thompson); 966-3518. **$$$$**
El Teddy's. *Mexican* 219 W. Broadway (bet. Franklin and White); 941-7070. **$$$**

The Villages

Angelica Kitchen. *Vegetarian* 300 E. 12th St. (bet. First and Second Aves.); 228-2909. **$$$**
Benny's Burritos *Mexican* 93 Ave. A (at Sixth St.); 254-2054. **$$**
Bouley. *Gourmet* 165 Duane St. (bet. Greenwich and Hudson); 608-3852. **$$$$$**
Brunetta's. *Cheap Eats* 190 First Ave. (bet. 11th and 12th Sts.); 228-4030. **$**
Cafe Loup. *French* 105 W. 13th St. (bet. Sixth and Seventh Aves.); 255-4746. **$$$**
Il Cantinori. *Italian* 32 E. 10th St. (bet. Broadway and University Pl.); 673-6044. **$$$$**
Chez Brigitte. *Cheap Eats* 77 Greenwich Ave. (at Seventh Ave.); 929-6736. **$**
Christine's. *Cheap Eats* 208 First Ave. (bet. 12th and 13th Sts.); 254-2474. **$**
Chumley's. *Tavern* 86 Bedford St.; 675-4449. **$$**
Corner Bistro. *Cheap Eats* 331 W. Fourth St. (at Jane St., near Eighth Ave.); 242-9502. **$**
Cowgirl Hall of Fame. *Tex-Mex* 519 Hudson St. (10th St.); 633-1133. **$$$**
Elephant & Castle. *American* 68 Greenwich Ave. (Seventh Ave. and 11th St.); 243-1400. **$$**
Flamingo East. *American* 219 Second Ave. (bet. 13th and 14th Sts.); 533-2860. **$$$**
Florent. *Round-the-Clock* 60 Gansevoort St. (bet. Washington and Greenwich Sts.); 989-5779. **$$$**
Frank's Restaurant. *American* 431 W. 14th St. (bet. Ninth and Tenth Aves.); 243-1349. **$$$**
Gotham Bar & Grill. *American* 12 E. 12th St. (Fifth Ave. and University Pl.); 620-4020. **$$$$**
Indochine. *Other Ethnic Fare* 430 Lafayette St. (bet. Fourth St. and Astor Pl.); 505-5111. **$$$**
Japonica. *Japanese* 90 University Pl. (bet. 11th and 12th Sts.); 243-7752. **$$$**
John's Pizzeria. *Italian* 278 Bleecker St. (bet. Sixth and Seventh Aves.); 243-1680. **$$$**
Lion's Head. *Tavern* 59 Christopher St. (bet. Sixth and Seventh Aves.); 929-0670. **$$$**
McSorley's Old Alehouse *Tavern* 15 E. Seventh St. (bet. Second Ave. and Bowery); 473-9184. **$$**
Mesa Grill. *Southwestern* 102 Fifth Ave. (at 15th St.); 807-7400. **$$$**
Il Mulino *Italian* 86 W. Third St. (bet. Thompson and Sullivan Sts.); 673-3783 **$$$**
Old Homestead. *American* 56 Ninth Ave. (bet. 14th and 15th Sts.); 242-9040. **$$$$**
Second Avenue Deli. *Deli* 156 Second Ave. (at 10th St.); 677-0606. **$$$**
Sucelt. *Cheap Eats* 200 W. 14th St. (at Sixth Ave.); 242-0593. **$**
Sugar Reef. *Other Ethnic Fare* 93 Second Ave. (bet. Fifth and Sixth Sts.); 477-8427. **$$**
Two Boots. *Cheap Eats* 37th Ave. A (bet. Second and Third Sts.); 505-2276. **$**
Veselka. *Other Ethnic Fare* 144 Second Ave. (at Ninth St.); 228-9682. **$**

Chelsea, Gramercy Park, Murray Hill

America. *American* 9 E. 18th St. (bet. Fifth Ave and Broadway); 505-2110. $$$

Blue Moon. *Mexican* 150 Eighth Ave. (bet. 17th and 18th Sts.); 463-0560. $$

Canastel's. *Italian* 229 Park Ave. South (at 19th St.); 677-9622. $$$

Christine's. *Cheap Eats* 438 Second Ave. (at 25th St.); 684-1879. $

Coffee Shop. *American* 29 Union Square West (at 16th St.); 243-7969. $$$

Friend of a Farmer. *American* 77 Irving Place (bet. 18th and 19th Sts.); 477-2188. $$

Health Pub. *Vegetarian* 371 Second Ave. (21st St.); 529-9200. $$

Jackson Hole. *American* 521 Third Ave. (at 35th St.); 679-3264. $$$

La Luncheonette. *French* 130 Tenth Ave (at W. 18th St.); 675-0342. $$$

Le Madri. *Italian* 168 W. 18th St. (at Seventh Ave.); 727-8022. $$$$

Old Town Bar. *Tavern* 45 E. 18th St. (bet. Broadway and Park Ave. South); 473-8874. $$

Periyali. *Other Ethnic Fare* 35 W. 20th St. (bet. Fifth and Sixth Aves.); 463-7890. $$$$

Pete's Tavern. *Tavern* 129 E. 18th St. (at Irving Pl.); 473-7676. $$$

Union Square Cafe. *Gourmet* 21 E. 16th St. (bet. Fifth Ave. and Union Sq.); 243-4020. $$$$

The Water Club. *Views and Ambience* 500 E. 30th St. (on East River); 683-3333. $$$$

Midtown and Times Square

Ben Benson's. *American* 123 W. 52nd St. (bet. Sixth and Seventh Aves.); 581-8888. $$$$

Brasserie. *Round-the-Clock* 100 E 53rd St. (bet. Park and Lexington Aves.); 751-4840. $$$

Cabana Carioca. *Cheap Eats* 123 W. 45th St. (bet. Sixth and Seventh Aves.); 581-8088. $

Cafe Un Deux Trois. *Cafes and Bistros* 123 W. 44th St. (bet. Sixth and Seventh Aves.); 354-4148. $$$

Carnegie Deli. *Deli* 854 Seventh Ave. (bet. 54th and 55th Sts.); 757-2245. $

Dock's Oyster Bar. *American* 633 Third Ave. (at 40th St.); 986-8080. $$$

The Four Seasons. *Classic New York* 99 E. 52nd. St. (Park and Lexington Aves.); 754-9494. $$$$$ (prix fixe $$$)

44. *American* Royalton Hotel, 44 W. 44th St. (bet. Fifth and Sixth Aves.); 944-8844. $$$$

Hard Rock Cafe. *Theme Restaurants* 221 W. 57th St. (bet. Broadway and Seventh Ave.); 459-9320. $–$$

Harley-Davidson Cafe. *Theme Restaurants* 1370 Sixth Ave.; 245-6000. $–$$

Le Bernadin. *Gourmet* 155 W. 51st St. (bet. Sixth and Seventh Aves.); 489-1515. $$$$$

Lutèce *Classic New York* 249 E. 50th St. (bet. Second and Third Aves.); 752-2225. $$$$$

Ollie's. *Chinese* 190 W. 44th St. (bet. Broadway and Eighth Ave.); 921-5988. $$

The Oyster Bar *American* Grand Central Station, Lower Level (bet. Vanderbilt and Lexington Aves.); 490-6650. $$$$

Peacock Alley. *French* Waldorf-Astoria Hotel, Park Ave. (bet. 49th and 50th Sts.); 872-4895. $$$$

P. J. Clarke's. *Tavern* 915 Third Ave. (at 55th St.); 759-1650. $$$

Planet Hollywood. *American* 140 W. 57th St.; 333-7827. $–$$

The Rainbow Room. *Views and Ambience* 30 Rockefeller Plaza, 65th floor (bet. 49th and 50th Sts.) 632-5100. $$$$$
The Russian Tea Room. *Classic New York* 150 W. 57th St. (bet. Sixth and Seventh Aves.); 265-0947. $$$$
Shun Lee Palace. *Chinese* 155 E. 55th St. (bet. Lexington and Third Ave.); 371-8844. $$$$
Supreme Macaroni Co. *Italian* 511 Ninth Ave. (bet. 38th and 39th Sts.); 502-4842. $$$
The "21" Club. *Classic New York* 21 W. 52nd St. (bet. Fifth and Sixth Aves.); 582-7200. $$$$$

East Side

Arizona 206 and Cafe. *Southwestern* 206 E. 60th St. (bet. Second and Third Aves.); 838-0440. $$$
Blue Moon. *Mexican* 1444 First Ave. (at 75th St.); 288-9811. $$
Boathouse Cafe. *Classic New York* E. Park Dr. N. and 72nd St.; 517-3623. $$$
Contrapunto. *Italian* 200 E. 60th St. (at Third Ave.); 751-8616. $$$
Elaine's. *Classic New York* 1703 Second Ave. (bet. 88th and 89th Sts.); 534-8103. $$$
Jackson Hole. *American* 1270 Madison Ave. (at 91st St.); 427-2820. $$$
Jackson Hole. *American* 1611 Second Ave. (bet 83rd. and 84th Sts.); 737-8788. $$$
Jackson Hole. *American* 232 E. 64th St. (bet. Second and Third Aves.); 371-7187. $$$
John's Pizzeria. *Italian* 408 E. 64th St. (bet. First and York Aves.); 935-2895. $$$
Le Cirque. *Gourmet* 58 E. 65th St. (bet. Fifth and Madison Aves.); 794-9292
Papaya King. *Cheap Eats* 210 E. 59th St. (at Third Ave.); 753-2014. $
Sign of the Dove. *American* 1110 Third Ave. (at 65th St.); 861-8080. $$$$$
Il Vagabondo. *Italian* 351 E. 62nd St. (bet. First and Second Aves.); 832-9221. $$$

West Side

Alcala. *Other Ethnic Fare* 349 Amsterdam Ave. (bet. 76th and 77th Sts.); 769-9600. $$$
Amsterdam's. *American* 428 Amsterdam Ave. (bet. 80th and 81st Sts.); 874-1377. $$$
Baci. *Italian* 412 Amsterdam Ave. (bet. 79th and 80th Sts.); 496-1550. $$$
Cafe Con Leche. *Cheap Eats* 424 Amsterdam Ave. (at 81st St.); 595-7000. $
Café des Artistes. *Classic New York* 1 W. 67th St. (bet. CPW and Columbus Ave.); 877-3500. $$$$
Carmine's. *Italian* 2450 Broadway (bet. 90th and 91st Sts.); 362-2200. $$$
Dock's Oyster Bar. *American* 2427 Broadway (bet. 89th and 90th Sts.); 724-5588. $$$
Fujiyama Mama. *Japanese* 467 Columbus Ave. (bet. 82nd and 83rd Sts.); 769-1144. $$$
Good Enough to Eat. *American* 483 Amsterdam Ave. (bet. 83rd and 84th Sts.); 496-0163. $$
Jackson Hole. *American* 517 Columbus Ave. (at 85th St.); 362-5177. $$$
John's Pizzeria. *Italian* 43 W. 65th St. (bet. Broadway and CPW); 721-7001. $$$
Memphis. *American* 329 Columbus Ave. (bet. 75th and 76th Sts.); 496-1840. $$$
Old Homestead. *American* 56 Ninth Ave. (bet. 14th and 15th Sts.); 242-9040. $$$$
Ollie's. *Chinese* 2315 Broadway (at 84th St.); 362-3712. $$
Shun Lee West. *Chinese* 43 W. 65th St. (bet. CPW and Columbus Ave.); 595-8895. $$$$

The Harlems

Ollie's. *Chinese* 2957 Broadway (at 116th St.); 932-3300. $$

Rao's. *Italian* 455 E. 114th St. (at Pleasant Ave.); 534-9625. $$$$

Sylvia's Restaurant. *American* 328 Lenox Ave. (bet. 126th and 127th Sts.); 996-0660. $$$

The Terrace. *Views and Ambience* 400 W. 119th St. (bet. Amsterdam Ave. and Morningside Dr.); 666-9490. $$$$$

■ TOURS

Adventures on a Shoestring. 265-2663. Theme tours such as "Big Apple Love Affairs" and "Haunted Greenwich Village," all priced at $5.00.

Big Onion Walking Tours. 439-1090. A wide range of offerings, from architectural and cultural tours, like "Historic Harlem," to gastronomical challenges like the "Multi-Ethnic Eating Tour."

The Central Park Rangers. 427-4040. Several excellent tours of Central Park, an ideal way to discover and enjoy Manhattan's greatest public space.

Circle Line Cruises. 563-3200. A three-hour, 35-mile cruise around Manhattan Island.

City Tour Packages. (800) 554-8687. Call for information and reservations.

Gray Line of New York. 397-2600. Bus tours for an overview of Manhattan.

Harlem Gospel & Jazz Tours. 757-0425 See Harlem and listen to great music.

History Walks with Joyce Gold. 242-5762. Intimate tours of individual neighborhoods.

Lower East Side Tenement Museum. 431-0233. Tour America's most famous immigrant neighborhood.

Madison Square Garden. 465-5800. Behind-the-scenes look at Knicks' and Rangers' home.

Museum of the City of New York. 534-1672 ext. 206. An excellent series of walking tours, with some of the most knowledgeable guides in the city.

Municipal Art Society. 935-3960. A superb schedule of both bus and walking tours, concentrating on architectural highlights but covering history and culture as well.

New York City Cultural Walking Tours. 979-2388. Architecture and history walking tours.

92nd Street Y. 415-5628 or 415-5599. Tours of a famous Upper East Side landmark.

Pride of 34th St. Tour. 868-0521. Learn about the Garment District.

River to River Downtown Walking Tours. 321-2823. See colonial New York.

Shortline Bus Tours. 397-2620. Bus tours for an overview of the city.

SoHo Art Tours. 431-8055. See galleries with a guide.

Times Square Exposé. 768-1560. Get the down and dirty on the crossroads of the world.

Urban Explorations. (718) 721-5254. Customized neighborhood walking tours.

■ Manhattan Calendar *Too Much to Do in Manhattan*

Monday	*Tuesday*	*Wednesday*
1 ★ Statue of Liberty and Ellis Island ◆ Dinner at Katz's on Lower East Side. ★ Stroll along Orchard St.; try piroshki; eat pickles at Guss's (Hollander's) on Essex	**2** ★ Wander through Village; watch street performers at Washington Square ◆ Mingle with models at Live Bait ★ Shop for shoes on Eighth St.	**3** ★ Metropolitan Museum of Art, European Collection ◆ Lunch at the Palm Court in the Plaza
8 ★ U.N. and U.N. Plaza ◆ Lunch at Oyster Bar; Grand Central Station ★ Shop at Bloomingdale's ◆ Drinks at Michael's Pub	**9** ★ Wander Upper West Side ★ Buy mysteries at Murder Inc. ◆ Eat dinner along Columbus Ave. at outdoor cafe	**10** ★ Go to Village; Visit St. Mark's Bookstore ◆ Tea at Cornelia Street Café, bring sketchbook ★ Evening jazz on Bleecker St.
15 ★ Walk across the esplanade of the Brooklyn Bridge ◆ Lunch at River Cafe ◆ Dinner: Korean barbecue in Little Korea	**16** ★ Visit SoHo galleries ★ Shop at Barney's ◆ Dinner at Bouley: pretend to be restaurant critic	**17** ★ Metropolitan Museum of Art, Egyptian Collection ◆ Drinks at White Horse Tavern; toast the ghost of Dylan Thomas ◆ Coffee at Caffè Reggio; smoke Galoise and read Camus
22 ★ New York Stock Exchange ◆ Lunch at Fraunces Tavern, where Washington bid his officers farewell ◆ Drinks at South Street Seaport ◆ Dinner in Chinatown	**23** ★ Museum of Modern Art ◆ Lunch in MOMA sculpture garden ★ American Ballet Theater (in season)	**24** ★ Take tram to Roosevelt Island ★ See Rockefeller Center (in winter, ice skate) ★ Score tickets for the Letterman Show

THURSDAY	FRIDAY	SATURDAY	SUNDAY
4 ★ Visit Radio City Music Hall and see the Rockettes ◆ Gin and tonic at Algonquin ★ Haircut at Astor Place in evening	**5** ◆ Dinner at Le Cirque to see rich and famous ★ Knicks game at Madison Square Garden (in season)	**6** ◆ Breakfast or lunch: H&H Bagels ★ Circle Line Tour of Manhattan Island ★ New York City Ballet (in season)	**7** ★ Tour St. Patrick's Cathedral ◆ Lunch at Tavern on the Green ★ N.Y. Shakespeare Festival in Central Park
11 ★ Visit Flower Market, North Chelsea ★ Whitney Museum ◆ Dinner at Russian Tea Room ★ Carnegie Hall concert	**12** ★ Visit Empire State Building ◆ Dinner at Indochine ★ Performance at Public Theater	**13** ★ Metropolitan Museum of Art, American Collection ◆ Pastrami on rye at Carnegie Deli ★ Broadway show	**14** ★ Hear Abyssinian Baptist Church gospel choir ◆ Brunch at Sylvia's ★ Jog reservoir, Central Park ★ Visit Grant's Tomb, walk in Riverside Park
18 ★ Guggenheim Museum ◆ Lunch at Lutèce ★ Evening performance at The Kitchen	**19** ★ Take a bus tour of Harlem and see Apollo Theater ◆ Drinks at Café des Artistes ★ New York Philharmonic	**20** ★ Wander through Marble Hill ★ Meander down Fifth Ave., visit bookshops ◆ Beer at McSorley's, oldest tavern in NYC ★ Off-Broadway show	**21** ★ Visit Church of St. John the Divine (the world's largest cathedral) ★ American Museum of Natural History ★ Shop at Orchard Street retail bazaars
25 ★ American Craft Museum ★ Shop at Bergdorf Goodman ★ See Bobby Short at the Carlyle	**26** ★ Tour Midtown skyscrapers: Chrysler Bldg., Lever Bldg., Sony Plaza, Trump Tower ◆ Drinks at Iridium ★ Metropolitan Opera (in season)	**27** ★ Frick Museum ◆ Seafood dinner at Le Bernadin ★ Off-Off Broadway show	**28** ★ Visit the Cloisters for medieval art ★ Row a boat on Central Park Lake **29** Crash on couch, order in Chinese food **30** Fly home

■ SPORTS

Sports in Manhattan—sports in New York in general—are a serious bone of contention, ever since the Brooklyn Dodgers baseball team decamped for Los Angeles. It started a rout: the New York Giants baseball team left the Polo Grounds in Harlem for the West Coast, and both the "New York" Giants and "New York" Jets football teams now play in New Jersey.

Despite these random betrayals, New York is a quintessential sports town, a place of rabid fans and foaming-at-the-mouth columnists and commentators. WFAN (660 on the AM dial) is an all-sports radio station, and a sampling of the call-in shows indicate the depth of passion for local teams.

For one thing, there will always be **the Knicks.** The New York Knickerbockers basketball team, 1994 NBA Eastern Conference Champions, play in Madison Square Garden, in front of a crowd of highly visible VIPs and a full house of thunderous fans. The 1994 Stanley Cup winners, the **New York Rangers** ice hockey team, also play at the Garden (obviously, never on the same nights as the Knicks).

The Bronx Bombers, a.k.a. the **New York Yankees**, continue to hold forth in the House That Ruth Built, Yankee Stadium, a classic piece of baseball architec-

Babe Ruth and Kate Smith surrounded by reporters in the stands at Yankee Stadium. (New York Municipal Archives)

ture. How much longer they remain there is subject to the determination of George Steinbrenner, owner of the Yankees and a man of many whims. The **New York Mets** are much more secure in Shea Stadium, beneath the thunderous flyovers from nearby La Guardia airport.

The **U.S. Open Tennis Championships**, in late August–early September, also play under the La Guardia flight path at Flushing Meadow Park, next door to Shea. A much-heralded agreement, brokered by then-mayor David Dinkins (a major tennis buff), re-routes the jet flyovers for the duration of the tournament. The Virginia Slims Women's Tennis Tournament comes to the Garden every November.

Outside of the Knicks, the most serious single sports event in Manhattan itself is probably the **New York Marathon,** run the first Sunday in November. The course kicks off on the Staten Island side of the Verrazano Bridge, enters Manhattan over the Queensboro Bridge, arcs briefly into the Bronx, and finishes up in Central Park. Call 860-4455 for information.

Other area sports teams include the **New York Islanders** (hockey) and the **New Jersey Nets** (basketball).

The 1937 "dream team" New York Yankees, who went on to win four consecutive World Series between 1936-1939. Joe DiMaggio is on the bench at the far left. (Underwood Photo Archives)

■ S P O R T S   V E N U E S

Madison Square Garden, Seventh Ave. and 32nd St.; 465-6000.

Shea Stadium, Roosevelt Ave. and 126th St., Flushing, Queens; (718) 507-8499. Take the number 7 train to the Willets Point/Shea Stadium stop.

U.S. Tennis Association National Tennis Center, Flushing Meadow Park, Queens, (718) 271-5100. Take the number 7 train to the Willets Point/Shea Stadium stop.

Yankee Stadium, West 161st and River Aves., Bronx. (718) 293-6000. Take the number 4 IRT subway from the east side of Manhattan, or the CC and D subways from the west side.

■ MUSEUMS

For descriptions of the collections at Manhattan's most famous museums—Frick Collection, Metropolitan Museum of Art, Whitney, Guggenheim, among others—see "Museum Mile" in the "EAST SIDE" chapter and refer to the index.

Abigail Adams Smith Museum
  Upper East Side 421 East 61st St. (bet. First and York Aves.); 838-6878
Alternative Museum
  SoHo 594 Broadway (bet. Houston and Prince Sts.); 966-4444
American Academy and Institute of Arts & Letters
  Upper Manhattan Audubon Terrace (Broadway and W. 155th St.); 368-5900
American Craft Museum
  Midtown 40 W. 53rd St. (bet. Fifth and Sixth Aves.); 956-3535
American Museum of Natural History
  Upper West Side CPW at 79th St.; 769-5100
American Numismatic Society
  Upper Manhattan Audubon Terrace (Broadway and W. 155th St.); 234-3130
Asia Society
  Upper East Side 725 Park Ave. (at 70th St.); 288-6400
Black Fashion Museum
  Harlem 155 W. 126th St. (bet. Adam Clayton Powell, Jr. and Malcolm X Blvds.) 666-1320
Children's Museum of the Arts
  SoHo 72 Spring St. (bet. Broadway and Lafayette); 941-9198
Children's Museum of Manhattan
  Upper West Side 212 W. 83rd St. (bet. Broadway and Amsterdam Aves.); 721-1223

China Institute
   Upper East Side 125 E. 65th St. (bet. Lexington and Park Aves.); 744-8181
The Cloisters
   Upper Manhattan W. 190th St. and Fort Washington Ave. (in Fort Tryon Park); 923-3700
Cooper-Hewitt Museum
   Upper East Side 2 E. 91st St. (at Fifth Ave.); 860-6898
Ellis Island Immigration Museum
   Lower Manhattan Ellis Island; 363-7620
Federal Hall National Memorial
   Lower Manhattan 26 Wall St. (at Nassau St.); 825-6888
Forbes Magazine Galleries
   West Village 62 Fifth Ave. (at 12th St.); 206-5548
Fraunces Tavern Museum
   Lower Manhattan 54 Pearl St. (at Broad St.); 425-1778
Frick Collection
   Upper East Side 1 E. 70th St. (at Fifth Ave.); 288-0700
Guggenheim (Solomon R. Guggenheim) Museum
   Upper East Side 1071 Fifth Ave. (at 88th St.); 423-3500
Guggenheim Museum SoHo
   SoHo 575 Broadway (at Prince St.); 423-3500
Heye (George Gustav Heye) Center of the National Museum of the American Indian,
   Smithsonian Institution, at the Alexander Hamilton U.S. Custom House
   Lower Manhattan 1 Bowling Green (at State St.); 668-2616
Hispanic Society of America
   Upper Manhattan Audubon Terrace (Broadway at W. 155th St.); 926-2234
International Center of Photography
   Upper East Side 1130 Fifth Ave. (at E. 94th St.); 860-1777
ICP Midtown
   Midtown 1133 Sixth Ave. (at W. 43rd St.); 768-4682
Intrepid Sea-Air-Space Museum
   Midtown Pier 86, Hudson River (at W. 46th St.); 245-2533
Jewish Museum
   Upper East Side 1109 Fifth Ave. (at E. 92nd St.); 423-3200
Lower East Side Tenement Museum
   Lower East Side 97 Orchard St. (bet. Broome and Delancey Sts.); 431-0233
Metropolitan Museum of Art
   Upper East Side Fifth Ave. at 82nd St.; 535-7710
El Museo del Barrio
   Upper East Side 1230 Fifth Ave. (at 104th St.); 831-7272

Museum at FIT, Fashion Institute of Technology
  Chelsea 27 W. 27th St. (at Seventh Ave.); 760-7970
Museum for African Art
  SoHo 593 Broadway (bet. Houston and Prince Sts.); 966-1313
Museum of American Financial History
  Lower Manhattan 24 Broadway; 908-4110
Museum of American Folk Art
  Upper West Side 2 Lincoln Square (Columbus Ave. at 66th St.); 595-9533
Museum of the City of New York
  Upper East Side 1220 Fifth Ave. (at 103rd St.); 534-1672
Museum of Modern Art
  Midtown 11 W. 53rd St. (bet. Fifth and Sixth Aves.); 708-9480
Museum of Television and Radio
  Midtown 25 W. 52nd St. (bet. Fifth and Sixth Aves.); 621-6800
National Academy of Design
  Upper East Side 1083 Fifth Ave. (at 89th St.); 369-4880
New Museum of Contemporary Art
  SoHo 583 Broadway (bet. Prince and Houston Sts.); 219-1355
New York City Fire Museum
  SoHo 278 Spring St. (bet. Hudson and Varick Sts.); 691-1303
New-York Historical Society
  Upper West Side 170 CPW (at 77th St.); 873-3400
New York Unearthed
  Lower Manhattan 17 State St.; 748-8628
Old Merchant's House Museum
  East Village 29 E. 4th St. (bet. Bowery and Lafayette); 777-1089
Pierpont Morgan Library
  Murray Hill 29 E. 36th St. (at Madison Ave.); 685-0610
Police Academy Museum
  Gramercy Park 235 E. 20th St. (bet. Second and Third Aves.); 477-9753
Roerich (Nicholas Roerich) Museum
  Morningside Heights 319 W. 107th St. (at Riverside Dr.); 864-7752
Roosevelt (Theodore Roosevelt) Birthplace
  Gramercy Park 28 E. 20th St. (bet. Park Ave. South and Broadway); 260-1616
Schomburg Center for Research in Black Culture
  Harlem 515 Lenox Ave. (at 135th St.); 491-2200
Society of Illustrators' Museum of American Illustration
  Upper East Side 128 E. 63rd St. (bet. Park and Lexington Aves.); 838-2560

Sony Wonder Technology Lab
Midtown 550 Madison Ave. (bet. 55th and 56th Sts.); 833-5414
South Street Seaport Museum and Marketplace
Lower Manhattan Fulton St. bet. Front and South Sts.; 669-9400/669-9416
Studio Museum in Harlem
144 W. 125th St. (bet. Lenox and Seventh Aves.); 864-4500
Ukrainian Museum
East Village 203 Second Ave. (bet. 12th and 13th Sts.); 228-0110
Urban Center Galleries
Midtown 457 Madison Ave. (bet. 50th and 51st Sts.); 935-3960
Whitney Museum of American Art
Upper East Side 945 Madison Ave. (at 75th St.); 570-3676
Whitney Museum of American Art at Phillip Morris
Midtown 120 Park Ave. (at 42nd St.); 878-2453
Yeshiva University Museum
Upper Manhattan 2520 Amsterdam Ave. (at W. 185th St.); 960-5390

■ PERFORMANCES AND NIGHTLIFE

No civilized man goes to bed the same day he wakes up.
—Mayor Jimmy Walker

The city that never sleeps offers a whole menu of choices for everyone from first nighters to night owls. The following selective listing includes concert venues, live music, dance clubs, jazz clubs, cabarets, and bars.

Concert Venues

The Apollo Theatre
Harlem 253 W. 125th St. (bet. Adam Clayton Powell, Jr. and Frederick Douglass Blvds.); 749-5838
Go for its famous Amateur Night every Wednesday and you may catch a rising star.
Beacon Theatre
Upper West Side Broadway at 74th St.; 496-7070
A somewhat shopworn but surprisingly intimate larger venue for major acts.

Bottom Line
West Village 15 W. Fourth St. (at Mercer); 228-6300
Classic rock.

Carnegie Hall
Midtown 57th St. and Seventh Ave.; 247-7800
You don't need any practice, practice, practice in order to hear a symphony there.

Irving Plaza
Gramercy Park 17 Irving Place (bet. 15th and 16th Sts.); 777-6817
Somehow, this antique Polish dance hall just feels right as the place to hear loud, hard-driving new rock acts.

Knitting Factory
TriBeCa 75 Leonard St. (bet. Broadway and Church); 219-3055
Come here to catch the newest and latest musicians and performing artists.

Lincoln Center for the Performing Arts
Upper West Side 62nd-66th Sts. (bet. Amsterdam and Columbus Aves.); 875-5400
Go for Verdi at the **Metropolitan Opera House,** *The Nutcracker* at the **New York State Theater,** a string quartet at **Alice Tully Hall,** the **New York Philharmonic** at **Avery Fisher Hall** or an outdoor concert at the **Damrosch Park** open-air bandshell. Afterwards, linger by the fountain in the center of it all.

Madison Square Garden
Chelsea Seventh Ave. and 32nd St.; 465-6741
Arena rock concerts (and circuses and dog shows and tractor pulls) in Manhattan.

92nd Street Y
Upper East Side 1395 Lexington Ave. (at 92nd St.); 415-5440
For solo recitals, chamber music, and classical performances, as well as literary readings.

Paramount Madison Square Garden
Midtown Seventh Ave. and 32nd St.; 465-6741
A medium-sized concert venue that's much loved by over-the hill superstars and up-and-coming talents.

Radio City Music Hall
Midtown 1260 Sixth Ave. (at 50th St.); 247-4777
If you're in the mood for Julio Iglesias or Bette Midler, this is where they'd take Manhattan.

Roseland
Midtown 239 W. 52nd St. (at Broadway); 247-0200
It's come a long way from its strictly mambo beginnings. Now you might find Deee-Lite one night, a mosh pit the next.

Summer Garden Concerts at Cooper-Hewitt Museum

Upper East Side 2 East 91st St. (at Fifth Ave.); 860-6868

For a serene, green listening scene, choose the free weeknight concerts in garden of Andrew Carnegie's mansion.

Summerpier

Lower Manhattan South St. Seaport, Pier 16, South and Fulton Sts.; 669-9480

Jazz, big band, and classical acts on warm Saturday nights at the Seaport. Bring a blanket.

Summerstage

Central Park Central Park Bandshell (mid-park at 72nd St.); 360-2777

An eclectic series put on by the Parks Department allows music fans to enjoy grand opera, the yiddish-inflected swing called "klesmer," and almost everything in between.

Symphony Space

Upper West Side 2537 Broadway (at 95th St.); 864-1414

All-day special-event concerts, readings, and more, off the beaten track.

Town Hall

Midtown 113 W. 43rd St. (between Sixth Ave. and Broadway); 840-2824

Refined ambiance with wonderful acoustics in a McKim, Mead & White showstopper.

Live Music and Dance Clubs

CBGB & OMFUG

East Village 315 Bowery (at Bleecker St.); 982-4052

The mystique is even thicker than the late-night air at this venerable punk club where bands like the Talking Heads, Patti Smith, and the Ramones first rousted audiences.

The Cooler

West Village 416 W. 14th St.; 229-0785

A hot live-music party in a former meat refrigerator.

Dan Lynch

East Village 221 Second Ave. (between 13th and 14th Sts.); 677-0911

After a couple of smokin' blues sets and a bunch of brews, you'll swear you're not in New York City.

The Grand

East Village 76 E. 13th St.; 777-0600

When you can't go to the Bronx for its hip-hop scene (if you can, try **The Fever** on

East Tremont Ave.), here's the next most-happening place, which showcases what its promoters call "hip hop for the fabulous."

Limelight
Chelsea 47 W. 20th St. (at Sixth Ave.); 807-7850
Formerly the Church of the Holy Communion, then a drug rehab center, then a theater and now the nightly haunt of myriad freaky souls.

Lone Star Roadhouse
Midtown 240 W. 52 St. (at Broadway); 245-2950
New York's premier venue for lonesome urban cowboys and cowgirls, it features chili, dancing, and occasionally Levon Helm or Hot Tuna.

Nell's Supper Club
Chelsea 246 W. 14th St. (between Seventh and Eighth Aves.); 807-7850
When Nell Campbell (remember her in *Rocky Horror?*) first opened the doors of her English-country-club-style joint in the mid-80s, she inspired scores of imitators. The real thing has outlasted them all.

Paddy Reilly's Music Bar
Murray Hill 495 Second Ave. (at 28th St.); 686-1210
Irish rock.

Palladium
Union Square 126 E. 14th St. (bet. Third and Fourth Aves.); 473-7171
No longer a trend-mecca, as it was when it opened, but still a good place to get an earful, get lost, and get down.

Pyramid
East Village 101 Ave. A (between Sixth and Seventh Sts.); 475-0069
Early on you'll get down on a postage-stamp dance floor. After midnight, let the drag shows begin.

Sound Factory
Chelsea 530 W. 27th St.; 643-0728
The ultimate hip-hop dance party for those who don't mind getting frisked at the door.

Sounds of Brazil
TriBeCa 204 Varick St.; 243-4940
Brazilian is only the beginning at this world-beat original, where you can hear anything from bossa nova to calypso to reggae. Ole Tunge on giant stilts, anyone? Prepare to sweat.

The Supper Club
Midtown 240 W. 47th St.; 921-1940
A cavernous setting for both live acts and dancing.

Tramps
Chelsea 51 W. 21st St. (bet. Fifth and Sixth Aves.); 727-7788
Cutting edge funk, some world beat, nothing less than genius scheduling all around. Pick anything and get plugged in.

Tunnel
Chelsea 220 12th Ave.; 695-7292
A literally cavernous disco installed in a section of old subway tunnel.

Webster Hall
East Village 125 E. 11th St.; 353-1600
One of the oldest original venues in New York, but always the freshest acts.

Wetlands
TriBeCa 161 Hudson St. (at Laight St.); 966-4225
A place that's proud of its hippie-dippie styling, where your fuel of choice can be beer, Ben & Jerry's, or "smart drinks."

Jazz Clubs and Cabarets

The Ballroom
Chelsea 253 W. 28th St. (bet. Seventh and Eighth Aves.); 244-3005
First-class tapas and cabaret make an improbably delightful combo.

Blue Note Jazz Club
West Village 131 W. Third St. (bet. MacDougal St. and Sixth Ave.); 475-8592
Just a room with great jazz.

Bradley's
Greenwich Village 79 University Pl.; 228-6440
Come here after hours: you might spot some jazz heavyweights just hanging out.

Cafe Carlyle
Upper East Side 35 E. Madison Ave. (at 76th St.); 744-1600
Classic cabaret for the uptown set.

Down Beat
West Village 101 Seventh Ave. South (at Grove St.); 620-4000
Another swanky new jazz club in a traditional mode has joined the long time duo of Sweet Basil and the Village Vanguard on the same stretch in Greenwich Village.

Downstairs at the Metropolis

Union Square 31 Union Square West (at 16th St.); 675-2300

Tucked into the basement of a popular restaurant-cafe overlooking Union Square, this new club sports a mammoth aquarium, home to one small but hungry shark, and name acts like McCoy Tyner and Jimmy Heath.

Fat Tuesday's

Gramercy Park 190 Third Ave. (bet. 17th and 18th Sts.); 533-7900

Rock 'n' roll stars make pilgrimages here on Monday nights to see electric guitar master Les Paul.

Fez

East Village 10 Great Jones St.; 533-7000

Satin and mosaic create a quasi-Moroccan ambiance for cool jazz.

Five Spot

Chelsea 4 W. 31st St. (at Fifth Ave.); 631-0100

A jazz venue and popular dinner joint in a turn-of-the-century ballroom.

Iridium Room Jazz Club

Upper West Side 44 W. 63rd St. (at Broadway); 582-2121

VERY SOPHISTICATED

*I*n case you don't live in New York, the Wicker Bar is in this sort of swanky hotel, the Seton Hotel. I used to go there quite a lot, but I don't any more. I gradually cut it out. It's one of those places that are supposed to be very sophisticated and all, and the phonies are coming in the window. They used to have these two French babes, Tina and Janine, come out and play the piano and sing about three times every night. One of them played the piano—strictly lousy—and the other one sang, and most of the songs were either pretty dirty or in French . . . .

It was pretty early when I got there. I sat down at the bar—it was pretty crowded—and had a couple of Scotch and sodas before old Luce even showed up. I stood up when I ordered them so they could see how tall I was and all and not think I was a goddam minor. Then I watched the phonies for a while. Some guy next to me was snowing hell out of the babe he was with. He kept telling her she had aristocratic hands. That killed me.

—J. D. Salinger, *The Catcher in the Rye*, 1951

This new venue in the basement of a trendy restaurant opposite Lincoln Center offers good sight lines, critically praised food, and swinging if somewhat mainstream jazz.

Michael's Pub
Midtown 211 East 55th St. (bet. Second and Third Aves.); 758-2272
Catch Woody on his clarinet in the New Orleans Funeral and Ragtime Orchestra.

Sweet Basil
West Village 88 Seventh Ave. South; 242-1785
Another of the greats for those who take their jazz straight.

Tavern on the Green
Upper West Side Central Park West at 67th St.; 873-3200
Best known as that twinkly restaurant in the park, but its Chestnut Room hosts serious jazz.

Village Vanguard
West Village 178 Seventh Ave. South; 255-4037
"Ur" jazz club.

Visiones
West Village 125 MacDougal St.; 673-5576
New and emerging jazz bands, with a reasonable cover charge.

West End Gate
Morningside Heights 2911 Broadway (bet. 113th and 114th Sts.); 666-8687
Where Columbia University graduate students unwind.

Zanzibar and Grill
West Village 73 Eighth Ave. (bet. 13th and 14th Sts.); 924-9755
Forties-style supper club with jazz, funk, fusion, and good old rhythm and blues.

Zinno
West Village 126 W. 13th St., 924-5182
Enjoy hearing a small jazz combo while you dine well on Italian food.

Bars

Coyote Ugly Saloon
East Village 153 First Ave.; 477-4431
A country-western jukebox provides the atmosphere in this laid-back neighborhood bar.

Dublin House
Upper West Side 225 W. 79th St. (at Broadway); 874-9528
Follow the glow of the giant neon harp suspended over the entrance to find a bar where the customers take their Guinness seriously.

Fanelli

Little Italy 94 Prince St. (at Mercer St.); 226-9412

For over a century this corner bar has beckoned Latin lovers.

Jeremy's Ale House

Lower Manhattan 254 Front St. (at Dover St.); 964-3537

The meeting place of junior Wall Street execs, where they can suck down a styrofoam pint and admire the ties and bras hung from the rafters.

Lucky Strike

SoHo 59 Grand St. (at West Broadway); 941-0479

A keeper in the trendy bistro-bar scene.

Manhattan Brewing Company

SoHo 42 Thompson St.; 925-1515

More than 50 beers are freshly brewed here—any takers for wildflower honey ale?—and you can order from a menu featuring beer-infused food.

Marion's

East Village 354 Bowery; 475-7621

On Sundays this restaurant hosts its "world-famous fashion brunches," but you can get a world-class martini anytime.

Max Fish

SoHo 178 Ludlow St. (at Houston); 529-3959

A bare-bones pool-table, pinball, and juke joint that happens to be the living center of New York's downtown art world.

Merc Bar

SoHo 151 Mercer St.; 966-2727

There may eventually be a fashionable SoHo hotel erected around this fashionable SoHo pub. But why wait to pay a visit?

No-Tell Motel

East Village 167 Ave. A; GRL-2172

New York's downtown sophisticates' interpretation of Middle-American turnpike tawdry. You have to see the X-rated wallpaper to believe it.

Oak Bar

Midtown W. 59th St. at Fifth Ave.; 759-3000

The Plaza Hotel's woody, impeccable, couldn't-be-anywhere-but-Manhattan retreat.

Puffy's

TriBeCa 81 Hudson St. (at Harrison St.); 766-9159

Artists crowd bikers off barstools at this TriBeCa mecca.

Vazac August
   East Village 108 Ave. B; 473-8840
   Where East Village denizens spend their evenings.

The View
   Midtown 1535 Broadway; 398-1900
   Only the vertigo-afflicted will be able to resist a trip to the only revolving bar in
   Manhattan, pitched high over the cacophony of Times Square in John Portman's
   Marriott Marquis.

■ INFORMATION RESOURCES

For hotel and event listings, travel packages, and brochures contact **New York
Convention and Visitors Bureau** (2 Columbus Circle, New York, NY 10019;
397-8222 or the **New York Division of Tourism** at One Commerce Plaza,
Albany, NY 12245; (518) 474-4116 or (800)225-5697.

A lot that goes on in Manhattan cannot be covered in the pages of any book,
simply because there are so many non-recurring and special events. Luckily, New
York is the ultimate media-savvy town, and there are a number of superb events
listings published on a daily or weekly basis.

One of the great delights of New York is that it is, more than any other place in
America, a newspaper town. This is largely a function of the peculiar nature of the
city's workforce, many of whom commute by train or buses to their jobs. Newspapers cater to those idle, commuting hands, especially the "tabs," or tabloids, designed to be easily read standing on the subway, or crowded onto the "Sardine
Express," as the Long Island Railroad is sometimes called.

At present, there are four major dailies in town, although that may change according to the whim of union contracts and the deep pockets of investors. The
New York Times presents itself as "the paper of record," and although there are a
few gaps, it generally lives up to the billing.

Tabloids include the *Daily News, New York Post,* and *New York Newsday.* All
four major dailies have extensive listings, with the *Times* Sunday edition especially
complete. The *Amsterdam News* is Manhattan's black-oriented daily, and *El Diario
La Prensa* is the highest circulation Spanish-language newspaper. The *New York
Observer* is a salmon-sheeted daily catering to what Jerry Brown used to call "the
chattering class"—the city's media elite.

The weekly publications covering New York are almost as numerous as the dailies, and often are better places to check for coming events. Leading the pack is the august *New Yorker,* recently infused with new life by the editorship of Tina Brown. *New York* magazine became the model for city-oriented publications the country over when it was started in the late '60s, and it, too, features extensive listings.

The *Village Voice* covers the cultural scene and the political landscape, and is by no means limited to Greenwich Village in its scope. *The Paper,* a Manhattan-oriented monthly, often spots trends before any other publication, and has a good listings section. But in order to keep current on what's happening, you need not spend a dime. The weekly *NY Press,* available free at street-corner newsboxes throughout Manhattan, is lively, credible, and inclusive.

■ R A D I O   C I T Y

Newcomers often bemoan the relative paucity of quality radio in New York, but with so much happening, who stays home to listen? A selective guide:

WFAN (660 AM) All sports, except for motor-mouthed iconoclast Don Imus in the morning.

WINS (1010 AM) Like they say, all news, all the time. A favorite of New York cabbies.

WKCR (89.9 FM) Columbia University's college station, specializing in excellent jazz. But
    word up—check out the Friday late night hip-hop show.

WFMU (91.1 FM) New York's best, and most eclectic, radio station actually broadcasts from
    East Orange, N.J.

WXRK (92.3 FM) "King of all media" Howard Stern in the morning, classic rock the rest of
    the time.

WNYC (93.9 FM/820 AM) Currently embattled, this city-owned radio station hosts a
    wide mix of classical, talk and special interest shows, along with the daily offerings of
    National Public Radio.

WQXR (96.3 FM) Owned by the *New York Times,* and currently the last bastion of classical
    music in New York.

WBAI (99.5 FM) Progressive, independent, *smart* radio.

WBLS (107.5 FM) Black-oriented music and talk, with some outrageous live club broad-
    casts.

RECOMMENDED READING

■ NON-FICTION

Allen, Irving Lewis. *The City in Slang: New York Life and Popular Speech*. Oxford: Oxford University Press, 1993. A love letter to the city disguised as an academic text.

Bayles, W. Harrison. *Old Taverns of New York*. New York: Frank Allaben Genealogical Company, 1915. Historic anecdotes about the city's oldest pubs.

Brecher, Charles and Raymond D. Horton. *Power Failure: New York City Politics and Policy since 1960*. Oxford: Oxford University Press, 1993. A scholarly guide through the labyrinthine world of local government.

Caro, Robert. *The Power Broker: Robert Moses and the Fall of New York*. New York: Viking, 1975. Moses was the man most responsible for the way New York looks and works today, and Caro is relentless in giving him his due.

Cudahy, Brian J. *Over and Back: The History of Ferryboats in New York Harbor*. New York: Fordham University Press, 1990. Ferries are coming back, and this book is a loving tribute.

Diamondstein, Barbaralee. *The Landmarks of New York II*. New York: Harry Abrams, Inc., 1993. The newly updated definitive study.

Dreiser, Theodore. *The Color of a Great City*. New York: Howard Fertig, Inc., 1987. These sociological essays portray New York just after the turn of the century, but those describing the chasm between rich and poor could have been written yesterday.

Friedman, Josh Alan. *Tales of Times Square*. Portland: Feral House, 1993. Disturbed, disturbing, gut-wrenchingly funny bulletins from the Crossroads of the World.

Gilfoyle, Timothy J. *City of Eros: New York City, Prostitution and the Commercialization of Sex, 1790–1920*. New York: W.W. Norton, 1992. The world's oldest profession, in a New York context.

Grannick, Harry. *Underneath New York*. New York: Fordham University Press, 1991. Just what the title says. Written in 1947 and a little dated now, but not much changes underground.

Hawes, Elizabeth. *New York, New York: How the Apartment House Transformed the Life of the City*. New York: Knopf, 1993. Lively chronicle of a social upheaval, forced by spiraling real estate values.

Hood, Clifton. *722 Miles: The Building of the Subways and How They Transformed New York*. New York: Simon & Schuster, 1993. Academic study on the subways, curse and salvation of Manhattan.

Howe, Irving, and Kenneth Libo, eds. *How We Lived: A Documentary History of Immigrant Jews in America 1880–1930*. New York: Richard Marek Publishers, Inc., 1979. Short personal accounts and descriptions as told by Jewish immigrants of their early days in the new country.

Kinkead, Gwen. *Chinatown: A Portrait of a Closed Society*. New York: Harper Collins, 1992. It may be closed to most people, but not to her. Excellent.

Lebowitz, Fran. *Metropolitan Life*. New York: Dutton/New American Library, 1988. Insights into New York style, art, and pop culture in the form of entertaining—often snippy—tales.

Lewis, David Levering. *When Harlem Was In Vogue*. Oxford: Oxford University Press, 1979. A social history of the Harlem Renaissance and the New Negro Movement.

Lewis, Michael. *Liar's Poker*. New York: Penguin Books, 1989. A look inside the psyches of stockbrokers and bond traders at Salomon Brothers, one of New York's most famous brokerage firms.

Mackay, David A. *The Building of Manhattan*. New York: Harper & Row, 1987. With perfectly rendered line drawings, a chronicle of how the city was put together.

McNickle, Chris. *To Be Mayor of New York: Ethnic Politics in the City*. New York: Columbia University Press, 1993. Why would anyone want to be mayor? This book may not answer that question, but it tells you how mayors from O'Dwyer to Dinkins did it.

Miller, Terry. *Greenwich Village and How It Got That Way*. New York: Crown, 1990. Lavish, full-color treatment of everybody's favorite neighborhood.

Mitchell, Joseph. *Up in the Old Hotel*. New York, Pantheon Books, 1992. Beautifully drawn word-portraits of city folk, as you'll hope to meet them.

Morehouse, Ward. *The Waldorf-Astoria: America's Gilded Dream*. New York: M. Evans, 1991. If any hotel deserves to have a book written about it, the Waldorf is it.

Morris, Jan. *Manhattan '45*. Oxford: Oxford University Press, 1987. A snapshot of a golden time, by a consummate travel writer.

Moscow, Henry. *The Street Book*. New York: Fordham University Press, 1978. How the streets of Manhattan came to be named.

Riis, Jacob. *How the Other Half Lives: Studies Among the Tenements of New York.* New York: Hill & Wang, 1957. A book that changed New York's treament of its poor, with astonishing photos.

Salwen, Peter. *Upper West Side Story: A History and Guide.* New York: Abbeville Press, 1989. Well-researched study of a great residential neighborhood.

Sante, Luc. *Low Life: Lures and Snares of Old New York.* New York: Random House, 1991. Superb, rich, interpretive history, quirky and engrossing.

Schwartzman, Paul and Rob Polner. *New York Notorious.* New York: Crown, 1992. A borough-by-borough tour of the city's most infamous crime scenes.

Sleeper, Jim. *The Closest of Strangers: Liberalism and the Politics of Race in New York.* New York: Norton, 1990. Neo-conservative musings, on the order of "Can we all just get along?"

White, E. B. *Essays of E. B. White.* New York: Harper & Row, 1977. If you can only read one thing about the city, read "Here Is New York."

■ FICTION

Alford, Henry. *Municipal Bondage: One Man's Anxiety-Producing Adventures in the Big City.* New York: Random House, 1993. A highly amusing tale of woe about a wanna-be entrepreneur.

Auster, Paul. *The New York Trilogy: City of Glass, Ghosts and The Locked Room.* New York: Viking, 1991. Spooky, post-post-modernist thrillers, deconstructing Manhattan.

Baldwin, James. *Go Tell It on the Mountain.* New York: Doubleday & Co., 1985. The compelling story of a young black man growing up in Manhattan.

Cohn, Nik. *The Heart of the World.* New York, Viking, 1992. A journey up Manhattan's Main Street, with stories.

Crane, Stephen. *Maggie.* New York: Fawcett, 1960. Seminal realist studies of crime and degradation in turn-of-the-century New York, and the conditions that spawned them.

Doctorow, E. L. *The Waterworks.* New York: Knopf, 1993. With this book, and with *Ragtime, World's Fair,* and *Billy Bathgate,* Doctorow has been slowly assembling a dazzling fictional chronicle of New York.

Dos Passos, John. *Manhattan Transfer.* New York: Harper Bros., 1925. Jazz Age sketches of the city and its occupants.

Ellison, Ralph. *The Invisible Man*. New York: Random House, 1969. Being black in Harlem in the 1950s, with universal applications.

Hijuelos, Oscar. *Our House in the Last World*. New York: Pocket Books, 1978. Latino New York, centered on the post-war period. More recent years are described in Hijuelos's *The Mambo Kings Play Songs of Love* (New York: Farrar, Straus & Giroux, 1989).

Hughes, Langston. *Selected Poems of Langston Hughes*. New York: Knopf, 1929. Contains the poem "The Weary Blues." Hughes's poetic voice sings the blues of the Jazz Age.

Hustvedt, Siri. *The Blindfold*. New York: Norton, 1992. Weird, shimmering stories of a Columbia graduate student getting swallowed up by the city.

James, Henry. *Washington Square*. New York: Bantam, 1987. Incisive, drawing room drama of New York's patrician classes.

Janowitz, Tama. *Slaves of New York*. New York: Pocket, 1986. A collection of connected stores about a collection of disconnected people on the fringes of the '80s Manhattan cultural scene.

McInerney, Jay. *Bright Lights, Big City*. New York: Vintage, 1988. A phenomenon when it was published, it holds up today as a ironic portrait of urban alienation.

Runyon, Damon. *Guys and Dolls: Three Volumes in One*. Philadelphia: Lippincott, 1929. Peopling a vast and incomparable New York of the imagination.

Salinger, J. D. *The Catcher in the Rye*. New York: Little, Brown, 1991. The classic post-war coming-of-age story, when a student ventures into the big city and meets only "phonies."

Wharton, Edith. *The House of Mirth*. New York: Bantam, 1984. Along with *The Age of Innocence* (New York: Macmillan 1992) and other novels, Wharton's oeuvre represents a trenchant look at nineteenth-century Manhattan.

Wolfe, Tom. *Bonfire of the Vanities*. New York: Bantam, 1987. Marvelous fictional satire, puncturing the over-inflated balloon of the '80s.

■ GUIDEBOOKS

Eyewitness Travel Guides' New York. London: Dorling Kindersley, 1993. Countless snippets of information, including relevant architectural diagrams, neighborhood maps, restaurant listings, and a thorough index.

Flashmaps New York. New York: Fodor's Travel Publications, 1994. Maps of every Manhattan neighborhood, with numerous thematic maps including transportation, zip codes, restaurants, and nightlife. Also included are "street finder" charts and seating diagrams of sports and theater venues. A must-have for visitors and residents alike.

Fodor's New York City. New York: Fodor's Travel Publications, annually updated. Lots of useful information for the newcomer or first-time visitor.

Fodor's Sunday in New York. New York: Fodor's Travel Publications, 1994. Great ways to spend a Sunday, with information about what's open on this quietest day of the week.

Insight Guide: New York City. Hong Kong: APA Publications, 1994. With each neighborhood described by a different author and pictures taken by a team of photographers, this guide provides a wide range of text and illustration. It's also a pretty good read.

Miller, Bryan. *The New York Times Guide to Restaurants in New York City.* New York: The New York Times Co, 1992. An exhaustive guide to the best eateries in the city, with thorough descriptions and numerous cross-reference listings.

NYC Access. New York: Richard Saul Wurman and HarperCollins, 1991. New York City block by block. Easy to use, with color codings for restaurants, historic sites, etc., and important signs and logos reproduced for quick spotting.

Schwartz, Sam. *Shadow Traffic's New York Shortcuts and Traffic Tips.* New York: Fodor's Travel Publications, 1994. "Gridlock Sam" Schwartz, former Chief of New York City's Traffic Bureau, gives detailed directions for shortcuts within the five boroughs and escape routes to help you get out of town or to the airport.

I N D E X

COMPASS AMERICAN GUIDES

Comprehensive, literate, and beautifully illustrated guides to the individual cities and states of the United States and Canada, Compass American Guides are unparalleled in their cultural, historical, and informational scope. They are to the 1990s what the WPA guidebook series was to the 1930s — insightful, resourceful, and entertaining.

"Each [Compass American Guide] pairs an accomplished photographer with a writer native to the state. The resulting pictures and words have such an impact I constantly had to remind myself I was reading a travel guide." — National Geographic Traveler

"Entertaining and well-illustrated with maps and photographs, in color and vintage black and white...good to read ahead of time, then take along so you don't miss anything." —San Diego Magazine

"You can read [a Compass American Guide] for information and come away entertained. Or you can read it for entertainment and come away informed . . . an informational jackpot." —Houston Chronicle

"Wickedly stylish writing!" —Chicago Sun-Times

Compass American Guides are available in general and travel bookstores, or may be ordered directly by calling 1-800-733-3000; or by sending a check or money order, including the cost of shipping and handling, payable to: Random House, Inc. 400 Hahn Road, Westminster, Maryland 21157. Books are shipped by USPS Book Rate (allow 30 days for delivery): $2.00 for the 1st book, $0.50 for each additional book. Applicable sales tax will be charged. All prices are subject to change. Or ask your bookseller to order for you.

"Books can make thoughtful (and sometimes even thought-provoking) gifts for incentive travel winners or convention attendees. A new series of guidebooks published by Compass American Guides is right on the mark." —Successful Meetings magazine

Consider Compass American Guides as gifts or incentives for VIP's, employees, clients, customers, convention and meeting attendees, friends and others. Compass American Guides are available at special discounts for bulk purchases (100 copies or more) for sales promotions or premiums. Special editions, including personalized covers, excerpts of existing guides, and corporate imprints, can be created in large quantities for special needs. For more information, write to Special Marketing, Fodor's Travel Publications, 201 E. 50th St., New York, NY 10022; or call 800/800-3246. Inquiries from the United Kingdom should be sent to Fodor's Travel Publications, 20 Vauxhall Bridge Rd., London, England SW1V 2SA.

COMPASS AMERICAN GUIDES

Critics, Booksellers, and Travelers All Agree You're Lost Without a Compass.

"Highly evocative...the
chapter on food forced me
to stop reading and go eat."
—*New York Times*

"This is my kind of
guidebook."
—*David Laird,
Books of the
Southwest*

"Canada goes a long way in
presenting this country in
all its complex, beautiful
glory."
—*Toronto Sun*

"Great to send to
anyone coming to
Chicago."
—*Chicago Sun-Times*

"A literary, historical and
near-sensory excursion
across the state."
—*Denver Post*

"Bold yet artful in
its photography."
—*Albuquerque Journal*

"A good guide to send to a
friend or relative — laced
with original maps,
historical and literary
excerpts."
— *Register-Guard*

"Compass Guides capture the
true spirit of a place from its
early settler days to modern
times."
— *America Online*

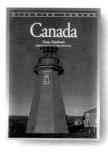

**Arizona
(2nd Edition)
1-878-86732-6**
$16.95 ($21.50 Can)

**Canada
1-878-86712-1**
$14.95 ($19.95 Can)

**Chicago
1-878-86728-8**
$16.95 ($21.50 Can)

**Maine
1-878-86751-2**
$16.95 ($22.95 Can)

**Manhattan
1-878-86737-7**
$16.95 ($23.50 Can)

**Montana
(2nd Edition)
1-878-86743-1**
$17.95 ($25.00 Can)

**South Carolina
1-878-86766-0**
$16.95 ($23.50 Can)

**South Dakota
1-878-86726-1**
$16.95 ($22.95 Can)

**Texas
1-878-86764-4**
$17.95 ($25.00 Can)

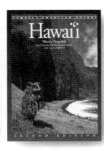
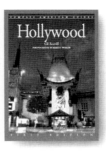

**Colorado
(2nd Edition)**
1-878-86735-0
$16.95 ($21.50 Can)

**Hawai'i
(2nd Edition)**
1-878-86769-5
$16.95 ($23.50 Can)

**Hollywood
(2nd Edition)**
1-878-86771-7
$16.95 ($23.50 Can)

**Las Vegas
(3rd Edition)**
1-878-86736-9
$16.95 ($22.50 Can)

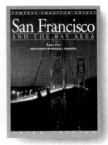

New Mexico
1-878-86706-7
$15.95 ($19.95 Can)

New Orleans
1-878-86739-3
$16.95 ($21.50 Can)

Oregon
1-878-86733-4
$16.95 ($21.50 Can)

**San Francisco
(3rd Edition)**
1-878-86770-9
$16.95 ($23.50 Can)

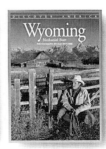

Utah (2nd Edition)
1-878-86731-8
$16.95 ($22.95 Can)

Virginia
1-878-86741-5
$16.95 ($22.95 Can)

Wisconsin
1-878-86744-X
$16.95 ($22.95 Can)

**Wyoming
(2nd Edition)**
1-878-86750-4
$17.95 ($25.00 Can)

■ ABOUT THE AUTHORS

Gil Reavill is a journalist, screenwriter, playwright, and novelist. His last book for Compass American Guides was *Los Angeles,* 1992 (second edition, 1994). He is currently writing a book on black police officers.

Jean Zimmerman, his wife, grew up 25 minutes north of Manhattan and has made her home in the city for the last 17 years. Her next book, on women in the U.S. Navy, is scheduled for publication in fall 1995.

■ ABOUT THE PHOTOGRAPHER

Photographer Michael S. Yamashita has been shooting pictures for National Geographic Society magazines and books since 1979. He is a frequent contributor to *Travel & Leisure* and *Portfolio,* and his work has been exhibited at the Smithsonian Institution's Museum of American History, the National Gallery in Washington, and Kodak's Professional Photographer's Showcase at EPCOT center in Florida. Mr. Yamashita's photography is also featured in the *San Francisco* and *Las Vegas* titles from Compass American Guides.